Praise for
The Best Spiritual Writing 2010

"Like a very fine friend returned from a year's voyaging, laden with delights and treasures to share, Philip Zaleski brings us, here again, another trove of well-wrought, luminous, soul-bracing gifts. Few books can be so certainly counted on to restore, renew, challenge, and uphold the quester and pilgrim as *The Best Spiritual Writing*."

—Thomas Lynch, author of *The Undertaking*
and *Apparition & Late Fictions*

"There is enough here to feed the hungry heart for years to come. Hats off once again to Phil Zaleski, whose genius it is to employ his critical knowledge of spiritual literature with generosity of heart and a sustained appreciation of our mystery."

—Phyllis Tickle, author of *The Great Emergence*

The Best Spiritual Writing

2010

Edited by

PHILIP ZALESKI

Introduction by

PICO IYER

PENGUIN BOOKS

PENGUIN BOOKS

Published by the Penguin Group

Penguin Group (USA) Inc.,

375 Hudson Street, New York, New York 10014, U.S.A.

Penguin Group (Canada), 90 Eglinton Avenue East, Suite 700, Toronto,

Ontario, Canada M4P 2Y3 (a division of Pearson Penguin Canada Inc.)

Penguin Books Ltd, 80 Strand, London WC2R 0RL, England

Penguin Ireland, 25 St Stephen's Green, Dublin 2,

Ireland (a division of Penguin Books Ltd)

Penguin Group (Australia), 250 Camberwell Road, Camberwell,

Victoria 3124, Australia (a division of Pearson Australia Group Pty Ltd)

Penguin Books India Pvt Ltd, 11 Community Centre,

Panchsheel Park, New Delhi – 110 017, India

Penguin Group (NZ), 67 Apollo Drive, Rosedale, North Shore 0632,

New Zealand (a division of Pearson New Zealand Ltd)

Penguin Books (South Africa) (Pty) Ltd, 24 Sturdee Avenue,

Rosebank, Johannesburg 2196, South Africa

Penguin Books Ltd, Registered Offices:

80 Strand, London WC2R 0RL, England

First published in Penguin Books 2010

5 7 9 10 8 6 4

Copyright © Philip Zaleski, 2010

Introduction copyright © Pico Iyer, 2010

All rights reserved

Pages 249–51 constitute an extension of this copyright page.

ISBN 978-0-14-311676-9

Printed in the United States of America

Set in Adobe Garamond

Designed by Elke Sigal

Contents

Foreword

ONE OF THE BEST TALES ABOUT THE DESERT FATHERS, THOSE MONKS and hermits who prayed, fasted, and battled demons in the Egyptian and Syrian wastelands of the third and fourth centuries A.D., recounts the last request of the venerable Abba Paphnutius. We read that on his deathbed, Paphnutius asked God to disclose to him whether any saints still lived upon the earth. God answered by sending a vision of three holy men: a reformed robber, a humble village headman, and a powerful merchant. Truly, Paphnutius reported to his fellow monks, "no one in this world ought to be despised . . . for in every condition of human life there are souls that please God and have their hidden deeds wherein He takes delight."

Hiddenness is rarely sought, often imposed, and almost always, if assumed with humility and thanks, a sure path to wisdom. This truth lies at the heart of Jesus's beatitudes, it shapes many scriptural images (the Garden of Eden sealed with the cherubim's flaming sword, the "garden enclosed" of the Song of Songs), it shines forth in mythological and fairy-tale motifs (the stranger who knows the way to paradise, the prince disguised as a pauper, the forest concealing the kingdom of the elves). To be concealed, forgotten, overlooked can be a great blessing, granting freedom to the oppressed, protection to the innocent, room to ripen to the immature, time to repent to the sinner.

As yesterday, so today; as in myth, so in life: even now—and even among spiritual writers—one can find, undetected in the bulrushes, those whose hidden deeds bring delight to heaven. The most famous example of sequestered literary holiness may be that of Thomas Traherne (1637-1674), the metaphysical poet who published while alive only a single minor theological treatise, and who remained more or less forgotten until 1897, when a scholar rummaging through a bin of secondhand books at a London shop discovered the manuscript of what has come to be known as *Centuries of Meditations,* Traherne's astonishing prose poems of ecstasy and wonder. Traherne has many close kin in the worldwide clan of spiritual writers. Two of them, living much nearer to our own time, have kept me company over the past year: Writers who lived and died in obscurity, whose testament belongs not to their own age but to the ages.

The first is a Catholic priest and poet by the name of Allan MacDonald (1859–1905). Father Allan, as he liked to be known, passed most of his life caring for the impoverished inhabitants of Eriskay, a bleak island in Scotland's Outer Hebrides. Always ready to sacrifice himself for others, he laid aside his native English tongue to write in the Gaelic—then a despised language, excluded from fine society—of his flock. *Maighistir Ailein,* his people called him in thanksgiving. Fr. Allan's poems tell of the rough life of fishermen and weavers, of their unbreakable faith in the invisible world, of the love of God that mantles them from birth to death. I can't judge his Gaelic, for I don't read that wonderful tongue; English translations give the impression of a soul humble and hardworking, filled with charity, in love with both natural and supernatural things. His characteristic sayings include "Be watchful always" and "God have mercy." Fr. Allan was also a folklorist, who compiled a dictionary of Gaelic sayings and collected the vanishing tales, songs, and prayers of his people; some of them appear in Alexander Carmichael's magisterial compilation of Scottish folklore, *Carmina Gadelica.* They are well worth seeking out, as are his poems, available on the Internet and from specialty publishers. This great poet-priest died at the age of forty-six, worn out by his labors. On Eriskay and throughout the Outer Hebrides he is revered to this day.

My second literary companion during the past year has been an English housewife, that most invisible of creatures. Lilian Staveley (1878–1928) wrote three books—*The Golden Fountain, The Prodigal Returns,* and *The Romance of the Soul*—about her remarkable mystical experiences. All were published anonymously. This reclusive woman guarded her inner life so well that even her husband, a brigadier general in the British army, didn't learn of her visions or her writings until after her death. From the few available, skimpy accounts of her life, we learn that Staveley was, outwardly at least, a typical English belle, educated at boarding schools, practiced in ballroom dancing and parlor chatter; inwardly, however, she traversed the spiritual landscape from pole to pole, embracing first atheism and then a cloudy nature mysticism before being swept off her feet by a life-changing rapture. This cataclysmic event occurred during the First World War, on a deserted hillside, when God descended upon her in the form of a mysterious white light that "hid all my surroundings from me, thought I stood there with my eyes wide open." The intense illumination penetrated her until "the Wall, the dreadful Barrier, between God and me, came down entirely, and immediately I loved Him. I was so filled with love that I had to cry aloud my love, so great was the force and the wonder and the delight and the might of it." Staveley lived for another decade after this epiphany, filling her hours with prayer, devotion, and the writing of spiritual memoirs. Her books are enthralling, passionate, with a fine sense of spiritual niceties: of the soul's dance between self-will and self-surrender, of the differing but parallel inner paths of men and women. Like Fr. Allan's, her works are hard to find but worth the effort.

Fr. Allan and Lilian Staveley have this in common—and this is why I bring them to your attention—both knew whereof they wrote, yet both remain largely unknown. Their names escape us; their writings flicker in and out of print. They had much to teach, and they chose to do so in obscurity, in anonymity. They sought out what the world ridicules or condemns—isolation, destitution, extinction—and in that void they found the precious pearl. As the classic formulation has it, they led lives hidden in God, and it was from this peculiar vantage point, that of souls enfolded by grace, that they wrote and transmitted their works of power and beauty. Their books, in the words of Abba Paphnutius, are "hidden deeds, wherein He takes delight." Both had the skill to triumph in the artistic salons of twentieth-century Europe. But had they done so, they would have produced nothing but literature. As it is, they gave voice to holiness. The lessons they teach are unmistakable: that each of us must determine, apart from the clamor and enticements of the world, his own spiritual ground and there take his stand; and that while fame and fortune may be secondary incentives, only those who write for heaven leave a worthy legacy upon earth.

This is not to suggest, of course, that a writer must be unknown to be on the side of the angels. John Updike and Fr. Richard John Neuhaus belonged to the company of heaven, not only in their dazzling literary skills but in their spiritual allegiances. We have lost both since the last volume in the Best Spiritual Writing series appeared. I wish to thank them once again for their frequent contributions to and ardent support of the series. May it be that, in the sublime world to which they have passed, their golden pens flow as generously as ever! *Resquiescant in pace.*

My thanks also, this year, to Pico Iyer; to Carolyn Carson and all the folks at Viking Penguin; to my agents Kim Witherspoon and David Forrer; and to Carol, John, and Andy, beloved inhabitants of my own garden enclosed.

PHILIP ZALESKI

Introduction

The Leopard on the Mountain Path

Spiritual writing cannot be mere religious writing, and it is something much more and much quicker than theological tract or philosophical inquiry; it is—as the name suggests—something that comes from, and goes to, the spirit, which is to say, the human being (or that part of us that communes with what's beyond us). It is therefore nearly always something faltering and finite and intermittent, and the more joyous for its intermittency, and being found again. Spiritual words do not come, in my experience, from someone who's constantly and calmly seen the light, so much as from someone who's seen it and then lost it, who's beset by shadows or imperfect refractions, who wrestles with her angels daily, but who knows, deep down, that somewhere our original radiance can be recovered.

Graham Greene, rooting his faith in the church of humanity, to expound a gospel for the fallen, shows us men in holy dress who are fallible, terrified, as confused and alone as the rest of us—but who earn the robes they sometimes shed by suddenly acting better than they expect or have a right to. The Zen monk, cultivating a transparency and attention that means that just sweeping leaves or cooking lunch or washing dishes in the kitchen are a form of meditation—of kneeling before the present tense—reminds us that everywhere is perfect if only we have the eyes to see it ("Look beneath your feet," says the sign at the entrance to many a Zen temple). I go to the cinema, and Terrence Malick shows us huge canvases of ancient rites and Old Testament forces—even plagues of locusts in his *Days of Heaven*—that tell us that we are tiny figures in a larger frame, and all our small dramas are nothing next to a higher logic enforced by Nature or Providence or Time.

Spirituality, I mean to say, arises out of the disjunction between us and the transcendent as much as out of the occasional union; it lies, as in any love affair, in the attempt to draw closer to a reality that we sense inside ourselves (though sometimes, in our uncertainty, we call it only "possibility"), and in our longing to live in the truth that is self-evident whenever we're where we ought to be.

It follows, then, as Emerson or Melville show us, in their different devotions to light and dark, that spiritual writing relies on energy, on movement, and on the intensity of our interaction with the Real; it is not stasis or assurance, any more than a love affair could or should be, but rather a permanent approach and retreat that can look to outsiders like an argument. Now we see the things we know; now we don't. Now our eyes are clouded over; and now, for just as little reason, they're awakened. Annie Dillard rages against her God at times—how can He allow children to be born deformed, or one hundred twenty thousand innocents to be swept away in a single flood?—as only a friend or a lover can; love has to have a flame burning at its core, or it is nothing.

That is why Flannery O'Connor gave us a character, Hazel Motes, who is so obsessed with Jesus that he shouts out his unbelief and sets up the Church Without Christ; to assert so relentlessly absence of a God is at heart to entertain the notion that some feel His presence. To say that the world lacks spiritual depth at any moment is to acknowledge that the chance for such depths exists; as with anyone who gives his heart over to some Other, the very act of surrender is an act of faith in the conviction that something true and beautiful exists beyond the chimera of all our projections and delusions and wishful hopes. The singer Bono, of the rock group U2, is one of the exalting spiritual writers of our time, for me, because the issue of faith is always so alive in him, even if as something that he is failing or traducing or not managing to live up to; onstage, he sometimes incarnates the devil, to give fleshly, firsthand body to all the temptations of power, glamour, or messianism that afflict even the most sincere or ardent spirits, the leopards that stand along our path.

The spiritual writer for me is, in other words, one driven not by certainties, but their absence; doubts, questions, tremors are his lifeblood. He does not belong in some other world, above the clouds, amid the boxed reassurances of some of the Anglican hymns I sang at school; he's in the middle of our world, where often it seems that nothing can be counted upon or is permanent. I've spent much of the last thirty-five years in conversation with the Fourteenth Dalai Lama, as grounded and wise and clear-sighted a man (and therefore as completely open and compassionate a soul) as it has been my fortune to meet. But what speaks to most of us about His Holiness's experience is precisely the fact that he has never been able to be a sage on a mountaintop, in a faraway kingdom, calmly pronouncing on the laws of the mind and reality that his meditation and his philosophy have offered him; he is in our midst, entirely human, dealing with Realpolitik every day for more than sixty years and having suffered losses (of his homeland, of his people, of his external freedom) that are almost impossible for the rest of us to imagine.

What a figure like this is showing us is not how warm and clear-sighted and selfless he is, but how warm and clear-sighted and selfless any one of us can be, if so we choose to apply ourselves. The Dalai Lama's spirituality takes the form of insisting on his humanness, his frailty, his fallibility, and so bringing the potential he represents into the room that we inhabit. Not long ago, traveling with His Holiness across Japan for a week, I saw an interviewer come into the bullet-train carriage in which we were sitting and ask the Dalai Lama the question any of us might ask: "If you could wave a magic wand, what would you do to resolve the situation in the Middle East?"

The leader of the Tibetans looked at the young man with his usual attentiveness and directness and said, as warmly as an old friend might, "Silly question!" If he had a magic wand, he was implying, he would find a cure for cancer, bring us universal peace, resolve the Chinese-Tibetan tangle in an instant, and perhaps guarantee humanity the happiness that otherwise we have to work for. But he was just a human being like the journalist, he explained— prey to the same temptations, challenges, even sorrows. "I really think of the Buddha as a scientist," he went on, stressing that his original teacher was not above the realm of mortality, but also that his empirical researches, if rigorously supported and meticulously investigated, could offer us truths as important as the law of gravity, or the fact of light being both particle and wave.

Read Thomas Merton, too, and see how this monk of twenty-seven years was forever sharing his little cell not just with the conviction that his life was in and with God, but with perpetual doubts and hesitations, like any lovelorn suitor. What makes his writing speak is the very fact that he never tried to sidestep or cover up his fears, as most of us do, but made his confrontation with them his daily business; the life of spirit, he might have been telling us, is the encounter with the challenges we otherwise avert our eyes from. His sense of what is important and at the core of him and us—he called it "God"— is not a stillness, a fixed idea, a finished product; it is a presence constantly being revealed again, being denied, coming into clearer and more refined and lasting focus. No one laments the absence of a lover—or just of a state of clarity—so powerfully as someone who has known its presence.

If someone asks me about my "spiritual life," I am likely to fall silent—even, perhaps, to go into hiding, because of my sense that whatever is deepest in us is that which can rarely be spoken. It's too enormous or invisible for words. In love, in crisis, in moments of transport we lose words as we pass out of ourselves into a larger presence or identity that has no need of the quibbles or the qualifications that words give body to. I have no fixed spiritual practice, in terms of a single church I attend, a unique teacher I follow, even a one-and-only holy book I refer to; and yet sometimes I think that most of what I do is "spiritual" in that it has to do with trying to do justice to what our clearer moments have taught us; attending to the spirit that friends and circumstances bring me; being aware, always, that there is another world (some would say beyond, some would say within) the world we see and talk about.

I get into a car in Bolivia at twelve thousand feet and notice, at one terrifying moment, that the driver (who has spent the night in New Year's Eve revelry) is hurtling at high speed into the mountainside, having fallen asleep at the wheel. "Why is he trying to kill me?" flashes through my mind, nonsensically. "What have I done to earn such hate?" The car smashes into the rock and overturns. It bounces into a ditch and rolls over again. Just as I think the calamity is over, it hits its side and rolls over once more.

The silence on the deserted mountain road is acute. I get out of the fetal position into which I've reflexively put myself and crawl out through a shuttered window into a scene of blood and glass. The driver slithers out through the front windshield, arm bloody, and wails. A car stops in this desolation and a man steps out to help us (a bishop, as it happens, on his way to deliver a New Year's Mass two hours away). That night, back in my little hotel room, in a foreign town, I call my sweetheart in faraway Japan and hear the consolation of her voice.

Such spiritual moments happen to us often, and are everywhere: It is as if the spirit is divided between the confrontation with death itself, the hunger for the assurances of love, the gratuitous kindness of a stranger met along the road, and the fellow feeling that cataclysm brings us. A reverse epiphany like that has brought me into the presence of immensities as fully as—more rendingly than—the many days I spend on retreat in a monastery, listening to tolling bells in the ringing silence. Spiritual writing may, to mix a metaphor or two, have one hand extended toward heaven (or, other traditions would say, raised to Allah, or pointed toward the fact of our impermanence); but its other hand, the one we recognize, the one that tells us what to do, is extended to another mortal, the bishop's hand of disinterest telling me that, at such moments, he or she is you and pronouns disappear.

For as long as Philip Zaleski has been bringing out these annual anthologies, they have been my daily sustenance in my two-room cell in rural Japan, along with the autumn that sings, in its turning leaves, its first intimations of coldness and the dark, its shining afternoons, of transience (yet speaks, too, in the depthless blue intensity of its skies, of what seems to outlast our changes). Each year I read anew of Islam's lovers longing to draw closer to their Beloved and recall that, in the time of our war against radical Islam, the best-selling poet in America is a thirteenth-century Islamic mystic, Rumi; I read memoirs that tell of a soul's confusion, its furies, its losses; and I find my mind concentrated to the point of dissolution by poems that, in observing the material world, celebrate it and its cycles, even when those cycles take its blessings away from us. The pieces come to me as psalms, cautionary tales, moments of comfort and doubt—and as simple reminders that to believe genuinely in a god is, almost inevitably, to believe in His shadow side, too; His inversion; and our inability to see Him clearly, often.

My heart always leaps when I find a piece in this anthology (as I do every year) that broadens, elevates, or brings to earth our notion of the "spiritual." So often we accord the term a solemn big *S* and assume that it is something that looms over us instead of living inside us. But the truest works tell us that it's in our daily lives, or it is nowhere; it is in our breathing in and out, and in the space where we leap and don't know what we'll find. Whatever is beyond us finds us in those moments when we're beside ourselves. We throw our arms, our hopes around it, and find that, as in any marriage, it comes and goes. Something is always there, but the certainties we seek are not.

It is a pleasure, in this year's volume, to meet certain wise spirits who have sustained many of us for years with their accounts of the travails, the sudden transports of our dailiness; and when I meet Philip Levine drinking his chocolate milk atop a hill in Dearborn, or the electric and radical Richard Rodriguez finding meaning in the baubles of Jerusalem, and all that isn't there, I am reminded of how and why our most soaring celebrant of spirit, Emerson, said he longed to ban the words "spiritual life" and "soul" from all accounts of religious experience. It is storms—wild prophets and a fire raging in the next valley down—that bring Floyd Skloot and Rick Bass to their senses here, and it is a leopard that Rodriguez's guide hopes to see in the desert, and Mary Jo Bang's Dante meets at the midpoint of his life's journey.

"Spiritual writers have a limited purpose," I remember Flannery O'Connor writing in a letter, "and can be very dangerous, I think"; I recall, too, Dostoevsky, in perpetual conflict with his faith, and Kierkegaard, placing us inside a seducer's mind. None of these were figures who could take their belief for granted; all were too self-aware, or exacting in their definition of the spirit, ever, perhaps, to call themselves "spiritual" beings or writers. But the followers of the great religious traditions—those of the Old Age, I'm tempted to say, rather than of the New Age—know that their quest is concerned not with simple affirmations or "positive thinking," but with suffering and reality and conflict and death.

As Thomas Merton wrote, in his *Bread in the Wilderness,* there is an important difference to be drawn between devotional and religious poetry. Devotional works are usually written for and by believers, to comfort them in their faith; religious works are, I think, aimed at every human being. And spiritual works touch on the darkness where we reach for what we know and find it absent. I didn't, I should stress here, select the piece in this book on Peter Matthiessen, by me, on leopards yet again (Philip Zaleski chose it before he decided to ask me to write this introduction); but I'm very glad it's here because Matthiessen happens to be at once a great naturalist and describer of the physical world and a Zen monk, and probably makes no distinction between the two. Spirituality—or happiness or daylight—exists precisely where we didn't think to look for it, he reminds us.

He never saw the snow leopard, and we are all the richer for the loss.

PICO IYER
Nara, Japan/New Camaldoli, California

DIANE ACKERMAN

The Thisness of What Is

FROM *Shambhala Sun*

MOST PEOPLE KNOW THAT SIX MILLION JEWS WERE KILLED DURING World War II, but most don't know that nearly all of the Orthodox community perished. Among them were many who had kept alive an ancient tradition of meditation and mysticism reaching back to the Old Testament world of the prophets. "In my youth," Rabbi Abraham Heschel wrote of his childhood in Warsaw, "there was one thing we did not have to look for, and that was exaltation. Every moment is great, we were taught, every moment is unique."

Heschel was fortunate enough to get out of Warsaw a few months before the war began and escape to the United States, where he became a charismatic teacher, writer, and social activist, renowned for his unflagging sense of wonder. He was among tens of thousands of Jews, aided by friends on "the Aryan side," who managed to escape from the Warsaw ghetto. But some famously chose to stay, including Henryk Goldzmit, a pediatrician and author, and Kalonymous Kalman Shapira, the ghetto's Hasidic rabbi.

Where can one find exaltation in a mutilated world? Shapira's hidden sermons and diary, unearthed after the war, reveal a tigerish struggle with faith, a man wedged between his religious teachings and history. How could anyone reconcile the agony of the Holocaust with Hasidism, a dancing religion that teaches love, joy, and celebration? Yet one of his religious duties was to help heal the suffering of his community—not an easy task given the magnitude of the suffering, and with all the trappings of piety outlawed.

Shapira's Hasidism included transcendent meditation—training the imagination and channeling the emotions to achieve mystical visions. The ideal way, Shapira taught, was to "witness one's thoughts to correct negative habits and character traits." A thought observed will start to weaken, he explained, especially negative thoughts, which he advised students not to enter into but to examine dispassionately. If they sat on the bank watching their stream of thoughts flow by, without being swept away by them, they might achieve a form of meditation called *hashkatah*, silencing the conscious mind. He also preached "sensitization to holiness," a process of discovering the holiness within oneself and the natural world. This included mindfully attending to everyday life, as the eighteenth-century teacher Alexander Susskind had taught: "When you eat and drink, you experience enjoyment and pleasure from the food and drink. Arouse yourself every moment to ask in wonder, 'What is this enjoyment and pleasure? What is it that I am tasting?'"

The etymology of the Hebrew word for prophet, *navi,* combines three processes: *navach,* "to cry out"; *nava,* "to gush or flow"; and *navuv,* "to be hollow." The task of this meditation was to open the heart, to unclog the channel between the infinite and the mortal, and to rise into a state of rapture known as "Great Mind."

"There is only one God," Hasidic teacher Avram Davis writes, "by which we mean the Oneness that subsumes all categories. We might call this Oneness the ocean of reality and everything that swims in it [which abides by] the first teaching of the Ten Commandments, 'there is only one *zot,* thisness.' '*Zot*' is a feminine word for 'this.' The word '*zot*' is itself one of the names of God—the thisness of what is."

. . .

The weak, sick, exhausted, hungry, tortured, and insane all came to Rabbi Shapira for spiritual nourishment, which he combined with leadership and soup kitchens. How did he manage such feats of compassion while staying sane and creative? By stilling the mind and communing with nature. He gathered this teaching "from the world as a whole, from the chirping of the birds, the mooing of the cows, from the voices and tumult of human beings; from all these one hears the voice of God. . . ."

All our senses feed the brain, and if it dieted mainly on cruelty and suffering, how could it remain healthy? Rabbi Shapira's message was that even in the ghetto, common people, not just ascetics or rabbis, could temper their suffering through meditation.

It's especially poignant that he chose for meditative practice the beauty of nature, because for most people in the ghetto nature lived only in memory—no parks, birds, or greenery existed in the ghetto—and they suffered the loss of nature like a phantom limb pain, an amputation that scrambled the body's rhythms, starved the senses, and made basic ideas about the world impossible for children to fathom. As one ghetto inhabitant wrote:

> In the ghetto, a mother is trying to explain to her child the concept of distance. Distance, she says, "is more than our Lezno Street. It is an open field, and a field is a large area where the grass grows, or ears of corn, and when one is standing in its midst, one does not see its beginning or its end. Distance is so large and open and empty that the sky and the earth meet there. . . . [Distance is] a continuous journey for many hours and sometimes for days and nights, in a train or a car, and perhaps aboard an airplane. . . . The railway train breathes and puffs and swallows lots of coal, like the ones pictured in your book, but is real, and the sea is a huge and real bath where the waves rise and fall in an

endless game. And these forests are trees, trees like those in Karmelicka Street and Nowolipie, so many trees one cannot count them. They are strong and upright, with crowns of green leaves, and the forest is full of such trees, trees as far as the eye can see and full of leaves and bushes and the song of birds.

Before annihilation comes an exile from nature, and then it is only through wonder and transcendence, the ghetto rabbi taught, that one could combat the psychic disintegration of everyday life.

Somewhere along the line, Shapira acquired medical training, and people from all over Poland made pilgrimages to him for physical and spiritual healing. During the war, he suffered the same torment, fear, pain, and loss as other residents of the ghetto, and came to know the agony of howitzers bombarding friends and loved ones with shrapnel—in one week, he lost his mother, only son, daughter-in-law, and sister-in-law. His beloved wife of many years, whom he regarded as a soul mate (he delighted in telling people how, on at least one occasion, she finished writing his sermon), fell ill and died.

Finding scope for the mind while the body remained enslaved, that was the challenge. Nowhere in his writings does one read the factual reality of life for Jews in occupied Poland, nor even the words "Nazi" or "German." Instead, his mission was compassion—"to project the supernatural powers of kindness into the realm of speech, so that they might take on concrete, specific form."

Today most of us, though not all, have the luxury of experiencing merely mild chronic stress, an ensemble of real and imaginary worries that spike the road of everyday life with tiny aggravating tacks. But for four years, people in the Warsaw ghetto endured both acute and chronic stress, with its suite of body-killers from diabetes and heart disease to the erosion of neurons from sheer overfiring.

Typically, high stress saps energy, slows thinking, depresses the psyche, and rachets up one's base level of fear and anxiety. Common antidotes are numbing one's ability to feel, selective forgetting, or imaginative escapes (sometimes to the striped mesas of psychosis). Another antidote is stilling the mind.

Even when saturated by more suffering than we bipeds were ever meant to feel, by paying deep attention the brain enters a state of vigorous calm, especially if one can meditate on joy, compassion, or gratitude. In the ghetto, meditation helped by tugging the mind from its sorrow and limiting rumination, and by giving practitioners a sense of agency that was scarce, allowing them to take charge of their own well-being and to create moments of tranquility, wonder, and occasionally something even rarer: pleasure. This cloud ride through suffering resonates strikingly with the Buddhist dictum of accepting life just as it is, without grasping at elsewheres or elsewhens, without judgment, viewing moment to moment as a changing flux of sensations.

Another man who, like Rabbi Shapira, chose to stay when offered escape, was pediatrician Henryk Goldzmit (pen name: Janusz Korczak), who wrote autobiographical novels, and books for parents and teachers with such titles as *How to Love a Child* and *The Child's Right to Respect*. To the amazement of his fans and disciples, Korczak abandoned both his literary and medical careers in 1912 to found a progressive orphanage for one hundred boys and girls, ages seven to fourteen, at 92 Krochmalna Street in Warsaw. There, with wit, imagination, and self-deprecating humor, he devoted himself to a "children's republic," complete with its own parliament, newspaper, and court system. Instead of punching one another, children learned to yell, "I'll sue you!" And every Saturday morning, court cases were judged by five children who weren't being sued that week. All rulings rested on Korczak's "Code of Laws," the first one hundred of which parsed forgiveness. He once confided to a friend, "I am a doctor by training, a pedagogue by chance, a writer by passion, and a psychologist by necessity."

In 1940, when Jews were ordered into the ghetto, the orphanage moved to an abandoned businessman's club in the "district of the damned," as he described it in a diary written on blue rice-paper pages that he filled with details of daily life in the orphanage, imaginative forays, philosophical contemplations, and soul-searching. It's the reliquary of an impossible predicament, revealing "how a spiritual and moral man struggled to shield innocent children from the atrocities of the adult world during one of history's darkest times." Reportedly shy and awkward with adults, he created an ideal republic with the orphans who called him "Pan Doctor."

At night, lying on his infirmary cot, with remnants of vodka and black bread tucked under his bed, he'd escape to his own private planet, Ro, where an imaginary astronomer friend, Zi, had finally succeeded in building a machine to convert radiant sunlight into moral strength. Using it to waft peace throughout the universe, Zi complained that it worked everywhere except on "that restless spark, Planet Earth," and they debated whether Zi should destroy bloody warmongering Earth, with Doctor Pan pleading for compassion given the planet's youth.

His blue pages stitched together sensations, fancies, and marauding ideas alike, but he didn't relate sinister ghetto events, for example, the deportations to the death camps that began on July 22, 1942, his sixty-fourth birthday. Instead of all the clangor and mayhem on that day, he wrote only of "a marvellous big moon" shining above the destitute in that unfortunate, insane quarter.

By then, as photographs show, his goatee and mustache had grayed, bags terraced beneath intense, dark eyes, and though he often endured "adhesions, aches, ruptures, scars," he refused to escape from the ghetto, despite many offers of help from disciples on the Aryan side. It creased him to hear the starving and suffering children compare their ills "like old people in a sanitarium," he wrote in his diary. They needed ways to transcend pain, and so he encouraged prayers like this one: "Thank you, Merciful Lord, for having arranged to provide flowers with fragrance, glow worms with their glow, and make the stars in the sky sparkle." By example, he taught them the mental salve of mindful chores, like the slow, attentive picking up of bowls, spoons, and plates after a meal:

> When I collect the dishes myself, I can see the cracked plates, the bent spoons, the scratches on the bowls. . . . I can see how the careless diners throw about, partly in a quasi-aristocratic and partly in a churlish manner, the spoons, knives, the salt shakers and cups. . . . Sometimes I watch how the extras are distributed and who sits next to whom. And I get some ideas. For if I do something, I never do it thoughtlessly. The waiter's job is of great use to me, it's pleasant and interesting.

Anticipating their calamity and fright when deportation day came, on August 6, 1942, he joined the children aboard the train bound for Treblinka, because, he said simply, he knew his presence would calm them. A photograph taken at the Umschlagplatz shows him marching, hatless, in military boots, hand in hand with several children, while 192 other children and 10 staff members follow, four abreast, escorted by German soldiers. Silently, Korczak and the children boarded red boxcars not much larger than chicken coops, usually stuffed with 75 vertical adults, though all the children easily fit.

In 1971, the Russians named a newly discovered asteroid after him, 2163 Korczak, but maybe they should have named it Ro, the planet he dreamed of. The Poles claim Korczak as a martyr, and the Israelis revere him as one of the Thirty-Six Just Men, whose pure souls make possible the world's salvation. According to legend, these few alone, through their good hearts and good deeds, keep the too-wicked world from being destroyed. For their sake, all of humanity is spared. The legend says that they are ordinary people, not flawless or magical, and that most of them remain unrecognized throughout their lives, while they choose to perpetuate goodness, even in the midst of inferno.

MARY JO BANG

Dante's The Inferno, Canto I:
A New Translation

FROM *New Letters*

Stopped mid-motion in the middle
Of what we call a life, I looked up and saw no sky—
Only a dense cage of leaf, tree, and twig. I was lost.

It's difficult to describe a forest:
Savage, arduous, extreme in its extremity.
I think and the facts come back, then the fear comes back.

Death, I think, can only be slightly more bitter.
Good comes from bad but before getting there,
I have to describe in detail what else I saw.

I can't say for certain how I entered it;
I must have become so tired
I ended up following a bad path.

The wooded valley I'd just plodded through
In heart-rending terror,
Dead-ended at the foot of a hill.

I looked up and saw the sun
Was on the body of the hill's high spot:
A torch for the path to the lost.

The lake of fear that had filled my heart
In the night I had passed in such sadness,
Calmed somewhat when I saw it.

Like someone breathless after an escape
From deep water who stands at the side of the pool
And looks back on the danger and trail of close calls,

That's how I looked back—my mind a stopped top
In the middle of a turn—for a glimpse of where I'd been,
A place no one has ever survived alive.

I rested for a while and then
Started up the sandy slope. My willful left foot rose
While the right foot trailed behind.

Suddenly, at the foot of a rise, just where the hill begins
Its steep incline—I saw a mottled leopard,
Light, agile, and very fast.

It shadowed the future so closely, that it kept blocking the way
And time and again I thought I should go back
And retrace my steps to where I'd been.

It was daybreak, the sun in the sign of Aries, the same
As it was when the first clock started, the spring
Set by the hand of a love supreme

Who set in motion all beautiful things. All this
Disarmed my fear of the beast with the freckled coat.
I was reassured by the fact of morning

And the hint of spring—
But the promise hollowed
When I caught sight of nothing less than a lion.

He seemed to be dead-set against me, head high
And ravished with hunger. It made not only me
But even the air around him seem nervous.

And after him, a she-wolf appeared, her frame so emaciated
Her body seemed defined by the cravings
That had caused so many to live in misery.

Looking at her bitch-kitty face,
I felt a sense of solid defeat, and lost sight of the hope
Of climbing any higher.

Like one who at a casino wheel whispers sweet nothings
To his winnings but when it's his turn to lose whimpers,
"How did we come to this?" and wrings his hands,

So was I, just like that sad sack, as the impossible beast
Inch by inch, drove me back into the shadows
Where the sun keeps a stopper in its mouth.

I was rushing backward into ruin
When I saw one whom, given I'd been alone for so long,
Seemed no more than a mirage.

There on that waste land, I called out,
"Take pity on me, please, whatever you are,
Ghost-man or tangible man."

"I was once a man," he said, "but now I'm not.
Both my parents, both Lombardi, were born
In Mantua. I was born late in the day

Of Julio Caesar and lived in Rome under the sword
Of good Augustus, back when the gods were false
And told sweet-talking lies.

I was a poet, singing songs of Aeneus—son
Of honest Anchises—who found his way back by boat
From Troy after vain Ilium had been burned to black ash.

But you, why are you returning to this tedious plain?
Why not climb the peaked mountain
Ahead of you. It's the ultimate end and means of all pleasure."

I said, "You're Virgil, aren't you? You're that rainmaker
Who creates a torrent of speech that turns into a riptide."
Then I felt bashful and hung my head.

"The best and the brightest in the class
Of poets, a far-famed bell, I read you and loved you and hope
That what I learned from you then will now serve me well.

First of all the authors and Master of me, I borrowed from you
And to you I owe any inkling of the passing success
I've been lucky enough to accrue.

Can you see the beast I had to flee? Can you save me
From her? You, Mr. Ubermensch, you Mr. Man
Of the World. I'm trembling with fear."

When he saw that I was now in tears, he said,
"In that case, you must leave this rock
And no water and the sandy road.

The cat that drove you back and made you cry
Ends the life to any who try
To pass her on their way through.

She's insane and insatiable. She eats more
And that just makes her more malignant with craving.
She kills all she comes in contact with. All with whom she comes.

She takes many to her bed and many more are coming
Until the day the big dog comes
And tracks her down and dastardly does her in.

The dog doesn't need property or money but lives on
Knowledge, love, and truth. He'll come at the end of the year
When Castor and Pollux arrive dressed in matching felt caps.

He'll save a once-regal country, glimpsed in the distance
Of time, and once fought for by those who died
Displaying great gallantry, and those who were gorgeously loyal.

He'll search for her in this city and that, chasing the bitch
Back to the hole where Envy first undid her chain and choker
And pointed her to the brick road that beelines into the world.

As we go forward from here, stay at all times behind me,
And I'll play the part of your guide. It's my plan
To lead you through a place never-ending, i.e., eternal

Hell, where you'll hear the worst kind of wailing,
See the ageless shades writhing in pain,
Sense their vain request for a second death.

After that, you'll see those who are happy
In the heat of the fire because they hope at some point
To pursue the path to Purgatory and so achieve a Bible clerk's
      bliss.

To those, if that's where you would go, up and farther up,
You'll need another escort, one more honored
Than I am. When I leave you, I'll leave you

With her. I can't enter the city of the Emperor,
So says He, since I was pagan and outside His unbending laws.
      He says
I'm smudged by Adam's ink and ergo must live in Limbo.

He reigns in all parts of the empire.
His city is there; so is His chair, poised at the edge of heaven.
Happy are those He asks in."

And I said to him, "Poet, I beg of you,
By the God you never knew, help me out of this Denmark
Which threatens to go from bad to worse. Lead me

To where you just mentioned, so I can see the door
Of Purgatory and meet the angel at the Gate and, along the way,
See the dolorous souls who are designated DAMNED."

Then he set out, and I at his back.

RICK BASS

Fire Season

FROM *Portland*

THE FIRE IS JUST ONE VALLEY AWAY, AND COMING WITH THE WIND, we just don't know quite when. But fires or not, we're cresting the back side of summer and now passing berry season; the year's berries must still be gathered, if we are to have huckleberry jam in the coming year, and pancakes and muffins and milkshakes; if we are to have huckleberries on our ice cream; if we are to prepare huckleberry glazes for the grilled breasts of wild duck.

Will the berries have a slight taste of woodsmoke in them this year?

I sit in the middle of a rich huckleberry patch and pluck berries contentedly, falling quickly into that daydreaming lull, the satisfied trance that fills me, with its deeper echoes of older times, as if I am the vessel.

I pick for an hour, suspended in this lovely August grace, before I discern the change coming. I can feel the drop in barometric pressure almost as violently as when a plane in flight bumps and sags suddenly, pitching silverware and playing cards to the floor in a clatter. The wind of the coming storm is not yet here, but I can see it, dark in the distance. I can see the wall of dust and smoke it is pushing ahead of it, like a piston; and up on my berry mountain, in that compressing dead-air space caught between the approaching storm and the mountain, I can feel the vacuum that is being created, and it is as unsettling a feeling, physically and emotionally and even spiritually, as was the berry-picking of only a few minutes ago a settled and peaceful feeling.

Next I hear the wind, as the advancing plume of it slides in over the air sandwiched below—the air in which I am still sitting, trying to pick huckleberries, trying to gather up the last of the summer's harvest, sensing or suspecting somehow that this might be my last leisure-day in the woods for a while, my last leisure-hour—and as that first-approaching, upper tongue of wind slides in across the mountain, just above the mountain, it passes through the upper reaches of the Swiss-cheese excavations from all the many woodpeckers that have riddled the blackened, towering spars left over from the last fire, six years ago, through the fire-gnawed Rorschach shapes, the strange gaps and apertures left in the husks of those old tree trunks. The result is a kind of music like none I have ever heard before, somehow both somber and joyous, and intensely powerful, fueled by more wind than all the human lungs in the world could ever provide, and it is singing right here, right now, on this mountain, and I am in the center of it, and part of me is not frightened; and I keep picking berries, though now in the distance I can see tremendous bolts of lightning, and can hear the cannonade of thunder. There is no rain. The air is as void of moisture as a laundered sheet taken crisp and hot from the dryer.

The wind is still above me, and as it moans through those hollow burned-tree keyholes and pipe-flutes, it bangs and rattles also against the taut hollow hides of the larger snags and spars, creating a deep drumming resonance to accompany all the strange organ-pipe howling, which from a distance sounds like a thousand calliopes playing for some demented, wonderful, terrifying circus—though right here where I am, beneath and amidst the drumming and the howling, it sounds like tremendously amplified symphony music, a thousand of the world's largest chamber orchestras vying to play either their own version of Mozart's *Requiem,* and now the wind-beneath-the-wind is reaching me, splashing in over me like dry waves at the ocean, the wind coming so strong that when I stand up, I can lean downhill into it without falling down, suspended like a hawk, or a heavy kite, and this lower wind is carrying pine needles and grit, which stings my face and arms and bare legs, and I have to turn my face to shield my eyes against it, and I know more than I have ever known that there is no hand of mankind, no technology or science or knowledge, or management directives, that can influence this breath of a living, restless earth: And again I feel tiny, puny, even invisible, and it is exhilarating, and I am reminded intensely of what an astounding privilege it is to be alive; of how rare the circumstances are that conspire to bring life.

I can see the lightning walking up the valley from the south, striding toward me, and I hurry down the mountain, through the stinging needles and grit, with entire tree limbs torn loose from the canopy and floating feathery, lichen-laden, through the sky. Now entire treetops are snapping off occasionally, and being launched into the air a short distance, like failed rockets. Farther down the mountain, I can hear still more tree trunks snapping, a sound like cannons.

It seems to me that the earth beneath my feet is buzzing or trembling, and the sky is plum-colored now, but still there is no rain, only wind and fire, and boiling clouds of dust.

I hurry through the tangle of old blowdown, old fire-char and new berry bush, new green saplings, running as a deer might run, into the wind, hoping to weave my way unscathed through that maze of falling branches, and once I'm back at the truck, and driving down the logging road, hoping that no trees fall across the road, I'm disoriented by the way the entire forest around me seems to be waving like nothing more substantial than the undersea fronds of kelp or reed-grass; or like the thick hair on the back of an animal's back, pressing flat and then swirling in the wind.

What a revelation it is, to have one's perceptions, one's universe, so startlingly reordered, so corrected or amplified. Yes, the forests of immense trees are powerful and awe-inspiring, but yes, even they, even they, are tiny beneath these gusts of breath from a living, restless world.

And once I'm home, my daughters and I go out onto the porch and watch the lichens and limbs continue to sail through the sky, and to gaze at the strangely glowing sky, a greenish hurricane-sky, and to watch the streaks of lightning, and to count, with thumping hearts, the number of seconds before we hear each crack of thunder: And still there is no rain, not even a little spit of it, and like a beggar or a miser or even a rich man gone broke, I find myself remembering the blizzard from last New Year's Eve, and the heavy, wet late snows in April. I'm hoping that enough moisture has been retained to hold back some of the fire, even as I understand more clearly than ever that the fire must come, that it is no different from the wind or snow itself, that it has shaped and continues to shape, this landscape: that it is its own kind of season, and that the time for it has arrived; that in this regard it is as unstoppable as the wind and rain. It's simply, or not-so-simply, a part of the world out here; it helped make the world out here. How strange to think that the fire helped sculpt and create the very thing it occasionally consumes. What an amazing thing, to stand just out of harm's way, at the edge of a valley, and watch it pass through, as it always has, and always will.

DAVID BERLINSKI

The God of the Gaps

FROM *Commentary*

THE IDEA THAT HUMAN BEINGS HAVE BEEN ENDOWED WITH POWERS
and properties not found elsewhere in the animal kingdom—or, so
far as we can tell, in the universe—arises from a simple impulse: Just
look around. It is an impulse that handily survives the fraternal invi-
tation to consider the great apes. The apes are, after all, behind the
bars of their cages, and we are not. Eager for the experiments to be-
gin, they are also impatient for their food to be served, and they
seem impatient for little else. After undergoing years of punishing
trials at the hands of determined clinicians, a few have been taught
the rudiments of various primitive symbol systems. Having been
given the gift of language, they have nothing to say. When two sim-
ian prodigies meet, they fling their placards at each other.

More is expected, but more is rarely forthcoming. Experiments—
and they are exquisite—conducted by Dorothy Cheney and Robert
Seyfarth indicate that like other mammals, baboons have a rich in-
ner world. Simian social structures are often intricate. Chimpanzees,
bonobos, and gorillas reason; they form plans; they have preferences;
they are cunning; they have passions and desires; and they suffer. In
much of this, we see ourselves. But beyond what we have in com-
mon with the apes, we have nothing in common, and while the
similarities are interesting, the differences are profound.

If human beings are as human beings think they are, then questions arise about *what* they are, and so do responses. These responses are ancient. They have arisen spontaneously in every culture. They have seemed to men and women the obvious conclusions to be drawn from just looking around. Accordingly, an enormous amount of intellectual effort has been invested in persuading men and women *not* to look around.

"With all deference to the sensibilities of religious people, the idea that man was created in the image of God can surely be put aside." Thus stated *Nature* magazine in a recent editorial. As for those unwilling to put their "sensibilities" aside, the scientific community has concluded that they are afflicted by a form of intellectual ingratitude. After all, the same editorial insists, "The idea that human minds are the product of evolution is unassailable fact."

It is remarkable how widespread our ingratitude really is, and also how far back it goes.

II

Together with Charles Darwin, Alfred Wallace created the modern theory of evolution. He has been unjustly neglected by history—perhaps because, shortly after conceiving his theory, he came to doubt its veracity. Darwin, too, had his doubts; no one reading *On the Origin of Species* can miss its note of moral anxiety. But Darwin's doubts arose because, in considering his theory's implications, he feared it might be true. With Wallace, it was the other way around. Considering its implications, he suspected the theory might be false.

In an essay entitled "Sir Charles Lyell on Geological Climates and the Origin of Species" (1869), Wallace outlined his sense that evolution was inadequate to explain certain obvious features of the human race. The essay is of great importance. It marks a falling-away in faith on the part of a sensitive biologist previously devoted to ideas he himself introduced.

Certain of our "physical characteristics," Wallace observes in this essay, "are not explicable on the theory of variation and survival of the fittest"—the criteria of Darwinian natural selection. These characteristics include the human brain, the organs of speech and articulation, the human hand, and the external human form with its upright posture and bipedal gait. Thus, only human beings can rotate their thumbs and ring fingers in what is called "ulnar opposition" in order to achieve a grip, a grasp, and a degree of torque denied to any of the great apes. So, too, with the other items on Wallace's list. What remains is evolutionary fantasy, of the sort in which the bipedal gait is assigned to an unrecoverable ancestor wishing to peer (or pee) over tall savannah grasses.

It is with respect to the human mind that Wallace's argument gathers real force. Do we understand why, alone among the animals, human beings have acquired language? Or a refined and delicate moral system? Or art, architecture, music, dance, or mathematics? This is a severely abbreviated list. The body of world literature and philosophy offers an extended commentary on human nature, yet over the course of more than four thousand years it has not exhausted its mysteries.

And here is the curious thing. Wallace writes that, among human beings, there is no evident distinction between the mental powers of the most primitive and the most advanced. Raised in today's England instead of the Ecuadoran Amazon, a native child of the head-hunting Jívaro tribe, otherwise destined for a life loping through the jungle, would learn to speak perfect English and upon graduation from Oxford or Cambridge would enjoy the double advantage of a modern intellectual worldview and a valuable ethnic heritage. He might become a mathematician. Or, for all anyone knows, he might find himself a commentator on the BBC, lucidly defending the cultural value of head-hunting in the Ecuadoran jungle.

From this manner of observation it follows, Wallace argued, that characteristic human abilities must be latent in primitive man, existing somehow as an unopened gift—the entryway to a world that primitive man himself does not possess and would not recognize. But the idea that a biological species might possess latent powers makes no sense in Darwinian terms. It suggests the forbidden doctrine that evolutionary advantages were front-loaded, far away and long ago. It is in conflict with the Darwinian principle that just as useful genes are selected for cultivation and advancement, useless genes are subject to negative selection pressure and must therefore drain away into the sands of time.

Wallace identified a frank conflict between his own theory and what seemed to him to be obvious facts about the solidity and unchangeability of human nature. That conflict persists; it has not been resolved.

III

No one doubts that human beings now alive are connected to human beings who lived thousands of years ago. To look at Paleolithic cave drawings is to understand that the graphic arts have not changed radically in twelve thousand years. And no one doubts that human beings are connected to the rest of the animal kingdom. It is rather more difficult, however, to take what no one doubts and fashion from it an effective defense of the thesis that human beings are nothing but the living record of a random and extended evolutionary process. That requires a disciplined commitment to a point of view that owes nothing to the sciences, however loosely construed, and astonishingly little to the evidence.

Why, then, has the kinship between human beings and the apes been so avidly promoted in contemporary culture, and not just as an "unassailable fact" but as a positive moral virtue?

The reason is that it functions as a hedge against religious belief, in particular the belief in man's uniqueness. "Chimps and gorillas have long been the battleground of our search of uniqueness," wrote the late Stephen Jay Gould,

> for if we could establish an unambiguous distinction—of kind rather than degree—between ourselves and our closest relatives, we might gain the justification long sought for our cosmic arrogance.

Following Gould, whose "cool authentic voice" he finds irresistible, Christopher Hitchens has likewise declared against our cosmic arrogance and in favor of mere cosmic happenstance. "If the numberless evolutions from the Cambrian period could be recorded and 'rewound,'" Hitchens writes in *God Is Not Great*, "and the tape played again, he [Gould] established there was no certainty it would come out the same way."

Of course, having no access to the tape of life, Gould established nothing of the sort. Yet so committed is Hitchens to his tautology that he repeats it. Had an early vertebrate named Pakaia not survived, he reports in amazement, its survivors would also not have survived. One waits breathlessly for Hitchens to enlarge upon these exercises in just-so logic to encompass nonlinear dynamics and Heisenberg's uncertainty principle, totems that in his "scientific" defense of atheism he waves at the reader like a majestic frond.

WHEN OUR cosmic arrogance is not being dismissed as religious prejudice, it is dismissed as a celebration of mere trivialities. Writing about "our inner ape," the zoologist Frans de Waal is concerned to demonstrate "how much [they] resemble us and how much we resemble them." How much, then? De Waal's answer: "If an extraterrestrial were to visit Earth, he would have a hard time seeing most of the differences we treasure between ourselves and the apes."

Well, yes. If a fish were thoughtfully to consider the matter, it might have a hard time determining the differences we treasure between Al Gore and a sperm whale: both of them are large, and one of them is streamlined. But suppose the fish wanted a more detailed demonstration. Then it might profitably consult a fundamental paper on the subject published in *Science* in 1975. In it, M. C. King and A. C. Wilson provided for the first time an estimate of the degree of similarity between the human and the chimpanzee genome.

Far more than was thought possible, King and Wilson assert, human beings and chimpanzees do share the greater part of their respective genomes. But should we therefore conclude that if our genomes match up so nicely, we must *be* apes? In the second section of their paper, King and Wilson expound the deficiencies of that idea:

> Although humans and chimpanzees are rather similar in the structure of thorax and arms, they differ substantially not only in brain size but also in the anatomy of the pelvis, foot, and jaw, as well as in relative lengths of limbs and digits. Humans and chimpanzees also differ significantly in many other anatomical respects, to the extent that nearly every bone in the body of a chimpanzee is readily distinguishable in shape and size from its human counterpart. Associated with these anatomical differences there are, of course, major differences in posture, mode of locomotion, methods of procuring food, and means of communication. Because of these major differences in anatomy and way of life, biologists place the two species not just in separate genera but in separate families.

There is nothing in this that was not evident to Alfred Wallace—or to any student of comparative anatomy. King and Wilson go on to suggest that the morphological and behavioral differences between humans and the apes, if they are not due to variations between their respective genomes, must be due to variations in their genomic regulatory systems. These control the activities of the various genes by telling them when to sound off and when to shut up. They are of an astonishing complexity, if only because they themselves require regulation. Higher-order regulation in turn involves higher-order codes beyond the genetic code, and these codes then require their own regulation. Even the simplest cell involves an intricate, never-ending cascade of control and coordination of a sort never seen in the physical world.

It is entirely safe to assign the differences between human beings and the apes to their regulatory systems. But nothing is known about the evolutionary emergence of those systems, and we cannot describe them with any clarity. Whatever the source of the human distinction, however, its existence is obvious, and when it is carelessly denied, the result is a characteristic form of inanity.

Thus, an English professor named Jonathan Gottschall has recounted his experience reading Homer's *Iliad* while under the influence of Desmond Morris's *The Naked Ape*. "[T]his time around," Gottshall writes,

> I . . . experienced the *Iliad* as a drama of naked apes—
> strutting, preening, fighting, and bellowing their power in
> fierce competition for social dominance, beautiful women,
> and material resources.

Actually, social dominance and material resources are not quite to the point:

> Intense competition between great apes, as described both
> by Homer and by primatologists, frequently boils down to
> precisely the same thing: access to females.

The governing words in this quotation are "boils down." What is essential about the boiling process is not what has been distilled but what has evaporated—namely, everything that is of interest in the *Iliad*.

For those purporting to be worried about the cosmic arrogance of human beings, what this suggests is an obvious counsel of humility. Before putting aside so flippantly "the idea that man was created in the image of God," they might first consider the ideas they propose to champion in its place.

IV

"In much the same way as prophets and seers and great theologians seem to have died out," Christopher Hitchens claims in *God Is Not Great*, "so the age of miracles seems to lie somewhere in our past."

Prophets and seers? I would have thought that Einstein, Bohr, Gödel, Schrödinger, Heisenberg, Dirac, and even Richard Feynman were all, in their own way, prophets and seers.

And miracles? The word seems to engender its own current of contempt. If one demands of a miracle that it violate the inviolable, there can be, by definition, no miracles. Surely this is too infantile a victory to afford even Christopher Hitchens a sense of satisfaction; he does not deign to debate the proposition that what could not be cannot be.

A miracle is exactly what it seems: an event offering access to the divine. And if this is what miracles are, whether they are seen will always be contingent on who is looking.

The miracles of religious tradition are historical. They reflect the power the ancient Hebrews brought to bear on their experiences. They did what they could, they saw what they could see. But we have other powers. We are the heirs to a magnificent scientific tradition. We can see farther than men whose horizons were bounded by the burning desert.

In a remark now famous, Feynman observed with respect to quantum electrodynamics that its control over the natural world is so accurate that in measuring the distance from New York to Los Angeles, theory and experiment would diverge by less than the width of a human hair. Einstein's theory of general relativity is in some respects equally accurate. We cannot account for these unearthly results. The laws of nature neither explain themselves nor predict their success. We have no reason to expect such gifts, and if we have come to expect them, that is only because, as the saints have always warned, we expect far more than we deserve.

Foremost among the undeserving are evolutionary dogmatists of the brand represented by Richard Dawkins and Daniel Dennett and marketed by their apostle Hitchens. Although theirs is not an undertaking notable for imaginativeness, it does seem to have conjured up a kind of god. Unlike the God of old, who ruled over everything, this god rules over lapses in argument or evidence. He is a presiding god, but with limited administrative functions. With gaps in view, he undertakes the specialized activity of incarnating himself as a stopgap. He may be called the god of the gaps.

As a rhetorical contrivance, the god of the gaps makes his effect contingent on a specific assumption: Whatever the gaps, they *will* in the course of scientific research be filled. It is an assumption both intellectually primitive and morally abhorrent—primitive because it reflects an absence of curiosity, and abhorrent because it assigns to our intellectual future a degree of authority alien to human experience.

The truth is otherwise: Western science has indeed proceeded by filling gaps, but in filling them it has created gaps all over again. The process is inexhaustible. Einstein created the special theory of relativity to accommodate certain anomalies in the interpretation of Clerk Maxwell's theory of the electromagnetic field. Special relativity led directly to general relativity. But general relativity is inconsistent with quantum mechanics. Understanding has improved, but within the physical sciences, anomalies have grown great, and what is more, anomalies have grown great because understanding has improved.

The god of the gaps? Why not say with equal authority that, for all we know, it is the God of old who continues to preside over the bent world with His accustomed fearsome majesty, and that He has chosen to draw the curtain on His own magnificence at precisely the place where general relativity and quantum mechanics should have met but do not touch? Whether gaps in our understanding reveal nothing more than the god of the gaps or nothing less than the God of old is hardly a matter open to rational debate.

This, however, has hardly prevented peevish displays of vanity on the part of scientists. In considering the possibility that the facts of biology might suggest an intelligent designer—which surely they do, even if they do not prove the case—the Darwinian biologist Emile Zuckerkandl has found it difficult to contain his indignation. Writing in the journal *Gene,* he overflows with epithets:

> The intellectual virus named "intelligent design" . . . certainly is a problem in the country. . . . [T]he "creationists" . . . have decided some years ago . . . to dress up in academic gear and to present themselves as scholars. . . . [T]hey try to foster on society . . . some enterprising superghost. The "intelligent designers" theme song . . . guided by a little angel . . . medieval in concept . . . an intellectually dangerous condition . . . the divine jumping disease. . . . Feeding like leeches on irrational beliefs . . . offensive little swarms of insects . . . must be taken care of by spraying biological knowledge. . . .

And so forth. For his part, Daniel Dennett answers the proponents of intelligent design thusly:

> Contemporary biology has demonstrated *beyond all reasonable doubt* that natural selection—the process in which reproducing entities must compete for finite resources and thereby engage in a tournament of blind trial and error from which improvements *automatically* emerge—has the power to generate breathtakingly ingenious designs. (Emphasis added)

The self-confidence here is wonderful. Nothing in the physical sciences, it should go without saying, has been demonstrated beyond "all reasonable doubt." The phrase belongs to a court of law. As for the thesis that improvements in life appear "automatically," it represents nothing more than Daniel Dennett's conviction that living systems are like elevators: If their buttons are pushed, they go up. Or down, as the case may be. Although Darwin's theory is very often compared favorably with the great theories of mathematical physics, on the grounds that evolution is, in the hackneyed phrase, as well established as gravity, very few physicists have been heard observing that gravity is as well established as evolution. They know better, and they are not stupid.

Nor are all biologists. They know better, too. The greater part of the debate over Darwin's theory is not in service to the facts, or to the theory. The facts are what they have always been: unforthcoming. And the theory is what it always was: unpersuasive. "Darwin?" a Nobel laureate in biology once remarked to me over his bifocals. "That's just the party line."

The god of the gaps occupies a very considerable comfort zone in biology. We know better than we ever did that a great many aspects of biological behavior are innate. They arise in each organism. They are a part of its nature. This is certainly true of human beings. The point has been made with great force by the linguist Noam Chomsky. Just as children are not taught to walk, they are not taught to speak. The environment serves only to trigger an innate program for maturation. Human language is the very expression of human nature.

This is widely seen as offering dramatic confirmation of Darwinian evolution. It is easy to see why. What is "innate" in an organism, so it is claimed, reflects its genetic endowment, and its genetic endowment reflects the long process in which random variations were sifted by a stern and unforgiving environment. If we are born with the ability to acquire a natural language, the gift lies within our genes and our genes lie within the shifting tides of time.

The view is common; it is also incoherent. What is both interesting and innate in an organism cannot be explained in terms of its genetic endowment. If the concept of a gene has any content at all, it lies entirely within the context of molecular biology and biochemistry. The gene is a chemical, a part of the molecule deoxyribonucleic acid, or DNA. Its function is straightforward: It specifies the proteins needed by a living organism, and it specifies them by means of a remarkably complicated system of translation and transcription. To speak clearly of the genetic endowment of an organism is to speak *only* of the passage from one chemical structure to another, and nothing more.

But to speak of the genetic endowment of an organism in terms that answer any interesting question *about* the organism is to go quite beyond the coordination of chemicals. It is to speak of what an organism does, how it reacts, what plans it makes, and how it executes them; it is to assign to a biological creature precisely the properties always assigned to such creatures: intention, desire, volition, need, passion, curiosity, despair, boredom, rage.

These properties of a living system cannot be easily seen as the consequences of any chemical reaction. It would be like suggesting that a tendency toward kleptomania follows the dissociation of water into hydrogen and oxygen. If this were so—research is required!—

it would represent a connection that we do not understand and cannot grasp. The gap is too great. When Richard Dawkins observes that genes "*created* us, body and mind" (emphasis added), he is appealing essentially to a magical connection. There is nothing in any precise concept of the gene that allows a set of biochemicals to create anything at all. If no precise concept of the gene is at issue, the idea that we are created by our genes, body and mind, represents a far less plausible thesis than the correlative doctrine that we are created by our Maker, body and mind.

V

"The more comprehensible the universe becomes," the physicist Steven Weinberg has written, "the more it also seems pointless." This has struck many of his readers as an ungenerous attitude, and Weinberg has subsequently made every effort to cover his comment in confusion, chiefly by affirming that he considers the universe a fine place after all.

My sympathies are with the sour and unregenerate Weinberg. The arena of the elementary particles—his arena—*is* rather a depressing place, and if it resembles anything at all, it resembles a fluorescent-lit bowling alley as seen from the interstate highway, tiny stick figures in striped bowling shirts jerking up and down in the humid night.

What *is* its point?

We humans seem to live our lives in perfect indifference to the Standard Model of particle physics. Over *there,* fields are pregnant with latent energy, particles flicker into existence and disappear, things are entangled, and no one can quite tell what is possible and what is actual, what is here and what is there, what is now and what was then. Solid forms give way. Nothing is stable. Great impassive symmetries are in control, as vacant and unchanging as the eye of Vishnu. Where they come from, no one knows. Time and space contract into some sort of agitated quantum foam. Nothing is continuous. Nothing stays the same for long—except the electrons, and they are identical, like porcelain Chinese soldiers. A pointless frenzy prevails throughout.

Over *here,* thank God, space and time are stable and continuous. Matter is what it is, and energy is what it does. There are solid and enduring shapes and forms. The sun is largely the same sun now that it was four thousand years ago when it baked the Egyptian deserts. Changes appear slowly, but even when rapid they appear in stable patterns. There is dazzling variety throughout. The great river of time flows forward. We anticipate the future, but we remember the past. We begin knowing that we will end.

The god of the gaps may now be invited to comment—strictly as an outside observer, of course. He is addressing us, and this is what he has to say: You have *no idea* whatsoever how the ordered physical, moral, mental, aesthetic, and social world in which you live could have ever arisen from the seething anarchy of the elementary particles. It is like imagining sea foam resolving itself into the Parthenon.

And even though the god of the gaps is speaking strictly as an observer, perhaps he will be forgiven for borrowing some phraseology from the God of old and inquiring of Christopher Hitchens, who has wandered into this discussion prepared to dispute anyone at the bar: "Where wast thou when I laid the foundations of the earth? Declare, if thou hast understanding."

Such examples may be multiplied at will. They form a common pattern. No one has the faintest idea whether, in particular, the immense gap between what is living and what is not, between the organic and the inorganic, may be crossed by any conceivable means. That must be why the National Academy of Sciences has taken pains to affirm that it has *already* been crossed. "For those who are studying aspects of the origin of life," the Academy has proclaimed, "the question no longer seems to be whether life could have originated by chemical processes involving nonbiological components but, rather, what pathway might have been followed."

Unfortunately for the Academy, the view among biochemists actively engaged in research is different. "The de-novo appearance of oligonucleotides [some of the indispensable building blocks of life] on the primitive earth," Gerald F. Joyce and Leslie Orgel write in a volume entitled *The RNA World,* "would have been a near-miracle." A near-miracle is a term of art. It is like a near-miss. The theories that we have in our possession do what they can do, and then they stop. They do not stop because a detail is missing; they stop because we cannot go on.

Writing about the eye in *On the Origin of Species,* Darwin confessed that its emergence troubled him greatly. He was nonetheless able to resolve his doubts in his own favor. Ever since then, biologists have wrongly assumed that inasmuch as Darwin proposed a solution, they need not face a problem.

The solution that Darwin proposed and defended was to point to countless examples of intermediate visual structures scattered throughout the animal kingdom. His argument was interesting, but it did not touch the central issue. The eye is not simply a biological organ, although surely it is that. It is a biological organ that allows living creatures to *see.* If we cannot say what seeing comes to in physical or material terms, then we cannot say whether *any* theory is adequate to explain the appearance of an organ that makes sight possible.

And this is precisely what we cannot say: how the twitching nerves, chemical exchanges, electrical flashes, and computational routines of the human eye and brain provide a human being with his experiences. The *processes* involved in sight are biological, chemical, and in the end physical. It may well be that at some point in the future, a physicist, perhaps by using quantum electrodynamics, will be in a position to write down their equations. Whether such an equation will encompass our experiences—why, this is something we simply do not know.

"Today we cannot see whether Schrödinger's equation contains frogs, musical composers, or morality," Richard Feynman remarked in his lectures on turbulence. The remark has been widely quoted. It is honest. The words that follow, however, are rarely quoted: "We cannot say whether something beyond it like God is needed, or not. And so we can all hold strong opinions either way."

If we do not know whether Schrödinger's equation will one day accommodate our experience, we certainly do not know whether our experiences reflect anything less than a miracle. For the moment, if asked to stand and declare ourselves on the most elementary aspects of the world in which we live, we can say nothing.

For almost as long as the physical sciences have made their claims about reality, poets and philosophers have observed that there is something inhuman about the undertaking represented by these sciences. They are right. We gain purchase on the physical world first by stripping it to its simplest form, and second by emptying it of its emotional content. Whatever the elementary particles may be doing, they are not forming political alliances, or eyeing each other in mute incoherent longing, or casting an anxious glance at the clock, or awaking with a start in the early hours of the morning wondering what it all means, or coming to realize that they are destined to fall like the petals of the flower leaving not a trace behind.

These are things *we* do: It is in our nature to do them. But how do we do them? By what means accessible to the imagination does a sterile and utterly insensate physical world become the garrulous, never-ending, infinitely varied, boisterous human world? The more the physical world is studied, and the richer our grasp of its principles, the greater the gap between what it represents and what we embody.

We live by love and longing, death, and the devastation that time imposes. How did they enter into the world? And why? The world of the physical sciences is not our world, and if *our* world has things that cannot be explained in *their* terms, then we must search elsewhere for their explanation. We who are alive in the early twenty-first century may permit ourselves to deprecate the parting of the Red Sea and to regard with unconcern the various loaves and fishes mentioned in the New Testament. Yet we who are heirs to the scientific tradition have been given a priceless gift of our own: a vastly enhanced sense of the miraculous. This is something that the very greatest scientists have always known and always stressed.

We are where human beings have always been, unable to place our confidence completely in anything, unable to place our doubt completely in everything, unsure of the conveyance—and yet conveyed.

JOSEPH BOTTUM

The Judgment of Memory

FROM *First Things*

I

MY WIFE DREAMS OF BRAZILIAN CITIES: SALVADOR DA BAHIA, RIO DE Janeiro, enormous South American cityscapes of sunlit beaches and anonymity. She hasn't lived in Brazil since she was a child, and she still imagines those cities as entirely happy and unself-conscious—even childish. Places that seem to stand outside the curse of politics and history's big ideas. Cities content in their sunshine to let the future be something that happens altogether elsewhere.

I dream instead of the prairie, when I long for escape from the life we've lived in Washington, Boston, and now New York—America's busy east-coast cities, our home in the years since we were married in the small chapel at Georgetown after we finished college. A few years ago, when I was out West visiting my childhood home in Pierre, South Dakota, I drove up, in the late afternoon, to one of the river hills on the edge of town. Why is the sun so much bigger out on those plains than it is back East? Sitting on the hood of the car to watch the huge orange sunset beyond the Missouri, I thought: Here is where I ought to be, here is where I should stay—returning all those things that leaving here had turned.

Up North, *down* South, *back* East, *out* West: Our geographical prepositions have come adrift, even as we seem to have lost our national story. Some memory of their grandparents' arrival in the Dakotas, some last lingering sense of the westward course of history since Columbus, made my parents insist we say "back East" and "out West." "Back" was civilization, the old country, the origin. "Out" was the frontier, the undiscovered country, the goal.

In her early books about a child's life on the frontier, Laura Ingalls Wilder tells of her family's wanderings from a log cabin in the big woods of Wisconsin, to a little house on the prairie in southern Kansas, and on to a sod dugout on the banks of Minnesota's Plum Creek. Her later volumes, however, chronicle her pioneer girlhood once her parents had settled down, at last, in a farmhouse near De Smet, South Dakota. And when an old Kansas neighbor visits on his way out to the new territory opening up in Montana—stopping by on his journey farther west—the teenaged Laura cries that her family should be moving too. "'I know, little Half-Pint,' said Pa, and his voice was very kind. 'You and I want to fly like the birds.'"

But for me, East is where I flew away to, and West is back toward home. When I think about abandoning the life I have these days, I imagine living on one of those dry Dakota buttes overlooking the river, alone with my family, miles from the nearest neighbor—a final refuge from the noise and rush, a perpetual anti-Washington, anti–New York. An anti-East, forever set apart and free.

Then I shake myself awake and remember that I'd probably starve to death attempting it. Perhaps my dreams of the prairie—my wife's dreams of Brazil, for that matter—are merely the standard-issue reveries by which settled people imagine they might somehow throw off their responsibilities and make a change. Perhaps they're merely daydreams of difference: the perpetual illusion that life might be lived down some entirely other path, the mirage that promises we can find what our spirits are missing simply by relocating our tired bodies.

But there is also a current in the mind that seems, inevitably, to pull fantasies about the future down into the dangerous eddies of the past. I know that what we might call *second innocence*—our grown-up goodness, our adult perfection, if we could ever reach it—must be different from the first innocence we knew as children. What we lost when we were young is not what we should seek when we are old.

I know all that, and yet the logic of human imagination always joins what might be with what has already been, every possible future somehow dependent on the past. Anyone can cure a patient's neurosis, an old psychoanalysts' joke runs. All you have to do is travel back in time and change the way his parents were treated as children.

"It's in vain to recall the past unless it works some influence upon the present," Betsy Trotwood warns the young hero of Charles Dickens's *David Copperfield:* sound advice, but the damaged boy, Dickens's most autobiographical character, cannot take it. We do so much in vain, attempting with memory to repair the broken past—as though we might arrange thereby a perfect future, as though the Eden we lost at the beginning is the same as the Heaven we must find at the end.

In looking back we perform a kind of simulated eavesdropping: a listening-in, as adults, on what we experienced as children, but this time, we imagine, with understanding. This time, getting it right.

II

So, what's a memoirist to do? Every human situation, the Roman Stoic philosopher Epictetus once warned, is like a vase with two handles: If you have quarreled with your brother, you can grasp the handle that is the fact that you have quarreled, or you can grasp the handle that is the fact that he is your brother.

For a decade and a half, from the early 1990s on, America has seen the publication of innumerable memoirs and lightly fictionalized accounts of childhood. Such books as Mary Gordon's *The*

Shadow Man, Lois Gould's *Mommy Dressing,* Kathryn Harrison's *The Kiss,* Mary Karr's *The Liars' Club,* Jamaica Kincaid's *My Brother,* Jacki Lyden's *Daughter of the Queen of Sheba,* Frank McCourt's *Angela's Ashes,* and Michael Ryan's *Secret Life*—they appeared in such a ceaseless stream that even professional book reviewers felt flooded by them, and half the New York literary crowd swore they'd never read another, no matter what former best friend wrote it.

What's interesting, however, is that all these books are gripping accounts, beautifully told, of strangeness, peculiarity, and unpleasantness. And they are all deeply determined to be *revelatory,* as though the truth that hides beneath memory's evasions can be uncovered only by grasping what Epictetus would have called the handle of the quarrel: the quarrel of daughters with their mothers, the quarrel of brothers with their sisters, the quarrel of human beings with their existence.

Perhaps these recent authors are right in the way they approach memory. Some sixty years earlier, the nation suffered through a similar run of memoirs and lightly fictionalized books about childhood, from Betty Smith's Irish Catholic *A Tree Grows in Brooklyn* to Sydney Taylor's Jewish *All-of-a-Kind Family*—to say nothing of Laura Ingalls Wilder's eight *Little House on the Prairie* volumes.

It is unfair, of course, to lump these books together. Clarence Day's *Life with Father,* published in 1935, was wry—in those days' approved *New Yorker*-y way—about being a child back in the 1890s. But the Gilbreth children's *Cheaper by the Dozen,* published a decade later, seems oddly more old-fashioned, mostly because of its unabashedly Victorian worship of a dominating paterfamilias. (The authors' father, Frank Gilbreth, was the engineer who helped create the fad for efficiency experts and motion studies in 1920s American business; *therbligs,* the engineering units in which the elements of a mechanical task are measured, derive from his last name spelled backward, more or less.)

Still, however much the old-style memoirs and novels of American childhood varied from one another, they had certain things in common: a similarity of conceit, a determination to be generally pleased with the past, only one handle picked in the choice of Epictetus. Does anyone still read these forgotten bestsellers? Bellamy Partridge's *Country Lawyer* and its sequel *Big Family*, about being a lawyer's son in upstate New York? Hartzell Spence's *One Foot in Heaven* and its sequel *Get Thee Behind Me*, about being a preacher's son on the Methodist circuit in Iowa? Spence went on, while editing *Yank* magazine during World War II, to coin the noun "pin-up" to describe the weekly pictures he published of Rita Hayworth, Hedy Lamarr, and other Hollywood bathing beauties. One doubts, somehow, that this is quite what his Wesleyan parents had in mind for him.

But, then, few of us are all our parents hoped we'd be. Though often dismissed as unbearably sentimental, the earlier American memoirs are not, in truth, much more sentimental than their later counterparts. Both typically accept the picture of larger-than-life parents dominating the adult writer's memory of childhood. The newer books differ mostly by calling this a bad thing. In her 1997 memoir *The Shadow Man*, Mary Gordon, for instance, seems to believe that by being *anti*-sentimental about her father she can achieve the accuracy of the *un*sentimental—as though black-tinted lenses will see more clearly than rose-tinted ones.

There is some dispute about who coined the description of bad biographies as adding a "new terror to death." It may have been John Arbuthnot, describing the torrent of miserable, catchpenny books that eighteenth-century publishers issued immediately after the death of anyone famous. Regardless, the phrase ought to have been reserved for the way deceased parents have been treated in the recollections of childhood published over the last decade and a half. Who would risk bringing up literary children, if the reward is those children's adding this new terror to their parents' deaths?

A few years ago, reviewing for the *Los Angeles Times* a mild memoir by a woman who had adopted a disturbed boy, the poet Richard Howard wrote: "I must acknowledge an interest, or rather a dismay, in discussing this 'family memoir,' for from experience and observation I have come to regard the American Nuclear Family in the last fifty years as the enemy of individual determination, of personal autonomy—in short, as a disease."

It hardly seems necessary to point out that the old style of memoir held the opposite: Family was not the disease, but the cure. Probably that's why most of those accounts of pre–World War II childhood were determined *never* to grasp the handle of the quarrel. Believing the moral order interwoven with the facts of the physical universe, memoirs like Kathryn Forbes's 1943 *Mama's Bank Account* imagine that suppressing nearly everything personally unpleasant about parents is *truer* to reality—simply for being the moral thing to do in a world in which morality itself is true. Believing instead that facts are utterly divorced from the values of the moral order, memoirs like Lois Gould's 1998 *Mommy Dressing* hold that accurate reporting of the unpleasant is the only honest thing to do—at least in part because the fact of the unpleasantness loudly proclaims the honesty of the reporter.

Something self-serving exists in either form, of course. The whole idea of writing a memoir aims at a doubtful purpose, and autobiographies are rarely undertaken by the humble or the shy. But compelled to choose—forced to grasp only one of Epictetus's handles— we should pick, I have come to believe, the old style as the more honorable. Every memoir of childhood is necessarily overshadowed by parents, and I could find, were I to turn my mind that way, stories of my father's drinking, his pretension, his bounce.

But my father, being dead, is not here either to be triumphed over by my telling of those stories or to defend himself against them. The death of parents leaves their honor in their children's hands, and the cruel accuracies we might fling in anger against them while they are alive seem even more wrong to use against them once they are gone. "To the living, we owe respect; to the dead, only truth," Voltaire once opined. It's a good line: high-minded, confident, sententious in the way only enlightened French philosophes could manage with any aplomb. But it also feels exactly backward, particularly about those we knew and loved. To squabble with our vanished parents about how they lived their lives seems more than a metaphysical nullity. It is, in fact, a moral failing.

If love is true—that is to say, a true thing: a really existing object to which the universe itself must bend—then there remains a place for reticence, and secrets swallowed, and the dead allowed to keep their darkness to themselves.

III

Memory may be our best tool for self-understanding, but only when we remember how weak a tool it really is: prone to warping under the narrative drive of storytelling, vulnerable to self-interest, susceptible to outside influence.

Here, for example, is a memory: To visit that hard South Dakota country in which I grew up—coming upon each little town with its water tower, its white houses, and its cemeteries filled with upright headstones—is to recognize what price the homesteaders really had to pay, for each of those towns was claimed from the plains, grave by grave. Inside are carefully planted trees and tended hedges, small square parks, right-angled corners with stop signs and streets laid out true to the compass: an aiming at an ordered life. Outside lies the wilderness: not the manicured wilderness of postcarded rain forests and picturesque mountain peaks beloved by the designers of national parks, but the real thing. A cold that kills. Pestilence and blight. Plagues of locusts and blackbirds. A summer heat that turns the high-banked cattle reservoirs first into mud pits, then into cracked-earth packets that fall to dust and blow away.

In most of my recollections of the prairie, the wind is blowing. Sheltered down between the river hills—picking chokecherries with my grandmother in the hollows by the cemetery or crawling with my friends through the gullies left by the flash floods—we felt it less. But out on the giants' dancing plain, the wind seemed never to stop.

Sometimes in the fall the family would go rock collecting on the buttes north of town, looking for agates to tumble in the rock polisher we got for Christmas when I was six or seven. And I always wondered that my mother and father, even my sisters, didn't seem to hear how much the dry wind was filled with hate, stunting the trees and twisting the scrub, gouging at anything that stood upright, scaling our skin and eyes, screeching in our ears cruelties and obscenities just beyond the edge of hearing. I always came home sick and trembling.

Except that, in fact, the wind often wasn't north-northwesterly, grinding down against us from the Canadian plains. Leaping from a particular moment to some great universal claim about the way things *always* were, memory is false, even when it's true—maybe especially when it's true, maybe especially at the moment we think we've finally gotten the story right.

Partly that comes from the universal decay of reality that happens when we begin a story about the past, for everything runs a little smoother in the telling than it did in the living. I have a theory I sometimes put to friends late at night—one of those complicated theories you find yourself trying to explain only after you've had enough to drink that you can't explain anything complicated—and it goes like this: Each time you tell a story, it loses 10 percent of whatever truth it still had left in it. The first time you explain what happened (while the highway patrolman takes notes, for instance), the story is probably around 90 percent in contact with reality.

It's also not much of a story. It lacks a sharp beginning, sags in the middle, and sputters out to a weak conclusion. So, without really meaning to, just obeying the internal logic of the storytelling, you sand it off a little when you go over it again (while your lawyer grimaces and calculates the damages). You leave out what have come to seem the extraneous bits, you make your own role perhaps a little more central than it appeared the first time around, and you let stand out a shade more clearly the especially comic or dramatic moments.

And thus the tale loses in its second telling 10 percent of that 90 percent of the first telling, falling to around 81 percent accuracy. Tell a story ten or twelve times, and it's only a third true. Tell a story fifty times, and the accuracy plummets down pretty close to zero—*pretty close,* but never quite reaching the absolute zero of pure fiction. The nice thing about this theory of truth's geometric regression is that our anecdotes always retain some relation to the past as it actually happened, however diminishingly small that relation may become.

Meanwhile, somewhere along the line there enters the temptation to weave, into what actually was, a thread or two of what should have been. The French call it *l'esprit de l'escalier,* "the wit of the staircase," the clever thing you ought to have said, which only comes to you on the stairs as you're leaving, rather than back at the party when it might have done some good. And we aren't lying—well, yes, we *are* lying, but we aren't engaged in a full-blown, all-out deception for personal gain—when we let some of that *esprit* slip into a story the seventh or eight time we tell it. The story itself wants to run that way, and we find ourselves unable to thwart it.

So, in *The Wind in the Willows,* when Mr. Toad escapes from prison and returns at last to his friends, he tells Ratty "all his adventures, dwelling chiefly on his own cleverness, and presence of mind in emergencies, and cunning in tight places; and rather making out that he had been having a gay and highly-coloured experience." And mark the sequel, twenty-odd pages later, when he tells the whole tale over again to Mole:

The Mole was a good listener, and Toad, with no one to check his statements or to criticize in an unfriendly spirit, rather let himself go. Indeed, much that he related belonged more properly to the category of what-might-have-happened-had-I-only-thought-of-it-in-time-instead-of-ten-minutes-afterward. Those are always the best and the raciest adventures; and why should they not be truly ours, as much as the somewhat inadequate things that really come off?

IV

The danger in all this—but, then, storytelling has *lots* of dangers. There's something morally questionable about any activity that treats real human beings as pawns in a game whose goal is self-congratulation. "How great, my God, is this force of memory, how exceedingly great!" as the first great autobiographer, St. Augustine, observed sixteen hundred years ago in his *Confessions*. "It is like a vast and boundless subterranean shrine. Who has ever reached the bottom of it?" Preternaturally sensitive to the sneaks and shifts to which pride impels us, Augustine meant that word "shrine"—for he knew the temptation to use the carefully patched-up stories of the past as offerings to the god of the self, worshipped at the inner altar.

For that matter, every dishonesty weakens reality by one effect or another. In a book called *The Quintessence of Ibsenism,* of all unlikely places, George Bernard Shaw remarks that people who routinely lie suffer from more than merely having their friends and family cease to believe them. A habitual liar eventually comes to think that everyone else must also be lying, and human interaction turns ghostly and unreal.

The worst danger, however, may be when we stop remembering just how much an exaggeration is exaggerated. Stories can reach back to change the shape of memory, even while memory is providing the basis for those stories. When I was very young, I was an escaper: a prison-breaker of toddlerdom, a Houdini of the stroller, a scaler of stairs, a mountaineer of the barriers with which parents try to cage their children. I remember it clearly.

Or, at least, I remember later hearing stories about it—so many stories, and there was a photograph of me as well, one or two years old, with one leg up on the edge of the playpen at my grandparents' house in Rapid City. It's not as though I have no genuine recollections of those days. I can still close my eyes and *see,* in perfect fragments of undatable memory, the towering look of my grandparents' bookshelves. The long, parallel channels carved down the curved legs of the chairs, seen from under the dining-room table. The way the deep red in the borders of an oriental rug would blink, light to dark, dark to light, as I brushed the threads back and forth. But now I begin to doubt my vision of climbing from the playpen. I begin to suspect I have cobbled that would-be memory from listening to my father's stories of my childhood—illuminated by a photograph and the few surviving flashes of early recollection.

It could easily have been something worse. During the 1980s, a kind of madness seized American pop psychology—and a great deal of serious psychiatry as well. Suddenly, nearly everyone you met or saw on television was in therapy to recover "repressed memories." Is it significant that these were the years that set the stage for the more recent boom of unhappy childhood memoirs? A notion Sigmund Freud entertained briefly before abandoning it, the idea was resurrected decades later in America to become a national obsession. Major universities, teaching hospitals, and even the National Institute of Mental Health joined the craze for bringing forgotten horrors to consciousness. By 1991 commentators routinely claimed that half the patients in psychiatric care suffered repressed memories of abuse during childhood—a perfect circle in which the failure to recall abuse became proof that abuse had likely occurred.

The Harvard psychiatrist Richard J. McNally's 2003 book *Re-*

membering Trauma is a good account of the movement's mushroom growth and sudden collapse. It's typically American to take an interesting but untested idea and blow it up into full-blown nuttiness—which is how the diagnosis blossomed into claims of repressed memories of Satanic orgies and experiments aboard extraterrestrial spaceships. Eventually, that nuttiness helped create a reaction against repressed memories in the late 1990s (aided by a national recoil from the widely publicized convictions of day-care workers for rituals of Satanic rape, on the basis of testimony from children whose memories had been "recovered" by prosecutors' psychologists). A few large malpractice lawsuits followed, and the diagnosis rapidly faded away, leaving little to mark its passing—little, that is, but a vision of childhood as a land of horrors and tens of thousands of patients estranged from the families they had accused of sexually and physically abusing them.

Repressed-Memory Syndrome was only a brief episode in medical history, a classic instance of extraordinary popular delusion and the madness of crowds. It came, however, with a certain plausibility—or, at least, the appearance of plausibility—for it was, in one sense, merely an extreme version of a fairly common psychological transaction: blaming on the past the failures of the present.

Nearly every family I know has an adult sibling or two whose lives are dominated by memories of parents: all their stories and self-explanations looping back to some frightening or awkward moment of childhood. There is a disturbing quality about middle-aged people who still haven't quite taken responsibility for their world, and I often feel a stern judgment welling up in me while I listen to them. A few human beings truly have been damaged irrevocably by their childhoods, but a rule might be posited for the vast majority of us: At fifteen, we get to blame our parents for the way we are; at thirty, there's no one to blame but ourselves.

And yet, if a harsh judgment can be made here, I have to turn it on myself, for, like everyone else, I do it too from time to time:

chewing on the past, mulling my parents over and over, gnawing at childhood for an explanation of the way I live now. South Dakota: Ah, yes, all my failures come from that strange, windblown world of South Dakota—or maybe from my eccentric relatives, or maybe from the endless cycle of divorces and remarriages that plagued my parents' generation. And why not? If we could shove back into the past the causes of all our present anxieties and discontents, we might find them *finished:* There's a reason we've been behaving in certain immoral and self-destructive ways, but that reason belongs to a different time, and now we're free to move on.

And so each foray into childhood becomes a story, with all the usual temptations for shading the truth that storytelling offers—and also with the great additional temptation to blame the poison of the present on poisoners from the past: constructing not just *a* story but *the* story, the overarching master tale that explains everything away. The key, especially in the modern run of memoirs, is that the past gets explained *away:* lost somehow, used up, even while it is being recounted.

"It is quite true what philosophy says: that life must be understood backward," Søren Kierkegaard wrote in his journals about the use of memory. "But then one forgets the other principle: that it must be lived forward. Which principle, the more one thinks it through, ends exactly with the thought that temporal life can never properly be understood." Caught in this whipsaw, unable to make past, present, and future cut in the same direction, I suppose I could turn my generally happy recollections upside down, coming to believe the most horrible ideas about my upbringing.

But those notions would have to be recovered from the same vague level of memory that makes me imagine I was a jail-breaking child. And the price would be parents and past made ugly and unhappy forever. The price would be childhood itself, explained away.

V

"An autobiography can distort; facts can be realigned," the Nobel Prize–winning V. S. Naipaul once wrote, in a last grand defense of the traditional novel. "But fiction never lies; it reveals the writer totally." If what we want is to make the past meaningful, then memoirs—in either their sentimental or their antisentimental form—may not be the solution to the modern writer's peculiar situation.

Back in 1989, after the massive success of his novel *The Bonfire of the Vanities,* Tom Wolfe took to the pages of *Harper's* magazine with a "manifesto for the new social novel." In our "weak, pale, tabescent moment," he claimed, there's no one doing what Dickens and Balzac and Zola had done. We have plenty of talented writers, but the "American novel is dying of anorexia," because those writers won't go out and report on anything other than themselves. Looking around at the world of serious American literature, Wolfe saw a thousand authors all possessing a professional prose so finely honed it seemed capable of cutting to the heart of almost anything. And he couldn't understand why they wouldn't use it to carve up something important.

There have been some enjoyable childhood memoirs in recent years, of course. My own preference runs toward unpretentious Americana, like Homer Hickam's Coalwood memoirs, especially *Rocket Boys,* and Terry Ryan's *The Prizewinner of Defiance, Ohio: How My Mother Raised 10 Kids on 25 Words or Less.* Still, you understand Tom Wolfe's complaint about the perfect preciousness and self-absorption of America's high literary types. The sensitive setpieces of childhood memoir are their natural form—rehearsing old wounds in faultless prose, like precocious children picking delicately at the scabs on their pale knees.

In fact, the modern memoir was created the day the writing-teacher's slogan, "Write About What You Know," dandied itself up, bought some flowers, and went to call on Henry David Thoreau's defense of autobiography at the beginning of *Walden:* "I should not talk so much about myself if there were anybody else whom I knew as well. Unfortunately, I am confined to this theme by the narrowness of my experience. Moreover, I, on my side, require of every writer, first or last, a simple and sincere account of his own life, and not merely what he has heard of other men's lives."

Thoreau may have been trying to make a joke—did anyone ever read *Walden* for the comedy?—but after a decade and a half of the modern run of memoirs, Wolfe's protest seems more telling than ever: The last thing we need from writers is another simple and sincere account of their own lives; we'd love it if only they *would* go out to hear about people other than themselves.

Wolfe may have missed, however, the extent to which a specific kind of prose creates its own uses, the extent to which a particular style requires a particular sensibility. The problem, really, is that they write too well; our literary boys and girls. There's hardly a writer now alive whose schooled prose cannot paint in sharp detail almost anything you'd care to name: a catastrophic train wreck, the death of a giant redwood tree, the way the tone-arm on a 1960s hi-fi would quiver just before it settled on the spinning phonograph record. Without being witty, they know what humor looks like on a page; without being wise, they know what shape an insight has. They know how to handle a gangster's strongest curses, and they know how to capture a prima donna's flightiest moods. They have a literary instrument ready to say almost anything. And they have almost nothing ready to say with it.

Our age, in other words, is an age of the literary academy, and it has all the virtues and all the vices Matthew Arnold promised when he urged English literature to build itself a counterpart to the Académie Française. Its virtues are a teachable consensus about what constitutes good writing and a single-minded concentration on the art of it all. Its vices are harder to describe precisely: a certain ennui that infects all highly stylized human activities, a prose that takes the form of revelation more often than it actually reveals anything.

It's as though our authors have all been forced to absorb something as exquisite as, say, Annie Dillard's *Pilgrim at Tinker Creek,* a book of semimystical nature observation that's been mandatory at writers' workshops for years. And once an author's been annie-dillardized, the prose gets finer and finer, and the subject gets smaller and smaller. In a column for the *Wall Street Journal,* I once described Alice Munro— whose collection of stories, *The Love of a Good Woman,* had just won the National Book Critics Circle award—as having a prose so fine it can barely lift anything heavier than a small cup of tea. There's a description of a china cupboard in her story "Cortes Island," for instance, so beautifully detailed and so profoundly pointless that it has to be read to be believed.

Except that perhaps it isn't pointless. I begin to think that I have gotten this wrong—spent years, in fact, getting it wrong and railing against its practitioners for their cosseting of meaningless detail after meaningless detail. Dillard, Munro, and all the rest are not writing this way for no reason. They have some purpose in mind with those endless circumstantial tidbits, and they are making some attempt to solve the problem of modern writing.

Indulging an inventory of details is nothing new. Homer used it in the *Iliad* when he spent 296 lines cataloging the Greek ships piled against the Trojan shore. If nothing else, it bulks up the text while the author is trying to figure out what to say next. More, such detail-studded prose is fun to write, and maybe even fun to read, in short bursts.

Here, for instance: Every fall in Pierre, to mark the end of the summer's bare feet and sneakers, my mother would take us downtown to buy school shoes—those heavy, round-toed Buster Brown monsters that children used to wear: binding torture devices with slick tan soles that slid across the shoe-store carpet and needed a week's scuffing on the curbs back and forth from school to make them walkable. By spring—snickered through piles of leaves, stamped in puddles, the winter's first thin frosts shattered with their heels, salted with the deicing on the neighbors' snowy walks—the shoes had faded from their original chocolate-linoleum brown to a kind of colorless gray, the tape aglets on the ends of the laces long disappeared, the broken laces themselves knotted together down the tongue of the shoe, the once smooth brown toes roughened down to blotting paper.

But what advance is made by this sort of writing? All the endless focus on details in contemporary writing—it serves, mostly, as artistic expansion: the writer's equivalent of what modern painters do when they blow up on large canvases the tiny brush strokes that classical painters once used to fill in corners of the background or the drape of a green velvet dress. A Victorian like Charles Dickens would have thrown away all this kind of thing in a passing paragraph to describe a waiter he wouldn't even bother to name. Then he would have indulged a little facetiousness, then described in telling detail a few of the other waiters, then drawn a large moral, and then followed his story's hero out the inn's door, never to return.

Well, easy enough for Dickens. His prose is driven by the story he uses it to tell, and story is exactly what has become a problem for most high literature these days. Victorian novels dwell in a more complete world than ours, for they assume at least the possibility of what the scholastic philosophers would have called the *unity of truth*. Every art and every science has its own techniques and starting points. But in a universe of intelligibility—a world with a purpose, a goal for human life—we can feel the many arts and sciences bending toward a single, unified truth about human existence: the places that narrative wants to go, the judgments that ethics wants to make, and the brute facts of physical reality, all straining to become one. It is (or, at least, it is supposed to be) a world in which beauty is illuminated by morality, morality by rationality, and rationality by beauty.

One way to tell the literary history of the twentieth century is to follow the progression of an extremely bookish people who grew more and more uncertain, more and more diffident, more and more self-conscious about the entire idea of telling a story or using the narrative finality of stories to convey unified judgments about society, history, or even themselves. How could we do what the Victorians had done, when we were quickly losing confidence that the way a story works reflects, in some measure, the way the world actually is?

The American memoirs from the middle of the twentieth century were still story-driven, or, at least, anecdote-driven—still confident enough in the completeness of the universe to assume that narrative is a motor by which truth can run. The newer memoirs are detail-driven instead. They have their own set of moral certainties, of course: some worse, and some better, than their predecessors'. Their prose, however, always tends to convey events with floods of particular circumstance rather than a storyline—using details like a great and inarticulate ocean, throwing wave after wave of sharply observed fact against the shore in the hope of washing down to sea a stranded meaning.

And why exactly shouldn't we use this technique? Indeed, how could we use any other, these days? Details exist, in a way that stories don't, apart from moral judgment. They swim beneath the messy world of virtue and vice, down in the clear, clean waters of the purely physical, as though what confronts us in memory is not the assailant's pistol but merely molecules of blued steel arranged by some chance in a deadly way.

If stories are just about stories and contingent facts just about contingent facts—if, in other words, the moral order of meaningful narrative and the physical order of pure information can no longer be truthfully aligned—then honest writers have a responsibility to speak about only the fine details.

Those details can be used to draw a picture in such a way that readers will make moral judgments, of course. But the prose needn't make those judgments itself. And as for the rightness and wrongness of the things described in such detail, that's left a sort of epiphenomenon, a spume that plays above the facts—which is, perhaps, a perfect literary expression of the division the twentieth century suffered between the moral and the real.

I do not see clearly how to mend the rift between the moral and the real. Writers were once people who imagined that a king's madness should call forth echoes in a disordered kingdom and a mad storm upon a heath, while their audiences were once people who believed that the stars themselves have a story to tell.

They both may have been righter than we are today with our demythologized details and our mistrust of sentimental stories. Those old melodramatic plots had to come from somewhere. Poetic justice, the sense of an ending, a tale with a moral like the clicking shut of a well-made box: Perhaps it isn't that we look for them in life because we found them in stories; perhaps we look for them in stories because we saw them first in life. Forget ambiguity. The entire universe wants a neat and happy conclusion. Creation is God's own cliff-hanger, the *Perils of Pauline* in six hundred billion installments, played across the stars.

And yet, the simple truth of autobiography is this: The accurate details of memory do not come naturally packaged into stories. You have to take a hammer and beat them into shape, a little.

Besides, our modern memoirists are describing lives that don't actually feel story-shaped anymore, with some grand narrative marching from birth's beginning to the moral of old age. And when our recent autobiographers try to force an overarching plot onto their childhoods, it turns odd and dark in their hands, just as the 1980s fascination with repressed memories always seemed to do.

VI

I remember once climbing a hill with my grandfather on a warm October afternoon, up into that endless South Dakota wind. In truth, the wind may have been gentler than I recall it. When you're five or six, and carrying a large paper kite against your chest like a lateen sail, a simple breeze feels like a giant's hand that wants to pick you up and fling you back to the bottom of the hill.

Still, the details of that day remain perfect in memory. The heartsinking dip and the upturn's reprieve as the kite first found the wind. The burn of the twine as it raced between my thumb and the side of my fingers. The bright red diamond, crisscrossed with balsa sticks, against the pale blue sky, while the long knotted streamer spiraled below it. Then the slow, agonizing drift to the right I couldn't halt, and the tangle with the cord of my grandfather's own dark-green diamond. Back and forth like a broken fan my kite whipped while my grandfather strained to bring them both down intact. But the string wouldn't hold. A hundred feet of loose tether fluttered gently down from the sky, and the red paper kite dwindled in the distance, sailing east across the empty plains.

Maybe I remember this now because it seems a figure for the loss of meaning in contemporary writing, untethered from the earth. Or maybe I recall it in the way my wife thinks of Brazilian cities: as a metaphor for what we lost when we were young and why we need to revisit the past if we want to find some escape for the future.

Or maybe it stands, finally, only as a small set of incidental facts—detailed but empty, dense in recollection but signifying nothing. I don't know. But I do see clearly at least one fact about modern memory: Those who pick up the vase of the past by the darker of Epictetus's two handles have achieved no superior form of autobiography. Between the narratives of the old sentimental versions of family life and the details of the newer antisentimental accounts, we have still not found much of a way to write an American memoir or tell the story of an American childhood.

Perhaps we never will. The great tangle of weak words and warped memory and streamlined narrative offers no apparent solution. The knot will not be untied by any memoir or story—by any confession, for that matter, or affidavit, or psychiatric review. Greater and lesser honesty remains, of course: *This* happened, *that* did not. But untruth tinges all the threads. In the end, every sentence with the word "I" in it is a lie: self-justifying, self-righteous, self-conscious, self-sick.

Here, at last, is the theological point. Every story longs for closure, just as every human being hungers for understanding and every fact within us seems to ache for meaning. Locked down within ourselves, however, we cannot climb to the *memory* of memory—the place outside time from which to see time. The fact of God's judgment is not merely a promise descending from above. It is the great human prayer, rising from below. Judgment waits for us, because we need it.

Last fall I thought again about my grandfather. On a visit down to Washington, I took my daughter to a playground near our old house in Georgetown, catching the western breeze to float the complicated polychrome fabric of modern kites out over Rock Creek Park. But after an hour, the wind sheered around to blow from the east, and while she struggled to hold the spool, her kite began to drift across the sky toward the impassible maze of the city's houses and trees.

She seemed—oh, I can't quite describe it. Tense, perhaps, but also confident somehow that we could pull her multicolored kite back in time. More confident than I had been, years before on that yellow prairie hill. As we carried my daughter's saved kite back to the hotel, I remembered my own kite and the way my grandfather held my hand down the hill to the rose-brick house. Out of such pasts, what future? *Let thy heart cheer thee in the days of thy youth, and walk in the ways of thine heart, and in the sight of thine eyes: but know thou, that for all these things God will bring thee into judgment.*

NICHOLAS CARR

Is Google Making Us Stupid?

FROM *The Atlantic*

"Dave, stop. Stop, will you? Stop, Dave. Will you stop, Dave?" So the supercomputer HAL pleads with the implacable astronaut Dave Bowman in a famous and weirdly poignant scene toward the end of Stanley Kubrick's *2001: A Space Odyssey*. Bowman, having nearly been sent to a deep-space death by the malfunctioning machine, is calmly, coldly disconnecting the memory circuits that control its artificial brain. "Dave, my mind is going," HAL says, forlornly. "I can feel it. I can feel it."

I can feel it, too. Over the past few years I've had an uncomfortable sense that someone, or something, has been tinkering with my brain, remapping the neural circuitry, reprogramming the memory. My mind isn't going—so far as I can tell—but it's changing. I'm not thinking the way I used to think. I can feel it most strongly when I'm reading. Immersing myself in a book or a lengthy article used to be easy. My mind would get caught up in the narrative or the turns of the argument, and I'd spend hours strolling through long stretches of prose. That's rarely the case anymore. Now my concentration often starts to drift after two or three pages. I get fidgety, lose the thread, begin looking for something else to do. I feel as if I'm always dragging my wayward brain back to the text. The deep reading that used to come naturally has become a struggle.

I think I know what's going on. For more than a decade now, I've been spending a lot of time online, searching and surfing and sometimes adding to the great databases of the Internet. The Web has been a godsend to me as a writer. Research that once required days in the stacks or periodical rooms of libraries can now be done in minutes. A few Google searches, some quick clicks on hyperlinks, and I've got the telltale fact or pithy quote I was after. Even when I'm not working, I'm as likely as not to be foraging in the Web's info-thickets—reading and writing e-mails, scanning headlines and blog posts, watching videos and listening to podcasts, or just tripping from link to link to link. (Unlike footnotes, to which they're sometimes likened, hyperlinks don't merely point to related works; they propel you toward them.)

For me, as for others, the Net is becoming a universal medium, the conduit for most of the information that flows through my eyes and ears and into my mind. The advantages of having immediate access to such an incredibly rich store of information are many, and they've been widely described and duly applauded. "The perfect recall of silicon memory," *Wired*'s Clive Thompson has written, "can be an enormous boon to thinking." But that boon comes at a price. As the media theorist Marshall McLuhan pointed out in the 1960s, media are not just passive channels of information. They supply the stuff of thought, but they also shape the process of thought. And what the Net seems to be doing is chipping away my capacity for concentration and contemplation. My mind now expects to take in information the way the Net distributes it: in a swiftly moving stream of particles. Once I was a scuba diver in the sea of words. Now I zip along the surface like a guy on a Jet Ski.

I'm not the only one. When I mention my troubles with reading to friends and acquaintances—literary types, most of them—many say they're having similar experiences. The more they use the Web, the more they have to fight to stay focused on long pieces of writing.

Some of the bloggers I follow have also begun mentioning the phenomenon. Scott Karp, who writes a blog about online media, recently confessed that he has stopped reading books altogether. "I was a lit major in college, and used to be [a] voracious book reader," he wrote. "What happened?" He speculates on the answer: "What if I do all my reading on the Web not so much because the way I read has changed, i.e., I'm just seeking convenience, but because the way I THINK has changed?"

Bruce Friedman, who blogs regularly about the use of computers in medicine, also has described how the Internet has altered his mental habits. "I now have almost totally lost the ability to read and absorb a longish article on the Web or in print," he wrote earlier this year. A pathologist who has long been on the faculty of the University of Michigan Medical School, Friedman elaborated on his comment in a telephone conversation with me. His thinking, he said, has taken on a "staccato" quality, reflecting the way he quickly scans short passages of text from many sources online. "I can't read *War and Peace* anymore," he admitted. "I've lost the ability to do that. Even a blog post of more than three or four paragraphs is too much to absorb. I skim it."

Anecdotes alone don't prove much. And we still await the long-term neurological and psychological experiments that will provide a definitive picture of how Internet use affects cognition. But a recently published study of online research habits, conducted by scholars from University College London, suggests that we may well be in the midst of a sea change in the way we read and think. As part of the five-year research program, the scholars examined computer logs documenting the behavior of visitors to two popular research sites, one operated by the British Library and one by a U.K. educational consortium, that provide access to journal articles, e-books, and other sources of written information. They found that people using the sites exhibited "a form of skimming activity," hopping from one source to another and rarely returning to any source they'd already visited. They typically read no more than one or two pages of an article or book before they would "bounce" out to another site. Sometimes they'd save a long article, but there's no evidence that they ever went back and actually read it. The authors of the study report:

> It is clear that users are not reading online in the traditional sense; indeed there are signs that new forms of "reading" are emerging as users "power browse" horizontally through ti-tles, contents pages, and abstracts going for quick wins. It almost seems that they go online to avoid reading in the traditional sense.

Thanks to the ubiquity of text on the Internet, not to mention the popularity of text-messaging on cell phones, we may well be reading more today than we did in the 1970s or 1980s, when television was our medium of choice. But it's a different kind of reading, and behind it lies a different kind of thinking—perhaps even a new sense of the self. "We are not only *what* we read," says Maryanne Wolf, a developmental psychologist at Tufts University and the author of *Proust and the Squid: The Story and Science of the Reading Brain.* "We are *how* we read." Wolf worries that the style of reading promoted by the Net, a style that puts "efficiency" and "immediacy" above all else, may be weakening our capacity for the kind of deep reading that emerged when an earlier technology, the printing press, made long and complex works of prose commonplace. When we read online, she says, we tend to become "mere decoders of information." Our ability to interpret text, to make the rich mental connections that form when we read deeply and without distraction, remains largely disengaged.

Reading, explains Wolf, is not an instinctive skill for human beings. It's not etched into our genes the way speech is. We have to teach our minds how to translate the symbolic characters we see into the language we understand. And the media or other technologies we use in learning and practicing the craft of reading play an important part in shaping the neural circuits inside our brains. Experiments demonstrate that readers of ideograms, such as the Chinese, develop a mental circuitry for reading that is very different from the circuitry found in those of us whose written language employs an alphabet. The variations extend across many regions of the brain, including those that govern such essential cognitive functions as memory and the interpretation of visual and auditory stimuli. We can expect as well that the circuits woven by our use of the Net will be different from those woven by our reading of books and other printed works.

Sometime in 1882, Friedrich Nietzsche bought a typewriter—a Malling-Hansen Writing Ball, to be precise. His vision was failing, and keeping his eyes focused on a page had become exhausting and painful, often bringing on crushing headaches. He had been forced to curtail his writing, and he feared that he would soon have to give it up. The typewriter rescued him, at least for a time. Once he had mastered touch-typing, he was able to write with his eyes closed, using only the tips of his fingers. Words could once again flow from his mind to the page.

But the machine had a subtler effect on his work. One of Nietzsche's friends, a composer, noticed a change in the style of his writing. His already terse prose had become even tighter, more telegraphic. "Perhaps you will through this instrument even take to a new idiom," the friend wrote in a letter, noting that, in his own work, his "'thoughts' in music and language often depend on the quality of pen and paper."

"You are right," Nietzsche replied, "our writing equipment takes part in the forming of our thoughts." Under the sway of the machine, writes the German media scholar Friedrich A. Kittler, Nietzsche's prose "changed from arguments to aphorisms, from thoughts to puns, from rhetoric to telegram style."

The human brain is almost infinitely malleable. People used to think that our mental meshwork, the dense connections formed among the hundred billion or so neurons inside our skulls, was largely fixed by the time we reached adulthood. But brain researchers have discovered that that's not the case. James Olds, a professor of neuroscience who directs the Krasnow Institute for Advanced Study at George Mason University, says that even the adult mind "is very plastic." Nerve cells routinely break old connections and form new ones. "The brain," according to Olds, "has the ability to reprogram itself on the fly, altering the way it functions."

As we use what the sociologist Daniel Bell has called our "intellectual technologies"—the tools that extend our mental rather than our physical capacities—we inevitably begin to take on the qualities of those technologies. The mechanical clock, which came into common use in the fourteenth century, provides a compelling example. In *Technics and Civilization,* the historian and cultural critic Lewis Mumford described how the clock "disassociated time from human events and helped create the belief in an independent world of mathematically measurable sequences." The "abstract framework of divided time" became "the point of reference for both action and thought."

The clock's methodical ticking helped bring into being the scientific mind and the scientific man. But it also took something away. As the late MIT computer scientist Joseph Weizenbaum observed in his 1976 book, *Computer Power and Human Reason: From Judgment to Calculation,* the conception of the world that emerged from the widespread use of timekeeping instruments "remains an impoverished version of the older one, for it rests on a rejection of those direct experiences that formed the basis for, and indeed constituted, the old reality." In deciding when to eat, to work, to sleep, to rise, we stopped listening to our senses and started obeying the clock.

The process of adapting to new intellectual technologies is reflected in the changing metaphors we use to explain ourselves to ourselves. When the mechanical clock arrived, people began thinking of their brains as operating "like clockwork." Today, in the age of software, we have come to think of them as operating "like computers." But the changes, neuroscience tells us, go much deeper than metaphor. Thanks to our brain's plasticity, the adaptation occurs also at a biological level.

The Internet promises to have particularly far-reaching effects on cognition. In a paper published in 1936, the British mathematician Alan Turing proved that a digital computer, which at the time existed only as a theoretical machine, could be programmed to perform the function of any other information-processing device. And that's what we're seeing today. The Internet, an immeasurably powerful computing system, is subsuming most of our other intellectual technologies. It's becoming our map and our clock, our printing press and our typewriter, our calculator and our telephone, and our radio and TV.

When the Net absorbs a medium, that medium is recreated in the Net's image. It injects the medium's content with hyperlinks, blinking ads, and other digital gewgaws, and it surrounds the content with the content of all the other media it has absorbed. A new e-mail message, for instance, may announce its arrival as we're glancing over the latest headlines at a newspaper's site. The result is to scatter our attention and diffuse our concentration.

The Net's influence doesn't end at the edges of a computer screen, either. As people's minds become attuned to the crazy quilt of Internet media, traditional media have to adapt to the audience's new expectations. Television programs add text crawls and pop-up ads, and magazines and newspapers shorten their articles, introduce capsule summaries, and crowd their pages with easy-to-browse info-snippets. When, in March of this year, the *New York Times* decided to devote the second and third pages of every edition to article abstracts, its design director, Tom Bodkin, explained that the "shortcuts" would give harried readers a quick "taste" of the day's news, sparing them the "less efficient" method of actually turning the pages and reading the articles. Old media have little choice but to play by the new-media rules.

Never has a communications system played so many roles in our lives—or exerted such broad influence over our thoughts—as the Internet does today. Yet, for all that's been written about the Net, there's been little consideration of how, exactly, it's reprogramming us. The Net's intellectual ethic remains obscure.

About the same time that Nietzsche started using his typewriter, an earnest young man named Frederick Winslow Taylor carried a stopwatch into the Midvale Steel plant in Philadelphia and began a historic series of experiments aimed at improving the efficiency of the plant's machinists. With the approval of Midvale's owners, he recruited a group of factory hands, set them to work on various metalworking machines, and recorded and timed their every movement as well as the operations of the machines. By breaking down every job into a sequence of small, discrete steps and then testing different ways of performing each one, Taylor created a set of precise instructions—an "algorithm," we might say today—for how each worker should work. Midvale's employees grumbled about the strict new regime, claiming that it turned them into little more than automatons, but the factory's productivity soared.

More than a hundred years after the invention of the steam engine, the Industrial Revolution had at last found its philosophy and its philosopher. Taylor's tight industrial choreography—his "system," as he liked to call it—was embraced by manufacturers throughout the country and, in time, around the world. Seeking maximum speed, maximum efficiency, and maximum output, factory owners used time-and-motion studies to organize their work and configure the jobs of their workers. The goal, as Taylor defined it in his celebrated 1911 treatise, *The Principles of Scientific Management,* was to identify and adopt, for every job, the "one best method" of work and thereby to effect "the gradual substitution of science for rule of thumb throughout the mechanic arts." Once his system was applied to all acts of manual labor, Taylor assured his followers, it would bring about a restructuring not only of industry but of society, creating a utopia of perfect efficiency. "In the past the man has been first," he declared; "in the future the system must be first."

Taylor's system is still very much with us; it remains the ethic of industrial manufacturing. And now, thanks to the growing power that computer engineers and software coders wield over our intellectual lives, Taylor's ethic is beginning to govern the realm of the mind as well. The Internet is a machine designed for the efficient and automated collection, transmission, and manipulation of information, and its legions of programmers are intent on finding the "one best method"—the perfect algorithm—to carry out every mental movement of what we've come to describe as "knowledge work."

Google's headquarters, in Mountain View, California—the Googleplex—is the Internet's High Church, and the religion practiced inside its walls is Taylorism. Google, says its chief executive, Eric Schmidt, is "a company that's founded around the science of measurement," and it is striving to "systematize everything" it does. Drawing on the terabytes of behavioral data it collects through its search engine and other sites, it carries out thousands of experiments a day, according to the *Harvard Business Review,* and it uses the results to refine the algorithms that increasingly control how people find information and extract meaning from it. What Taylor did for the work of the hand, Google is doing for the work of the mind.

The company has declared that its mission is "to organize the world's information and make it universally accessible and useful." It seeks to develop "the perfect search engine," which it defines as something that "understands exactly what you mean and gives you back exactly what you want." In Google's view, information is a kind of commodity, a utilitarian resource that can be mined and processed with industrial efficiency. The more pieces of information we can "access" and the faster we can extract their gist, the more productive we become as thinkers.

Where does it end? Sergey Brin and Larry Page, the gifted young men who founded Google while pursuing doctoral degrees in computer science at Stanford, speak frequently of their desire to turn their search engine into an artificial intelligence, a HAL-like machine that might be connected directly to our brains. "The ultimate search engine is something as smart as people—or smarter," Page said in a speech a few years back. "For us, working on search is a way to work on artificial intelligence." In a 2004 interview with *Newsweek*, Brin said, "Certainly if you had all the world's information directly attached to your brain, or an artificial brain that was smarter than your brain, you'd be better off." Last year, Page told a convention of scientists that Google is "really trying to build artificial intelligence and to do it on a large scale."

Such an ambition is a natural one, even an admirable one, for a pair of math whizzes with vast quantities of cash at their disposal and a small army of computer scientists in their employ. A fundamentally scientific enterprise, Google is motivated by a desire to use technology, in Eric Schmidt's words, "to solve problems that have never been solved before," and artificial intelligence is the hardest problem out there. Why wouldn't Brin and Page want to be the ones to crack it?

Still, their easy assumption that we'd all "be better off" if our brains were supplemented, or even replaced, by an artificial intelligence is unsettling. It suggests a belief that intelligence is the output of a mechanical process, a series of discrete steps that can be isolated, measured, and optimized. In Google's world, the world we enter when we go online, there's little place for the fuzziness of contemplation. Ambiguity is not an opening for insight but a bug to be fixed. The human brain is just an outdated computer that needs a faster processor and a bigger hard drive.

The idea that our minds should operate as high-speed data-processing machines is not only built into the workings of the Internet, it is the network's reigning business model as well. The faster we surf across the Web—the more links we click and pages we view— the more opportunities Google and other companies gain to collect information about us and to feed us advertisements. Most of the proprietors of the commercial Internet have a financial stake in collecting the crumbs of data we leave behind as we flit from link to link—the more crumbs, the better. The last thing these companies want is to encourage leisurely reading or slow, concentrated thought. It's in their economic interest to drive us to distraction.

Maybe I'm just a worrywart. Just as there's a tendency to glorify technological progress, there's a countertendency to expect the worst of every new tool or machine. In Plato's *Phaedrus,* Socrates bemoaned the development of writing. He feared that, as people came to rely on the written word as a substitute for the knowledge they used to carry inside their heads, they would, in the words of one of the dialogue's characters, "cease to exercise their memory and become forgetful." And because they would be able to "receive a quantity of information without proper instruction," they would "be thought very knowledgeable when they are for the most part quite ignorant." They would be "filled with the conceit of wisdom instead of real wisdom." Socrates wasn't wrong—the new technology did often have the effects he feared—but he was shortsighted. He couldn't foresee the many ways that writing and reading would serve to spread information, spur fresh ideas, and expand human knowledge (if not wisdom).

The arrival of Gutenberg's printing press, in the fifteenth century, set off another round of teeth gnashing. The Italian humanist Hieronimo Squarciafico worried that the easy availability of books would lead to intellectual laziness, making men "less studious" and weakening their minds. Others argued that cheaply printed books and broadsheets would undermine religious authority, demean the work of scholars and scribes, and spread sedition and debauchery. As New York University professor Clay Shirky notes, "Most of the arguments made against the printing press were correct, even prescient." But, again, the doomsayers were unable to imagine the myriad blessings that the printed word would deliver.

So, yes, you should be skeptical of my skepticism. Perhaps those who dismiss critics of the Internet as Luddites or nostalgists will be proved correct, and from our hyperactive, data-stoked minds will spring a golden age of intellectual discovery and universal wisdom. Then again, the Net isn't the alphabet, and although it may replace the printing press, it produces something altogether different. The kind of deep reading that a sequence of printed pages promotes is valuable not just for the knowledge we acquire from the author's words but for the intellectual vibrations those words set off within our own minds. In the quiet spaces opened up by the sustained, undistracted reading of a book, or by any other act of contemplation, for that matter, we make our own associations, draw our own inferences and analogies, foster our own ideas. Deep reading, as Maryanne Wolf argues, is indistinguishable from deep thinking.

If we lose those quiet spaces, or fill them up with "content," we will sacrifice something important not only in our selves but in our culture. In a recent essay, the playwright Richard Foreman eloquently described what's at stake:

> I come from a tradition of Western culture, in which the ideal (my ideal) was the complex, dense, and "cathedral-like" structure of the highly educated and articulate personality— a man or woman who carried inside themselves a personally constructed and unique version of the entire heritage of the West. [But now] I see within us all (myself included) the replacement of complex inner density with a new kind of self—evolving under the pressure of information over-load and the technology of the "instantly available."

As we are drained of our "inner repertory of dense cultural inheritance," Foreman concluded, we risk turning into " 'pancake people'— spread wide and thin as we connect with that vast network of information accessed by the mere touch of a button."

I'm haunted by that scene in *2001*. What makes it so poignant, and so weird, is the computer's emotional response to the disassembly of its mind: its despair as one circuit after another goes dark, its childlike pleading with the astronaut—"I can feel it. I can feel it. I'm afraid"—and its final reversion to what can only be called a state of innocence. HAL's outpouring of feeling contrasts with the emotionlessness that characterizes the human figures in the film, who go about their business with an almost robotic efficiency. Their thoughts and actions feel scripted, as if they're following the steps of an algorithm. In the world of *2001,* people have become so machinelike that the most human character turns out to be a machine. That's the essence of Kubrick's dark prophecy: As we come to rely on computers to mediate our understanding of the world, it is our own intelligence that flattens into artificial intelligence.

JUDITH ORTIZ COFER

The Aging María

FROM *Image*

SHE STANDS IN MY MOTHER'S FRONT LAWN, FORBEARING THE ELE-
ments, the yearly tropical depressions and occasional hurricanes,
calm blue gaze cutting through time just as she had in my grand-
mother's *jardín,* where she stared perpetually at the avocado tree.
Santa María, sole witness to the mature fruit's mysterious plunging
off the branches in the night, explosions on the zinc roof of my first
bedroom, the abrupt starts of my awakenings on the island. The
paint on her plaster face is now cracked so that she seems wiser,
somehow marked by lines of pain and laughter. Her blue-and-white
gown is worn through to the raw material of her making, as if she
had been neglected by busy offspring in her waning years, living on
a fixed income, no daughters checking in on her from time to time,
no new robes or sandals on Mother's Day. Now in direct contact
with the ground, her naked feet have yellowed. The cloud she once
stood on is half buried in the fertilized soil where my mother grows
her high-maintenance roses. The Queen of Heaven is aging on a
Caribbean island, sustained only by the collective memory of her
one year of living dangerously, and the still popular assumption that
glory clings to her presence. Her new smile may be the irony created
by loss, the real revelation: She is beyond repair. Yet year after year a
tiny crèche is placed before her in December, as if her arms could

still hold a child, although it is plain to see that her fragile fingers are chipped at the tips and broken at the joints. In fact, all that is unsustained by cast or mold has begun to fall away. Still, year after year, she stands firm in my mother's garden. In crepuscular light, her still regal form acquires a certain luster, the yellow patina of age briefly turning to a luminous gold, as though she were lit, as she is, from within.

BILLY COLLINS

Searching

FROM *The Atlantic*

I recall someone once admitting
that all he remembered of *Anna Karenina*
was something about a picnic basket,

and now, after consuming a book
devoted to the subject of Barcelona—
its people, its history, its complex architecture—

all I remember is the mention
of an albino gorilla, the inhabitant of a park
where the Citadel of the Bourbons once stood.

The sheer paleness of him looms over
all the notable names and dates
as the evening strollers stop before him

and point to show their children.
These locals called him Snowflake,
and here he has been mentioned again in print

in the hope of keeping his pallid flame alive
and helping him, despite his name, to endure
in this poem, where he has found another cage.

Oh, Snowflake,
I had no interest in the capital of Catalonia—
its people, its history, its complex architecture—

no, you were the reason
I kept my light on late into the night,
turning all those pages, searching for you everywhere.

CHRISTI COX

The Dalai Lama Spends the Night

FROM *Snow Lion*

MY FATHER LAUGHED WHEN I FIRST TOLD HIM THAT THE DALAI Lama was going to spend a couple of nights at my house. Really, Dad, no kidding. Yes, *that* Dalai Lama. Tibet.

He was thinking that if anyone had predicted, when he was a young man growing up in Europe, that one day his daughter would run bath water for the near-mythical Tibetan leader, he would have thought that they were crazy. Meshuga. He rotated his fingers expressively at his temple and rolled his eyes.

And truly it was unlikely. First, I was not even a Buddhist. Not yet.

And second. At the time I was living in the most economically depressed county in New York State, home to rusting cars abandoned in backyards. My neighbors lived in an alarming, corrugated metal building—and turned out to be the kind of people who shot each other. It was not an environment that most people would imagine to be appropriate for a dignitary of any kind, let alone a major world leader.

But he came. Looking back, it all seems pretty unbelievable: the amiable sheriffs in the kitchen, the lentil casseroles I made for dinner, and the unexpected transformation of my life.

If you've been around the Dalai Lama lately you'll understand the significance of the amiable sheriffs. These days the security presence around His Holiness is not amiable. It is serious indeed, involving the FBI and State Department, as well as local and state law enforcement. The cost of security for a few days can run close to a million dollars. Each public and private moment is scheduled—and double-scheduled.

But back in 1979, the Dalai Lama's first trip to the United States, he traveled light. The U.S. government had not yet figured out that it had a superstar, semipolitical entity on its hands who needed to be protected.

This is the short version of how it happened.

A friend who knew the tour planner brought him to see my house as one of several options in the area. The planner was a European sophisticate with impeccable manners and an appreciable amount of exhaustion. This was to be His Holiness's first U.S. trip, and he wanted everything to be perfect. But being a Buddhist and a realist, he knew that would be impossible. After a quick, discreet examination of the small, simple house, he suggested that His Holiness would like to spend a few days of rest there. Perhaps his exhaustion had worn him down; I don't know. But it was to be. I had a few months to prepare.

In a way the outer sequences of events that brought the Dalai Lama to the guest room of my funky ranch house don't quite add up. The mathematics is off, doesn't seem quite sound when I look back. Why would a trip planner decide to house a world-class spiritual leader in a house like mine? It made no sense then; it makes no sense now. The facts followed the logic of myth rather than that of any kind of Western science: the miraculous manifests inexplicably out of the void into a small, unlikely structure. It seems that's just how grace works. Always did; probably always will.

I began to clean my house—seriously, absurdly, endlessly. Armed with a crisp toothbrush I vigorously scrubbed all my plastic spice boxes, and then—in a fit of utter irrationality—went on to bleach the underside of the sofa. Rectangles of sponge sprawled, ready for immediate action, on windowsills in every room. Cleaning like this—actually *any* cleaning beyond the cursory tidying triggered by impending guests—was not my usual style: I had always been a devotee of the minimalist school of dusting. But now things had shifted: I *had* to scour, scrub, and disinfect, moved by something ineffable.

"The Dalai Lama doesn't care about your canning jars, for God's sake," a friend said in some exasperation, as he watched me wipe two years of basement dust off them. Of course I knew that. The spiritual leader of Tibet wasn't going to march into my house and then demand a tour of my basement or ask to review my pots and pans.

Of course not. Even as I scrubbed, I suspected that I was acting out a kind of archetypal urge for inner purification, one that most often precedes a spiritual initiation. I had read many religious writings—both Eastern and Western—explaining that significant spiritual events are often marked by a symbolic outer cleansing. Baptism, immersion in the Ganges. Sprinkling with holy water. I, however, had apparently been seized by a hapless, suburban cleansing ritual—purification by Pine-Sol.

And then, one fall evening, he was there at the front door. There was a maroon robe, a shaved head, and a pair of very serious black oxfords. Also a high-tech watch and jaunty spectacles. A hand reached for mine and grasped it firmly. And then there were the eyes. They locked into mine briefly, knowingly. They released; the hand released. And the Dalai Lama walked past me into the living room.

Now, decades later, I still don't know how to explain what happened in that brief interchange. There was no blinding light, no profound insight into the nature of the universe, no visions of the future. But it was the single most transformative moment of my life. One moment I was a woman with a sponge, the next I was a fully ecstatic woman with a sponge.

This woman stood in shock in the doorway. Gently, a young monk who had been standing behind the Dalai Lama touched her on the elbow. "Could you show His Holiness to his room?" he prompted softly. The housewifely necessities of the moment called me back into a minimal congruence with this body, this room, this man. I managed to lead the way down the hall and swing wide the door to the compact room where the Dalai Lama would sleep. He walked in, surveyed the new orange pillows, the new creamy curtains, the new brown sheets on the bed. "Good," he said, guttural and noncommittal, and closed the door.

The young monk was tapping me on the arm again. His Holiness needs another towel, he said, and something to eat. He could see I needed prompting. "He likes bagels best," he advised, "lightly buttered."

With that mechanical oddness of people who have experienced trauma or some profound inner dislocation, I rummaged in the freezer for bagels. I *had* been traumatized, wonderfully, deliciously, profoundly. It was trauma stripped of its pejorative overlay. Outrageous, positive trauma. Balancing the bagels on a plate, I negotiated through the crowd of sheriffs and monks arrayed throughout the house, knocked on the door at the end of the hall, and waited.

The young monk opened the door; I could see the Dalai Lama sitting back against the cushions of the bed. "Thank you," said the monk, but I was looking beyond him into the room. From the orange cushions an arm with a high-tech watch raised into the shining air, and waved.

That night, as I lay awake in a lumpy borrowed bed, I noticed that every cell in my body seemed to be involved in some rhythmic, celebratory dance, vibrating so energetically that sleep was impossible. But I didn't care. The sense of fulfillment was so extreme that it occurred to me that I could die without regret right there and then on the broken springs. "Trite thought," I said out loud, and laughed because I did not need to forgive myself for it. Trite or not, it felt truer than almost anything else in my life. That cool, miraculous night I would have given my life for the Dalai Lama instantly, without question. I felt utterly transformed and utterly baffled. And, apparently, madly in love. What had happened to me? What had happened after I opened the door?

The next day, and the next, the ecstasy continued. Each morning I began my part in the tight scripting of the visit. I laid out the meals that had been prepared—according to schedule—by friends who brought them steaming and fragrant to the door. Chocolate cakes, cherry pies, and vast bowls of cashews and dried fruit displayed their allure shamelessly along the kitchen counter. I often observed the attendant monks succumbing eagerly and happily to the gustatory seduction. But what the Tibetan leader chose to eat—besides bagels— I don't know. This was because, after making sure that the food was where it should be, I usually left the house to give the visitors—and the Visitor—privacy.

After the meals, teams of my friends arrived in the best cars they could borrow to transport the Tibetans to the halls where His Holiness was scheduled to speak. And, in a piece of elegant choreography, other friends let themselves into my house to clean it and wash the dishes while the guests were away. It was heaven: I didn't have to hoist a broom or heft a sponge.

How homey and casual it was, despite the valiant organizing and planning. Just a group of friends, making it happen. Drawing straws for the plum jobs, such as driving His Holiness. Baking their best barley casseroles. Even doing the laundry. These monks had been traveling for a while and, of course, their robes needed a wash. There's something strangely intimate about washing someone else's clothes. And something strangely wonderful about throwing several maroon robes—including one belonging to the Dalai Lama—into your washing machine. One sentimental friend, whose machine it was, kept the lint as a memento.

These days the Dalai Lama travels with several sets of men in expensive dark suits and gun holsters. When he gets in or out of his limousine, entire city blocks are closed down; sometimes when he stays in a hotel, brand-new plates and silverware are required—not because he's fussy, but because his security detail is concerned about poisoning. At my house, way back before we all knew better, we managed with home-baked pie, ancient cups, and a few stalwart sheriffs sitting uneasily in the flowerbeds at night.

Three days passed and it was time for the entourage to move on. We drove through cool sun to the small airport where a private aircraft had been hired to take the group to the next stop. Stepping out of the car, the Dalai Lama pulled his robe tight against the wind, shook each of us by the hand, and strode toward the puny plane that lay on the runway. His attendant was visibly unhappy. Only one propeller. So small. But the Tibetan leader bounded up the two steps, turned in the low doorway, waved buoyantly, and was gone.

I returned home. Returned to the clean house still laden with carrot cake and casserole. Took my collection of sponges and threw them in the garbage. Lay down on the bed with the brown sheets and orange pillows. And understood, for the first time, that from here on out, I was on my way to becoming a Buddhist.

LOUISE GLÜCK

Before the Storm

FROM *The New Yorker*

Rain tomorrow, but tonight the sky is clear, the stars shine.
Still, the rain's coming,
maybe enough to drown the seeds.
There's a wind from the sea pushing the clouds;
before you see them, you feel the wind.
Better look at the fields now,
see how they look before they're flooded.

A full moon. Yesterday a sheep escaped into the woods,
and not just any sheep—the ram, the whole future.
If we see him again, we'll see his bones.

The grass shudders a little; maybe the wind passed through it.
And the new leaves of the olives shudder in the same way.
Mice in the fields. Where the fox hunts,
tomorrow there'll be blood in the grass.
But the storm—the storm will wash it away.

In one window, there's a boy sitting.
He's been sent to bed—too early,
in his opinion. So he sits at the window—

Everything is settled now.

Where you are now is where you'll sleep, where you'll wake up in
the morning.

The mountain stands like a beacon, to remind the night that the
earth exists,

that it mustn't be forgotten.

Above the sea, the clouds form as the wind rises,
dispersing them, giving them a sense of purpose.

Tomorrow the dawn won't come.

The sky won't go back to being the sky of day; it will go on as
night,

except the stars will fade and vanish as the storm arrives,
lasting perhaps ten hours all together.
But the world as it was cannot return.

One by one, the lights of the village houses dim
and the mountain shines in the darkness with reflected light.

No sound. Only cats scuffling in doorways.
They smell the wind: time to make more cats.
Later, they prowl the streets, but the smell of the wind stalks
them.

It's the same in the fields, confused by the smell of blood,
though for now only the wind rises; stars turn the field silver.

This far from the sea and still we know these signs.
The night is an open book.
But the world beyond the night remains a mystery.

SEAMUS HEANEY

The Whisper of Love

FROM *Granta*

IN ANTONIO DEL POLLAIUOLO'S PICTURE OF APOLLO AND DAPHNE IN the National Gallery in London, the god appears like a bare-legged teenage sprinter who has just managed to lay hands on the fleeing nymph. Myth requires her to take root on the spot and begin to sprout laurel leaves and branches, so her loosely robed left leg does appear to be grounded while two big encumbering bushes have sprung from stumps on her shoulders. But her face between the laurel boughs looks back without panic at the face of her pursuer, just as the inside of his left thigh is making contact with the bare calf of her right. Intact she may be, but she remains forever touched and susceptible.

Laurel as emblem of a chaste escape makes sense, especially nowadays when the bush belongs so brightly and trimly in the domestic hedge. Daphne's two sky-besoms do signify her joy at being out of reach, but a part of her is still reluctant to be free, the part suggested by bare legs at full tilt, the part where the erotic vies with the ethereal, the part that is more a birch tree than a laurel.

Birch is the tree of desire, ashimmer with sexual possibility even when it arrives swathed in botanical Latin. *Betula pendula* and *Betula pubescens,* names of the silver and the downy birch, have an indolent sensual loll to them; and technical descriptions of their various characteristics are equally suggestive, the silver variety having "young twigs hairless, with white warts," the downy having "young twigs with velvety white hairs, without warts." No wonder the tree reminded the poet Louis Simpson of "a room filled with breathing, / The sway and whisper of love," where arms being raised to unclasp an earring are like a sallow trunk dividing into pale, smooth, slender branches.

Simpson's birch is warmly and consentingly adult, as if it were a grown-up member of the group Robert Frost saw once after an ice storm in a New England wood, bowed down like girls on their hands and knees, throwing their hair "before them over their heads to dry in the sun." And the first time I entered a New England wood I too was full of the stir of poetry, and much else besides. I had read in Robert Graves's *The White Goddess* that *beith*/birch was the synonym for *B* in the Ogham alphabet, and had translated Mad Sweeney's praise of the trees of Ireland, where the blessed, smooth-skinned *beithe bláith bennachtach* sways magically in the breeze, under its crown of plaited twigs. But there and then all that airy, erotic energy and association got captured and confined (much as Ariel was by Sycorax in a cloven pine) in a section of birch trunk I found on the wood floor.

This was a thick-stemmed piece of sapling about ten inches long and as thick as a nymph's leg above the ankle, in the shape of a Y that had been pruned. Just above where the young trunk divided, the two branches had snapped off, and afterward the thing lay marinating in a compost of old leaves and moss until the heartwood turned altogether soggy. When I discovered it, the innards had actually decayed to the point where I was able to clear out the mush and was left holding an open-ended sheath of bark, flecked and grained, warted, dampish, a little bit tufty-downy at the cleft.

This was in May 1979, beside Eagle Pond in New Hampshire, where I had gone with my family to visit the poet Donald Hall, friend of Louis Simpson, disciple of Frost, and the inheritor of his grandfather's farm, to which he had only recently returned. Eventually, therefore, my chance find became a memento of our visit to his poetry station, the memento became a keepsake, and when I read that the birch is "a light-demanding tree and will not grow in the shade of others," the keepsake began to shine in my mind like a Platonic idea.

At the end of the weekend I took it back to Harvard and have not parted with it since. First I let it dry (when it stiffened, it was as if the word "birch" were turning into the older "birk"); then I stood the blunted Y shape upside down so that it became a little torso agleam in its own whiteness, a *puella* forever *pubescens,* an armless, legless Venus de New Hampshire, as disinclined to move as Daphne was desperate to flee. A form that seems to ponder Rilke's response to the archaic torso of Apollo—"You must change your life"—before answering wistfully, "Yes, perhaps, but first you have to live it."

JANE HIRSHFIELD

Vinegar and Oil

FROM *The Atlantic*

Wrong solitude vinegars the soul,
right solitude oils it.

How fragile we are, between the few good moments.

Coming and going unfinished,
puzzled by fate,

like the half-carved relief
of a fallen donkey, above a church door in Finland.

PAULA HUSTON

The Kingdom of the Eternal Heaven

FROM *Image*

WE ARE ROCKETING THROUGH THE STEPPES INTO THE EYE OF THE setting sun. To the east of us, the great thrusting shoulders of the Tian Shan, or "Celestial Mountains," are burnished with the deep rose gold you see on icons from the Sinai or tanka paintings from Nepal. According to local lore, deep within the range, at the far eastern border of Kyrgyzstan, towers "Ice Mountain," a confluence of mighty glaciers. It is said that there are seventy-eight hundred of these glaciers in the Tian Shan, and on the high ridges that run above them lives the ghostly snow leopard. The fifteen-hundred-mile-long range flows south between Kyrgyzstan and Kazakhstan, where it spirals into the Himalaya and the Hindu Kush at the Pamir Knot, the meeting place of the loftiest mountains in the world.

Far to the north of us lie the Altai Mountains of Siberia—according to Indian legend, home of the mystical kingdom of Shambala. East of the Altai is Baikal, the oldest and deepest lake on the planet and, since ancient days, mother to the reindeer-herding, earth-worshipping Evenk. Their heirs, the Mongolian Buryat, still practice a peculiar sort of Lamaist Buddhism—which is to say, Tibetan Buddhism tempered with a strain of much older, indigenous shamanism. North of the Altai and Baikal sits the vast Siberian taiga, a thick-growing coniferous forest of stone pine and larch that runs six thousand miles across Russia from sea to sea. The taiga is the traditional home of the Goldi, an aboriginal tribe of shamans and far-ranging hunters. It was also the wandering space of the stranniks, the nineteenth-century Orthodox Christian pilgrims who trudged through its deep green silence seeking the hidden hermitages of starets, or holy men.

We ourselves are in the vast grassland known as the steppes, heading southwest from Almaty to Taraz, down the eastern border of Kazakhstan.

Our driver, Ivan, clearly a descendent of Turkic-Mongol warriors, is maneuvering his "machina" one-handed at what must be top speed—the dial reads 160 kilometers per hour. He hangs his free arm across the top of the seat and turns to see how I am doing in my nest of pirated videotapes. Next to him, spectacular Alina, born to be the mistress of a billionaire but condemned instead to the life of an English teacher in the heart of crime-ridden Central Asia, rolls her eyes. She is disgusted at this blatant display of bravado, and I can't blame her. Ivan is putting all three of us at risk. Yet in spite of my anxiety about crashing out here in the middle of nowhere, I can't help but like Ivan and his gold-studded teeth. When he is not showing off, he is bashfully kind to me, and I am very far from home.

Every few minutes we hit a pothole and the machina lurches, springs from the asphalt, and crashes back to the road, usually in the other lane. Aside from the wrenching to our necks, this is no problem, for there are few vehicles in this part of the world. And aside from the occasional twist and turn, we can see forever; we are racing over potholes across a fifteen-hundred-mile expanse of ancient nomadic herding land. We fly past grazing sheep and dark yurts, people on horseback, carts. We fly through small villages with candlelight glimmering in the windows. The sun flares behind the massed rainclouds in the west, then disappears below the horizon. Suddenly, we are skimming through violet twilight into flocks of blackbirds ex-

ploding skyward. Ivan reaches down and pops in a cassette, Simon
and Garfunkel's *Sounds of Silence*. For an eerie moment it's the late
sixties, and I'm a high school junior in Southern California who has
never heard of Central Asia, much less Kazakhstan.

Then we come to a big curve. Ivan lifts his black shoe from the
accelerator and puts his free hand on the wheel. Around the bend we
enter upon disaster. A pickup has hit a horse and rider, then flipped.
People have gathered from nowhere. The crowd gazes down at the
motionless herder. Off to the side lies the still-saddled horse, with its
head flung back like the anguished beast in Picasso's *Guernica* and
most of its neck missing. I feel hot, then icy, then sick. My eyes fill
with tears of nauseated shock. Ivan glances at Alina, who is studiously
avoiding the grisly mess in the road, then gives me an apologetic shrug
and speeds up again to get us out of there. No one says a word.

Kazakhstan is a stopping place for me, a week out of the months I
will spend on this round-the-world journey. In some ways, though I
will also visit India and Nepal, this Central Asian interlude is my
most exotic. Not many Americans have been here, far fewer of them
than, say, go trekking in the Himalayas or study with gurus in Vara-
nasi. What is there to see, after all? Kazakhstan is a third the size
of the United States and is bounded by, among other remote places,
Mongolia, Siberia, and the Chinese far western frontier. There are few
highways. Fewer than three people per square mile. A lot of grass.

Yet Taraz, where I'll be staying in a small apartment owned by
Alina's family, was in ancient times known as Talas, a Silk Road trad-
ing post in the middle of the vast stretch of plains that lie between
Europe and Asia. For more than fifteen hundred years before the
Renaissance, whatever cultural exchange took place between the East
and West happened here on the steppes. In the first century, the road
started in Antioch, crossed the Euphrates River, passed near modern
Teheran, and headed east to the Pamir Mountains, where a stone

tower marked the exchange zone. Farther on, the road split into a northern and southern route, both running toward China. Taraz, or Talas, was on the northern leg. Wooly, double-humped Bactrian camels, roped together and loaded with Chinese silk or Persian rugs or Indian spices, crossed and recrossed the sea of grass in undulating lines. Missionaries and pilgrims from opposite ends of the civilized world followed in their tracks.

In A.D. 630, Hsüan-tsang, a Buddhist pilgrim from China, passed through Talas on his way west. His return journey followed the southern leg of the Silk Road, and he recorded what he'd seen as he traveled through the Tarim Basin oases on the edge of the Gobi: a meld of Greek, Roman, Iranian, Indian, and Chinese religion, philosophy, and art. Sanskrit texts were being translated into Indo-European languages. Nestorians and Byzantines mingled with Hellenes, Levantines, Tibetans, and Chinese, here at the far western edge of the Orient.

But the true masters of this land were neither merchants nor pilgrims but mighty warrior nomads. From the notorious Bronze-Age Scythians of the western steppes to the infamous Turkic-Mongol Huns of the East, Central Asia was dominated until the late eighteenth century by the mounted archers of the plains. When they weren't at war, they were following the grass with their vast herds of horses, goats, sheep, and camels, migrating with the seasons in great wagon trains. They scorned city life and destroyed it systematically. They scorned agriculture, too, and decimated cropland wherever they found it in order that the grass might grow unimpeded. And they periodically struck like wolves at the great civilizations that lay on their borders: Rome, Byzantium, Persia, India, China.

The ferocity of these warrior nomads is legendary. Herodotus, for example, records that a favorite Scythian practice was to saw horizontally through the skull of the enemy, cover the half skull with leather and gold, and use it for a drinking cup. Huns sealed a contract by imbibing human blood. They also honored their dead chiefs by cutting the throats of their wives and servants—sometimes as many as a thousand of these at a time—on the tomb of their departed leader. In mourning, they slashed their faces with knives so that blood would mingle with their tears.

At midnight we are still driving. From Almaty, where my Lufthansa flight out of Frankfurt landed at the nearly lightless airport, to Taraz, where Alina and Ivan have lived in neighboring houses since they were children, is an eight-hour trip. I am not asleep but not fully awake either when we hit a monster pothole. Ivan fights the gyrating wheel as we reconnect with the road. Safely down, we hear it: a wheeze like someone dying of TB. The car begins to slow of its own accord. We enter a dark village under a full moon, and stop. From out of nowhere a car filled with Kazakh men materializes beside us, calling in Russian out of their open window: "Your fuel pump fell out! Your fuel is running out on the road!" Then they are gone, their red blaze of taillights winking, fading, then snuffing out. We are alone in this sleeping village on the steppes.

Ivan sighs, opens the car door, climbs out. Alina, curiously unconcerned, is inspecting her nails by moonlight. "What's going on?" I croak. "Have we broken down? Are we stranded?"

She gives me an airy wave. "Do not worry," she says. "He will think a little. Then he will fix it."

Ivan, who has been crouching silently at the rear of the car, now crunches around to Alina's open window, murmuring something in Russian. "He wants to know if you have a torch," she tells me.

"I do!" I begin digging through the pile of videotapes in search of my buried backpack. I unzip the side pocket and pull out the small flashlight Mike slipped inside at the last minute, a husband's last-ditch effort to protect his crazy wife on her solo trip around the world. It flickers, then goes out. I jiggle it, but nothing. Ivan takes it apart, finds a loose lightbulb, twists it, then puts everything back together. I show him how to turn it into a lantern. His eyes widen appreciatively in the face of this small miracle. Then he crunches back around the car to set up shop.

Alina begins a long story I have heard before, the story of Ivan and what a good, noble, truehearted friend he has always been to her, and why, tragically, she can never marry him. At this point, however, I am far more interested in the fate of our machina. I hold up one hand, telling Alina I want to see if I can help. She shakes her head—these American women, so strangely masculine—and goes back to inspecting her nails. I trudge to the back of the car where Ivan is lying on his side on the cold asphalt.

The fuel pump dangles in two pieces. Ivan dries them with a rag, then tests them for leaks. No leaks. A fortuitous sign. He puts them back together but has no way to secure them. I remember Mike's emergency kit, a pencil with duct tape wrapped around it. Also a fairy ring of thin wire. I go back to my pack and dig them out, then present them to our mechanic. Ivan tests the duct tape and declares that it is "harasho"—good. He does some magic with the wire to reattach the pipe, and soon we are on our way, though at a more sedate speed. He murmurs something to Alina, and she translates, though in a bored way—these mechanical problems are of no interest to her—"He says that you are unusually prepared."

Not me, I think. I prefer clinging to the happy illusion that nothing bad will ever happen to me. It is Mike, with his uncanny ability to forecast trouble, who takes such precautions on my behalf.

Taraz is actually a new name for a city long known as Dzhambul. Since the collapse of the Soviet Union, Kazakhstan has been consciously returning to its roots, and Taraz is simply another pronunciation of the ancient name of Talas, which for several hundred years sat at the heart of the khanate of the Western Tu-Chüeh. In the sixth century, the head of the Western Tu-Chüeh, a Turkic khan called Istämi, regularly wintered near the springs of Talas. His people were like Attila's people, and also like those for generations to follow. Cropless and cityless, they were always on the move, sheltering in transportable felt yurts, trailing their vast herds through seasons of grass, seasons of drought. Istämi wore his hair long and flowing, held back from his forehead by a ten-foot length of silk. His flagstaff was crowned with a golden she-wolf's head; his men-at-arms were known as *fu-li*, "the wolves."

Istämi belonged to the cult of Tängri, or "The Eternal Heaven," a demanding god who required regular sacrifice of sheep, oxen, and horses. The Tängrian cosmos consisted of seventeen realms of light and nine realms of darkness—Turkic heaven and hell. Dealing with Tängri required powerful, prophetic shamans whose legacy still shapes Central Asian culture. Even today the arts of leaving and returning to one's body, casting the evil eye and healing with one's hands are said to exist in the remote regions north of Irkutsk.

Seven hundred years after Istämi, when Genghis Khan's massed archers burst forth across the steppes toward medieval Europe, their worldview was much the same. As in the ancient days of Attila, Tängri ruled the heavens, sacrifice was mandatory, fire and running water were to be venerated, and hundreds of *yer-sub* (genies) lurked among the hills and springs. Genghis, too, relied heavily on shamanistic prophets. One of these, Kökchü, announced to a gathering of the clans that the Eternal Blue Heaven himself had appointed Genghis as universal khagan, or emperor over all Turkic-Mongolian people. The shaman, who was famous for traveling to the realms of light on a dapple-gray horse in order to consult with the spirits, inspired such awe with his prowess as a magician that no one dared object.

Genghis himself made pilgrimages to the holy mountain of Burqan Qaldun to pay homage to Tängri before major campaigns. There, the grand emperor of all Central Asia submissively removed his cap and lay his belt over his shoulder, genuflecting nine times and sprinkling *kumiss*—fermented mare's milk—in offering to his holy lord. Like all warriors of the steppes, he hid when it thundered—a sign of Tängri's wrath. More, he was always prudently respectful of other arbiters of supernatural power: Muslim mullahs, Tibetan lamas, Nestorian priests, Franciscan missionaries, Buddhist monks, Taoist magicians.

Alina and I are sitting across a lace-covered table piled with dumplings, blingees, hard white cheese, borsht, home-canned wild mushrooms, spicy tomatoes, and herbs. Given the ongoing energy crisis in Taraz, she and her sister are masterful cooks. For years there has been no gas in their part of the city, so they can their fruits and vegetables on a wood-burning stove and heat water for chai with a dangerous-looking electric wand. Hot water is centrally located in most former Soviet cities; with no gas, the huge tanks meant to supply the populace no longer provide. I have been in Kazakhstan long enough to catch up on some sleep, and to recover my appetite after my long flight and harrowing drive.

Alina, who was once nominated for the Kazakh national teacher of the year award, speaks English more gracefully than anyone I've met in America. Long ago, she traveled to England for a brief period of study, and this perhaps helps explain her passionate love of nineteenth-century British novels and her curiously Victorian air. She is both driven and judged by her own lofty standards, and as committed to personal honor as any warrior of the steppes. Her battlefield is the teacher's lounge where (as might be expected, given her startling beauty and her moral fastidiousness) she magnetically attracts the most vicious envy, spite, and conspiratorial nastiness. "Sometimes," she tells me, "they even cast the evil eye. I can feel it in the back of my head and neck, a lot of pain and heaviness."

"What does a person do about that?" I ask.

She gives me a somber look, then unbuttons the top two buttons of her blouse and draws it open so I can see her bra. Pinned over her right breast is a large safety pin. I take a sip of chai and try not to raise an eyebrow.

"Protection," she explains. "You should wear one also."

This is not a new theme for her. During the few hours we were in Almaty, while Ivan was busy buying and selling his illegal video-tapes, she took me shopping for amulets to bring home to my four kids. These turned out to be small, woven, multicolored diamonds of yarn, much like I'd seen in the marketplaces of Guatemala. She was especially adamant that I buy one for my tall son, Johnny. "Why?" I asked her. "Why him in particular?"

"Because," she said, as though it were obvious. "He is so very handsome and accomplished. He will attract a lot of evil."

Now she tells me, "You cannot simply wear the pin. You have to do a lot of prays. My mother learned them all when she was growing up in Azerbaijan, and she taught us how to do them correctly."

"Why can't you just ask God to protect you from harm?"

She reaches across the table and lays a firm hand on my forearm. "Listen," she says, "you must do them right, and there are a lot of them. Otherwise you are vulnerable."

"Is there a way besides feeling it in the back of your neck to know if someone is wishing bad luck on you?"

"Yes," she tells me. "You take a handful of flour and drop it in a pan of water. If the flour separates into small clumps, then someone has cast a spell on you. If it stays together, then all is well. But there are special prays for this also, and if you do them incorrectly, the ritual does not work."

I sit digesting this new information for a moment. After many years of cynicism about the so-called power of prayer, I've become an ardent believer. And this belief, curiously enough, has grown in me the way a physicist's or biologist's faith in a theory might—through the amassing of empirical evidence. Prayer has directly impacted my life through a myriad of unlikely events. I know, for example, that I was prayed by my sister back into Christianity after twenty years of angry agnosticism. I know that I was prayed by a friend through the doors of the Catholic Church. I am delighted by the landscape prayer has opened up for me: a novelistic space of conflict, epiphany, reversal, synthesis. A life of prayer, I've found, is a life of endless surprises.

But Alina is talking about something I've never thought of before: a prayer of evil, so to speak, that is meant to wreak havoc in another person's life. And as I mull this over, I realize how likely it is that the evil eye does indeed have the power to harm: focused malice, bolstered by the invoking of cruel spirits. This flusters me; I prefer to think of the spiritual as purely good, purely loving. But where, I now wonder, did I ever come up with *this* notion? Surely not from the Gospels, where one of Jesus's main occupations is the casting out of demons.

"So, Alina," I say cautiously, "what if someone casts the evil eye at you and something happens? Like, say, you get sick?"

She turns to gaze out into the twilight, and an unreadable look crosses her face. "There are healers," she says finally. "You must get to a healer right away."

"Have you been to one?"

"Oh, yes," she says, "many times. There is a Muslim woman at the school, for example, who is very well known."

"A teacher?"

"Yes. When she was young, a large bird appeared on her back and shoulders, and she knew it was the sign that she was meant to heal." She pauses and tears off a piece of bread.

"Like a tattoo, you mean?"

Alina nods. "But not in color—all dark markings. She showed it to the community of healers here in Taraz and they sent her up to Russia for evaluation."

I give her a puzzled look.

"By the great healers there," she explains. "They confirmed the sign was real and told her to go home and use her gift."

"And has she cured you of anything?"

Alina's face goes still at the memory, and I can see that she is still traumatized by what happened to her. She says, "The one who hates me most—that very Katya I told you about in America?—cast a very bad spell and I began to suffer with a large swelling on the side of my neck. I grew weak and it was hard to come to school or teach my classes because of the pain. Then I went to the healer, and she prayed over me and used her hands. I had to go back several times, but the lump disappeared. Without her, who knows what would have happened?" I am staring at her, unable to get inside this alien worldview but also unable to call it nonsense. She adds with a clear and child-like simplicity, "I might have died."

I ponder this for a moment. Then I cough.

Alina narrows her eyes at me. "Are you ill?"

I have been secretly fighting a sore throat for several days now, no doubt a relic of the long plane trip from Frankfurt to Almaty, but hoping to avoid a trip to the healer with the bird tattoo, I staunchly shake my head. Alina is nobody's fool, however, and she is studying me closely. I cough again and shrug. "Just a tickle," I say.

Shamans can be found throughout the world: among North American tribes, for example, and in Southeast Asia and Oceania. However, the term itself—*saman*—is Tungus, from the Altaic family of languages characteristic to Central Asia. And it is in Central Asia, especially Siberia, that shamanist ideology has traditionally characterized religious belief.

Shamans ferry souls. They are a living bridge between the land of spirit and the land of flesh. They heal by seeking out and returning souls who have wandered from their desperately ill owners. Sometimes, however, souls are stolen and imprisoned by demons, and in these cases shamans must descend to the land of the dead in order to free them. Shamans also escort the souls of sacrificial animals— horses or reindeer—to heaven, where they offer them to the gods. And they regularly accompany the souls of the dead to the Kingdom of Shadows.

This is not a job for the faint of heart, and not many seek out the profession on their own. Instead, they inherit the role or are chosen by a supernatural being. Following election, they enter a period of trial, which often means serious illness or the irresistible urge to wander alone in the wilderness. And during this dreamscape time, they undergo complete destruction and reconstruction: They are tortured by demons, dismembered, and finally brought back to life as entirely new creatures, far more like spirits than human beings. Only then does their shamanistic instruction begin.

The ecstasy or trance of shamans allows them to both transmigrate—leave their own bodies and travel to other realms—and be in turn possessed by powerful spirits, especially the *ayamis* who originally chose them. Helper spirits such as the bear or tiger can also penetrate them, entering their bodies like a mysterious vapor. Shamans have mystical vision; they can see into the supernatural realms and report back to those who have only human eyesight. But their greatest gift is the gift of healing.

Alina's healer, the woman with the great bird etched in black across her back, was no doubt sent to the Altai region of Siberia for confirmation of her divine election.

Genghis Khan's respect for the holy men of other religions did not prevent him from systematically decimating Muslim, Buddhist, and Christian populations if they failed to surrender in time. More often than not, a defeated city underwent total massacre. In one large Iranian city, the killing took a whole week, and when it was over, the army feigned departure in order to capture and destroy those few survivors who emerged from hiding. When Genghis himself died in 1227, forty of the most beautiful girls from the families of his ranking officers were given the honor of being slaughtered on his grave, along with the finest horses in the empire.

By 1230, Talas had become part of the Khanate of Jagatai, who was the second son of Genghis Khan. Northwest of Talas, stretching all the way to Kiev and Moscow, was that portion of the empire known as the land of the Golden Horde. To the east, taking in much of Siberia, Mongolia, Tibet, and China, lay the empire of the Great Khan. Mongolian reign over the steppes seemed near absolute. But in 1241, still in the early years after Genghis's death, Europe lay unconquered and alluring. During that Advent season, a Mongolian army surged from Kiev toward Vienna by way of Kraków and Hungary. If Genghis's successor had not died in Mongolia at this moment—December 11—necessitating an election back home, Europe might easily have been burnt back to grassland and forest.

Genghis and his fierce successors were followed in time by two more military geniuses: Kublai Khan and Tamerlane. Kublai was a masterful politician, who managed to reunite the fragmented Mongolian Empire, and was also a late-in-life convert to Chinese Buddhism. Tamerlane, for his part, was a highly skilled butcher who left pure devastation in his wake. He reinstituted the ancient terror tactics used by Attila: pyramids of human skulls; living bodies piled on living bodies then cemented into pillars; corpses whose hands, feet, and heads were systematically removed; total massacre, including infants. Ninety thousand here, seventy thousand there, seven hundred cities and towns razed to the ground in Russia alone. Some have compared him—quite aptly—to Hitler because of his savage love of killing. And because of the sheer numbers of his victims.

· · ·

Alina is thrilled. After some heavy machinations at school, she has wangled us an invitation to a Kazakh feast at a dacha in the region of the Talas springs. I am excited too, though with some trepidation: Mike has given me a briefing on such events, which often involve a slow-roasted sheep and dozens of cups of vodka. To complicate matters, I am sick; the sore throat has become bronchitis, and I am pretty sure I'm running a fever.

Yet when we arrive at the reedy lake shore, I find I am charmed. Tucked under the great leafy trees are simple green dachas, the traditional rural cottages used by people all over the former Soviet Union, both for vacationing and for supplementing their food supplies. Beyond the dachas lie gardens, fields of grain, grazing flocks. Herders in traditional Kazakh dress stand talking in a nearby pasture. And running toward us with welcoming cries are sun-flushed women with bowls and baskets in their arms.

The tables are already heaped with food: *lepyoshki* (wheels of bread), *halva* (crushed sesame seeds and honey), *plof* (rice cooked with mutton), *shurpa* and *lagman* (spicy soups with noodles), *manti* and *samsa* (meat-stuffed dough), *kishmish* (raisins), tomato and onion salad, fresh fruit. Men stand beside a fire tending roasting spits; another group of them watch smoke seeping from a pit, wherein lies a whole sheep or calf.

Eventually, we are seated at the head table on rug-covered benches beside the family patriarch, Molian. He turns his yellow cat's eyes on me in a long, unsmiling gaze. Then he begins to speak, and the other tables fall silent. Alina translates. I am most welcome. He hopes I am enjoying my visit to Kazakhstan. They have few visitors from America, so this is a special day for his family. But he cannot understand why I don't eat meat.

"Tell him," I say, "that many Americans choose not to eat meat for health reasons."

He looks both amazed and dubious. He asks how this can be when it is meat that gives a man strength.

I turn to Alina. "Tell him that in Kazakhstan, it is still necessary for men to be men. In America, most people drive cars and sit behind desks—they don't need big Kazakh muscles. If they eat such rich food, they get sick." I am in earnest, here; this is not a joke.

But her translation earns me a roar of laughter. Molian is grinning and thrusting a full glass of vodka at me, shouting out a toast. For this clan of modern-day Turkic-Mongol descendents, I am a major aberration—a California vegetarian who has inexplicably wandered into the heart of carnivorous Central Asia—but somehow I am in. The thought fills me with a foolish, bashful joy. I ask about this startling hospitality of theirs, and Molian tells me it is a very ancient tradition going back to nomadic times, long before Islam. The stranger, he says, was considered a great gift, for he brought news of the world. And he could also, of course, be God in disguise.

Then a woman steps forward and begins to sing with the voice of a Vienna choir boy in a language that sounds like how cats would speak if they could form words. Iman, Alina tells me, is a Kazakh musician who lives far out on the steppes and rarely even speaks Russian. She sings, swaying, with her eyes closed, snapping her fingers to keep time, and the sun flashes against her earrings and necklace of malachite and silver.

Later, we walk arm in arm by the side of the lake, Iman and Alina and me. Iman confesses she has never seen a real foreigner before, that she was terrified to perform for me, but that our open faces put her at ease. When I tell her how much I admire her songs, she says that she often receives her music fully formed, as if from space. As if, she says, from Bog himself. Just then a thousand blackbirds take rushing flight from the branches above us. Our faces snap skyward: no birds. Iman whispers, "Druga," wind, but not a leaf is stirring. We turn in thoughtful silence and head back toward the tables.

A shout goes up at the fire pit—the sheep is finally done! Molian, softened by much vodka and long hours in the sun, gives me instructions. A platter containing the baked head of the sheep will be placed before me. I will carve off the left ear, hand it to the daughter of my hosts, and give her my blessing.

Dusk is now giving way to darkness, but the full moon has not yet risen above the tree line. A woman goes down the row of tables, lighting candles. Faces appear, vanish, reappear in the flickering glow. I am suffering from a great, happy feeling of love. Everything seems good, even the mutton grease snapping in the embers.

Then the platter is placed before me and I am staring into the astonished eyes of the sheep, who has been sacrificed for this feast and then roasted to a pliable leathery orange. The right ear has already been severed; this will be taken to the dacha afterward as an offering. The other ear is mine.

I close my eyes, thanking God for this generous animal and also for making me a vegetarian, then pick up the knife. The ear falls gracefully into my hand. I look up at bright-eyed Dinara, daughter of my hosts, and launch into my blessing. "May you be successful in school," I say, "and someday go on for higher education. May you work at a career you love. May you find a man who adores and respects you as much as you deserve, and may you have a wonderful, long marriage. May God keep you healthy and strong, and may you bear many fine children to make your parents proud."

Then I hand her the ear and shove the platter over to Molian, who pulls open the jaws of the sheep and carves out the tongue, a slab of wrinkled white cheese. This, he hands to Alina in honor of her translating abilities.

Serious meat-eating begins. Candlelight plays over faces happy and shiny with grease. The stack of bones grows higher. Finally, people are pushing back from the tables, laughing, moaning, patting their bellies. Bowls of fermented mare's milk—a great aid to digestion, I am told—make the rounds. Crossing my fingers and closing my eyes, I drink down two bowlfuls.

Then it is time to say farewell. The women form a line, hugging me and kissing me on the lips, some of them weeping. Suddenly, Iman stands in front of me, her eyes wet. She pulls me to her in a long, solemn hug, then stands back and removes her beautiful silver and malachite necklace and drapes it around my neck. Alina gasps. "She tells you that she has had this necklace for many years and it is very precious to her. She wants you to have it and take it with you in your travels."

There is no way to protest. Instead, I pull my turquoise rosary from my pocket and thrust it into her hand while tears pour from her dark and tilted eyes.

Contemporary DNA studies suggest that modern human beings evolved in Africa a hundred thousand years ago and arrived in Central Asia about fifty thousand years later. A gene called microcephalin, which emerged in Homo sapiens some thirty-seven thousand years ago, is a possible evolutionary explanation for the symbolic thinking that began to emerge in our species about this time. Another, younger, gene called ASPM—fifty-eight hundred years old, by now—is a primary evolutionary suspect in the mysterious and relatively sudden city-building that began to take place in the Near East shortly thereafter. Though the roots of the great world religions no doubt go back to somewhere near the emergence of microcephalin in the human brain, imperial warriorhood is of necessity far younger. There had to be cities before men thought of conquering them. And it did not take long for conquerors to seek religious justification for what they did.

Attila the Hun piously invoked the will of Tängri before his scorched-earth campaigns. So did his military heirs, including Genghis. Other khans converted to Islam, then wreaked destruction on their Sunni or Shi'ite brothers. Still others became Tibetan Buddhists and got caught up in the battle between the old Red Church, with its still-strong link to ancient Bon shamanism, and the Yellow Church of the khan-instituted line of Dalai Lamas. The Christians of the Byzantine Empire cut deals with the warriors of the steppes to protect their Silk Road trade. Nestorian Christians in the East, declared heretical by the Roman Church, became themselves military khans. Taoist magicians and Confucian wise men grew adept at Central Asian political intrigue.

Our history as a species—really, astonishingly brief—can from one perspective be summed up as a battle for power, the chief strategy employed being mass murder justified on religious grounds.

Alina is furious with me for gulping down a cup of cold orange juice when I am sick. "How can you drink something cold when you have a fever? Don't you know that this will make all your vessels tremble?"

She tells me about Pavlov's chicken experiment, one I've not heard about before. Apparently, he put one hen's feet in ice water and the other's in lukewarm water, then injected them both with the same germ. "And who do you think got sick?" She casts me a darkly triumphant look when she asks me this, as though she knows I know the answer whether I will admit it or not. "You must never allow yourself to be chilled when you are sick," she adds seriously, "either by what you eat and drink or by how you dress."

Then I am told to remove my shoes and put my bare feet into a pan of boiling water. I obey. While my feet are being destroyed, Alina helps me into my coat, wraps a heavy red Kazakh scarf around my neck, settles a wool hat on my head, and thrusts a tall glass of hot milk, honey, and cognac into my hand. "Drink!" she commands. I drink, and—feeling faint—break into a powerful sweat. "Harasho!" she declares. Very good. "Now take this." *This* turns out to be half of what looks like an antibiotic.

"Oh, no," I begin, holding up one sweaty hand. "No, Alina, I can't take that."

"Why not?" she demands.

"You can't just take half an antibiotic—it can work the opposite way and make the bug stronger. Do you know what I mean?"

Alina draws herself up and stares down at me and my wrinkled feet. I can hear the breath whistling, outraged, through her aristocratic nose. "You forget—my mother was a Soviet physician," she reminds me. "It is she who has made this prescription for you. The other half comes in the morning."

"One pill?" I say feebly. "That's it?"

"And after that we go to the healer."

I spend the night in a land of confusing, fevered dreams and wake feeling like a sodden log beneath the heaped woolen blankets. Alina is already up and dressed and waiting. "I think I'm good now," I say, as soon as I'm able. "Don't worry about the healer, okay?"

An hour later I'm standing with my legs apart and my hands away from my sides in front of a shy Kazakh woman who is briskly rubbing her palms together. Then she thrusts her right hand into the air, like a receiver, and places the other, flat-palmed, an inch above my abdomen, and begins tracing circles. Her eyes close. Her smiling face now looks remote. She says, in a strange, flat voice, "Normalna," and moves on to my kidneys, then my throat.

Alina keeps asking me if I feel heat—I don't. "Normalna," drones the healer, still circling with her palm. "Normalna, normalna." Everything, fortunately, seems to be normalna. My examination is complete. I will live.

Once again, we are hurtling across the steppes, with—who else?—Ivan once again at the wheel. We have been driving since two A.M. Alina and her mother and sister chose this time carefully, for the trip is hours-long with a border to cross illegally before I can board my flight to Delhi out of Tashkent. I had planned to fly Kaz Air, but

Kaz Air no longer travels, though I saw the planes sitting quietly and patiently on the tarmac at the airport in Almaty. My only option was Uzbekistan Airlines, but of course there was no time to get an Uzbek visa.

I have my instructions. Whenever we are stopped—either by the police, who stand by the road with batons, waiting for unsuspecting vehicles to dare pass them, or by border guards—I am to feign sleep. Under no circumstances, Alina tells me, am I to speak out loud. "The moment they realize you are a foreigner, especially an American, they will demand so many bribes you will not be able to pay." We have already been stopped three times. Ivan is good at this, this joking around and then slipping the bribe.

But now dawn is breaking and we are nearly to the border of Uzbekistan. My two friends are nervous, I can tell, though they stoically refuse to admit this. Suddenly, at the worst possible moment, for we are within sight of the guard house, a hubcap goes ringing off into the brush at the side of the road. Ivan cannot afford to lose a hubcap. He pulls over and we all get out and silently search in the half-light of early morning. I have no idea what will happen if we attract attention and are questioned. Will I wind up in a Uzbek jail? Will Alina and Ivan go with me?

Alina gives a soft whoop, then scuttles back to the car with the battered hubcap under her arm. Ivan kicks it back into place, then pulls back into the road and drives slowly to the guard house. I curl up and close my eyes, as though asleep, though I'm pretty sure the guard has seen me poking through the bushes.

Ivan takes my air ticket inside. We can hear the two of them, Ivan and the guard, joking and laughing. Then a long silence, then more laughing. Then he is back. I hold my breath, thinking that the guard has asked to see me, the woman whose name is on this ticket to India. But it is okay, Ivan tells us in a low voice: The guard couldn't even read. He held the ticket upside down.

"Then what were you laughing about?" asks Alina sternly. Ivan, looking only slightly abashed, tells us that the guard noticed two blondes in the car and wondered why a simple Kazakh should have both women and he, a good Uzbek, have none. She looks disgusted and I give a half-hysterical, relieved snort. I'm going to miss pragmatic Ivan and his gold-studded smile. We glide through the border crossing. We are early; my plane takes off in four hours. But we have no idea where the airport might be.

We drive through the early-morning streets of Tashkent, ancient home of the dreaded Scythians of Asia, looking for a control tower, anything that will lead us where we need to go. I wish we had more time to explore this Silk Road city. I wish I was legal.

Then we see it—a chain-link fence, a parking lot, and planes. Ivan pulls into a small parking lot with hardly any cars in it, and we lock my pack inside and head for the terminal to see if they'll let me check in. At the cash exchange window, I try to trade my eight hundred remaining Kazakh tengay for dollars but not only won't the clerk consider such an impertinent request, he won't exchange my tengay for *any* sort of money, even Uzbek. On this subject, he is entirely firm. In Uzbekistan, he informs me, tengay are worthless. Sighing, I hand the wad of bills to Alina; she, at least, can make good use of it back home.

We return to the parking lot for my pack. A short cop, churning with histrionic rage, is clearing out all the cars for some reason we cannot determine. He demands Ivan's Kazakh license and says he must wait for his ticket to be written up. Ivan quietly offers him the usual bribe, but he shouts that he does not take money, and besides, doesn't he know that tengay are worthless in Uzbekistan? Other people, looking resigned and defeated, are quietly waiting on the margins. Half an hour later, we are still standing around, hoping that the cop will stop shrieking at new cars entering the lot long enough to finish the tickets. Ivan, looking large, friendly, but cautious, goes up to him, hoping to plead my cause. "Do not approach me!" the cop screams, brandishing a gun. "For this, I am holding your license for two months!" Ivan steps back, then humbly asks if we can at least remove my luggage.

I can feel my vessels trembling under an onslaught of hopeless anxiety. This cop is not even the immigration officer. What will happen to me in the terminal? Will I ever get out of Central Asia?

But Ivan, in his kindly and inoffensive way, the way of people everywhere who are used to living under corrupt overlords, has managed to extract my luggage from the machina. We walk away from the parking lot, hoping not to be shot in the back, and enter the terminal, which by now is filled with people traveling who knows where. China, perhaps, or Afghanistan. Nepal or India. Russia or even Europe. We are in Tashkent, after all, the ancient crossroads between East and West.

We come to a barricade. Beyond it is a line. Hidden around the corner must be the immigration checkpoint. My hands begin to sweat again. I turn toward my two dear friends, these people who have driven me halfway across the steppes, who have risked their own security for mine. What to say? I pull Alina, who is by now fiercely resisting the tears that are splashing down the front of her coat, into my arms and hold her there. May God bless and keep you, I am thinking, from all danger and harm. From the evil eye. From corrupt police. From the KGB, who still haunt Taraz, and from the robbers who prey on those who still have jobs. From economic disaster and war and nuclear winter. In the name of the Father and the Son and the Holy Spirit, amen.

I kiss her wet cheek and turn to Ivan, whose fists are jammed in his pockets, whose feet are shuffling in uncertainty. I pull out one of his hands—he jerks in surprise—and turn it over, then lay Mike's magic flashlight, the one that turns into a tiny lantern, the one that saved us on the road from Almaty, across his palm. He stares down at it, then at me, then grins, and the light from the big gray bureaucratic fluorescents above us catches the gold in his teeth. "Thank you," he says, his first English words to me.

I pat them both blindly on the fronts of their coats, cross the barrier, and find my place in line. When I finally reach the corner—there is the immigration officer, waiting for me—I turn and look back. And there they are, still keeping their faithful watch, though they cannot possibly know, far less control, what will happen to me next.

PICO IYER

The Return of "The Snow Leopard"

FROM *The New York Review of Books*

THE SNOW LEOPARD IS AN ACCOUNT OF AN EXPEDITION HIGH INTO
the seldom-seen Himalayan land of Inner Dolpo, to record the hab-
its of the bharal, or rare Himalayan blue sheep, and, if possible, in
passing to glimpse the famously shy and evasive snow leopard. The
book, which is just being reissued by Penguin Classics, begins, as
most scientific logs do, with a precise map, and ends with scholarly
notes and an index. The leader of the climb is the eminent field bi-
ologist George Schaller (here known as "GS") and with him travel
various local porters and Sherpas and the writer who records the trip,
Peter Matthiessen. The author, a "naturalist, explorer," as his bio has
it, takes pains to note every "cocoa-coloured wood frog" the travelers
pass, and the "pale lavender-blue winged blossoms of the orchid tree
(Bauhinia)." He records altitudes and temperatures and the history
and geography of every region he visits. The human habitations he
describes are, typically, full of "vacant children, listless adults, bent
dogs and thin chickens in a litter of sagging shacks and rubble, mud,
weeds, stagnant ditches. . . ."

Yet even as it makes us feel every pebble and rag on the tough
journey, *The Snow Leopard* is the record of a different kind of ascent
as well, which the reader catches as a silent current pulsing just be-
neath the lines. "I climb on through grey daybreak worlds towards

the light," its author tells us at one moment, and a little later he is in a world of "snow and silence, wind and blue." The journey is clearly to places inward as well as up, and as the author climbs and climbs toward his final waystation, at eighteen thousand feet, near the Crystal Mountain, he seems so to disappear inside the vastness of the scene around him—the sharpened skies, the deep blue silences, the elegant clarity of a world of snow and rock—that it begins to feel as if those forces are speaking as much as he does. "The earth is ringing. All is moving, full of power, full of light."

The book is written, you begin to sense, by a serious self-taught scientist (who spent most of a year driving around his country and producing a near-definitive book, *Wildlife in America*). But it is also written, in the same breath, by a Zen student who will later become a priest, whose business it is to see past all the projections and delusions of the mind to the hard rock of unvarnished reality. It is written by a seasoned journalist of the old school whose range is so great that he can light up the paths he is taking by referring to Blake and Heisenberg and Sufi and Native American lore, drawing his epigraphs from a Hindu priest, a modern lama, Hesse and Rilke and Ovid; but it is, in those same sentences, being written by a novelist who seeks to track the nature within us as well as without, and, indeed, to link the two. The ascent is an attempt to chart what cannot be seen and recorded, and the sense of elevation we feel on reading the book is the one we know, perhaps, when we close our eyes and just sit still.

What comes to seem remarkable, and haunting, about the book has little to do with the fact that few travelers had been to Inner Dolpo in 1973, or even that no one, Peter Matthiessen suggests, had ever recorded the voice of the blue sheep before he did, as he's observed by the animals from a distance of ten yards. It comes, rather, from the sense that we feel, with him, the pulse-quickening sense of discovery that arises when you come upon passes and places that have almost never been seen before; and yet, in that very moment, you also feel a sense of loss—that excitements fade, that everything moves on, that animals and forests will soon be no more, and that even the epiphanies and discoveries that seemed so exhilarating yesterday will very soon be forgotten.

If you visit the high plateaus of the Himalayas—moved, perhaps, by the book to do so—you come upon great many-storied buildings on the hilltops that look out across the emptiness like fortresses and watchposts both at once. If you step into their chapels, you smell centuries of melted yak butter, make out frescoes barely visible in the faint light, feel coldness on the bare floors. The sun comes in shafts through the dust, lighting up the Buddhas. And as you walk around these cities on a hill, you begin to notice that each level is linked to the next by a short, steep ladder. You climb up, through terraces, past kitchens and altar rooms and schoolrooms, till finally you come to a flat rooftop from which nothing can be seen or heard but the snapping of prayer flags in the wind, the blue skies extending all around, the snowcaps in the distance. You have entered, as *The Snow Leopard* shows us, a realm of allegory.

When I return to Peter Matthiessen's silver account today—noticing how it grows as I do, giving back a different light every time I pick it up again—what I feel most is the sheer physicality of the climb, the return to something bare and essential behind or beneath the realm of thoughts. The author crops his skull as he sets out, and begins to walk barefoot as he leaves the world of roads. He makes me feel and flinch from the blisters on the climbers' feet, the leeches on their skin. I shiver, such is the transparent immediacy of the prose, when the temperature sinks to −20 degrees centigrade, and feel with the author how "I quake with cold all night."

Part of the beauty of such a trip is that it permits few vanities: The writer is reduced to scrambling on all fours and watches himself laboring under sixty pounds of lentils. He starts to go to sleep at nightfall and to awaken with first light, like the living things around him. His porters, at one precipitous moment, give themselves over to a silent trance. The trip is not taking him away from the real world, so much as deeper into it, the better to feel its sting; epiphanies, after all, are the easy part—it's the acceptance of the everyday that comes hard.

Yet always there is something pricking at the corner of the sentences that suggests a deeper trip. The first day the expedition leaves town, Matthiessen spots a corpse; he has come to Nepal by way of Varanasi, the ancient city in India where dead bodies are committed to the holy waters of the Ganges. Very soon after that, "I nod to Death in passing, aware of the sound of my own feet upon my path." One reason he has come on this journey, we see tucked into a tight-lipped sentence, is that his young wife, Deborah Love, has died of cancer the previous winter.

So as the climb proceeds, it becomes a trip into an understanding of the reality and suffering that lie at the heart of the area's philosophy. Siddhartha Gautama, the Buddha, was born just thirty miles from where the travelers pass, and he, too, was a "wanderer," the author tells us, whose path took him into "the unsentimental embrace of all existence." The Buddha had his first prompting toward awakening, we may remember, when he stepped out of the gilded palace in which his father tried to keep him, and encountered the abiding human truths of sickness, old age, and death.

Very soon, therefore, as the landscape begins to empty out—no roads, no watches, no reminders of the modern world—it becomes clear that the "path" Matthiessen describes is not completely unrelated to the paths of which the Buddha spoke. The journey will be not just a training in attention—and a hard slog—but an instruction in surrender. Matthiessen is not a "seeker," he reassures us, and he seems much too observant and unsparing to entertain romantic notions of a never-never land. Yet he is honest enough to acknowledge that he hears, every now and then, intimations of another world. "From the forest comes the sound of bells." At another point he notes that the things he's carrying along with him are "a dim, restless foreboding" and occasional glimpses of "the lost paradise of our 'true nature.'"

"It is not worth the whole to go round the world to count the cats in Zanzibar," Henry David Thoreau famously said, after completing his long journey to (and in) a place only one and a half miles from his home; you do not have to know that Thoreau helped bring Buddhism into America—through the Lotus Sutra whose translation from the French he oversaw in 1844—to see that Matthiessen is walking, to some degree, in his footsteps. Why go round the world to count the cats in Inner Dolpo—especially if, like this author, you are not a field biologist who has a professional need to do so, or a porter who can make a living only by carrying heavy loads?

Yet as he climbs, he begins to think back to the wife he's just lost, to the Zen discipline she introduced him to. He starts to look at the very tendencies in himself that he might be inclined to sidestep or cover up at home. It quickly becomes apparent that this author is in no hurry to gloss over anything in the inner, or outer, landscape. He wishes to push his friend GS, a famous naturalist, off a cliff at one point; he presents himself more and more as just a "haunted animal," who confesses, "my legs refuse to move and my heart beats so that I feel sick"; he even admits to a spiritual ambition, the hope that at some point he will come upon some magical teacher or revelation that will lay bare for him the secrets of the universe.

At one moment Matthiessen recalls his eight-year-old son back home, and quotes a letter—a touchingly charming letter—from the boy, Alex, who signs himself "Your sun." When Matthiessen had decided to take off into the Himalaya, his little boy's response had been "Too long!" and he had begun to tear up in spite of himself. The eight-year-old has already lost his mother, suddenly; now, he might reasonably feel he's losing his only other parent.

Matthiessen tells his boy that he'll be back by Thanksgiving. Yet as the journey progresses, we notice that the days are flying by and there is little hope of Matthiessen returning in time to spend Thanksgiving with his son. The quest for understanding has caused him to do one of the most difficult things a parent can do, which is not just to leave behind a child in need but to keep that child waiting. Matthiessen's trip, we begin to feel, will have to involve some very great revelations indeed in order to justify that letdown.

I have met a few readers over the years, especially mothers, who remain upset by that revelation, and choose not to recall that one of the hardest things about the Buddha's devotion to the truth is that he had to leave his beloved wife and son behind. Yet what moves me, every time I read the book, is that Matthiessen elects to include in his story a letter and a moment that will show him in an uncomfortable light. Most travelers are guilty of a kind of infidelity when they leave their homes and the people closest to them in order to undertake a long and perilous journey—and almost all of them (I know as someone who writes about travel myself) choose to keep out from their records the less exalted, human tradeoff. We like to present ourselves as conquering heroes or lone wolves; we will use any literary device we can to keep out of the text the ones waiting for us at home, or the truth of what is always an uneasy compromise.

Matthiessen, by contrast—and this is part of the honesty and unflinchingness that I take the book and the climb to be about—tells us whom he's letting down. He notes, unsentimentally, that he and his late wife had come close to divorce only five months before her death. And as the climb goes on, he keeps thinking back to Alex and Deborah, more and more, sees his boy dressing up (as a skeleton) for Halloween, is suddenly taken back to him even when he hears a woodpecker. Part of the tension of the book comes not in wondering if the team's provisions will run out, if the passes will be shut off by snow, if the porters will return—though all are real and vivid dangers—but in seeing what it is Matthiessen will find to bring back to compensate for his delayed return.

The Snow Leopard is a liberating book, in fact, in part because it is not about ordinary goodness. It features some of the most transcendent, crystalline moments in modern prose, and yet it is, at every turn, about anger and pain and fear, and its protagonist is as impatient and far from Buddhist tolerance on his way down from his transcendent moments as on his way up. In that sense, it's a journey into humanity, which Matthiessen is wise enough to see as lying on the other side of the mountains from sainthood (courage, as they say, refers not to the man who's never scared, but to the one who's scared and yet braves the challenge nevertheless). In all these regards, and as part of the doctrine of hard realism, it is only right that the door to the Crystal Monastery is locked when Matthiessen arrives, that the lama whom he has been longing to meet for so long turns out to be "the crippled monk who was curing the goat skin in yak butter and brains" that he walked past, and that it is only after the mists clear and his spirit, so he writes, is focused by the Crystal Mountain that "I feel mutilated, murderous; I am in a fury of dark energies, with no control at all on my short temper."

It is in that context that the most powerful character in the book is the stealthy, unassimilable presence among the party known as Tukten. A Sherpa among the porters, a spirit that no one is entirely comfortable with, a man who has the feel of a sorcerer and is accused of being a thief, Tukten is the most slippery and unsettling presence in the mountains, whose air of threat sometimes seems more charged and intense than that of the elements themselves. And yet he is the author's shadow, and, you could say, familiar. He is "somehow known to me, like a dim figure from another life," and the two of them seem linked, always aware of where the other is. Milarepa, the great poet-saint of Tibet, was said once to have converted himself into a snow leopard to confound his enemies; reading Peter Matthiessen, we begin to suspect that a snow leopard like the one he hopes to see has chosen to turn himself into Tukten, who always remains solitary and unknowable, "the most mysterious of the great cats." Matthiessen even calls Tukten—twice—"our evil monk," the "our" perhaps the most unnerving word of all ("This thing of darkness I acknowledge mine," as Prospero says of Caliban).

Tukten appeals to Matthiessen, even perhaps teaches him (more than does the obviously wise but matter-of-fact lama of Shey) by taking everything in his stride, as the way things are; he will look unmoved, Matthiessen says, on "rape or resurrection." Not the least of the charms of the book is how the author, who never gives himself the last word and who shows himself in all his foolishness and unfairness, is constantly learning from the people around him—noting how GS happily devours his last ration of chocolate, even as the author is protectively holding on to his; registering how a Sherpa, when his pack falls into a river, greets the catastrophe by laughing aloud. The lessons of the journey into the Himalaya come not just from the famously uplifting mountains, but from the fallen but steadfast, practical, down-to-earth people who walk among them.

The central feature of the practice of meditation and hard work known as Zen is that, as Matthiessen says, it "has no patience with 'mysticism,' far less the occult." Nor does it have any time for moralism, the prescriptions or distortions we would impose upon the world, obscuring it from our view. It insists that we take this moment for what it is, undistracted, and not cloud it with needless worries of what might have been, or fantasies of what might come to be. It is, essentially, a training in the real, what lies beyond our ideas (and they are only ideas) of good and bad. "The Universe itself is the scripture of Zen," as Matthiessen puts it, and the discipline initiates its practitioners in the clear, unambiguous realization that what is, is; the world (enlightenment, happiness) is just that lammergeier, or bearded vulture, in the sky, this piece of dung, that churning river, all of which have life and blood as our perceptions of them do not.

In that regard, *The Snow Leopard* records the story of a journey into precision, and all that lies on the far side of our thoughts, our ceaseless chatter. Up near the Crystal Mountain, creating a homemade meditation shelter for himself (and as he has said earlier, sometimes pushed to do Zen practice just because it is so cold), Matthiessen enters at last a moment that seems to open up unendingly. "These hard rocks instruct my bones in what my brain could never grasp." This involves, as he writes of the Buddha, a deeply unsentimental embrace of all existence: prayer flags are "worn to wisps by wind," the lama is dressed in "ancient laceless shoes" and a jacket "patched with burlap," feasts in this barrenness consist of "sun-dried green yak cheese," but for those few days in a "world above the clouds"—not having seen a mirror for weeks—the author enters a world that can't be argued away.

It can be so startling to enter this world that is at once as real as this blister and a subtle allegory that it is easy to overlook the extraordinary care and craft that underlie the book. And that is fine. William Shawn's *New Yorker,* which sponsored most of Matthiessen's natural expeditions, including this one, encouraged its writers to pay attention to the world they were reporting on, and not themselves; Zen does much the same, making the ego seem small and laughable in the context of the natural facts around it. The point of *The Snow*

Leopard is, much more than in most books, to lose sight of the author and his language so as to feel the silver light of the mountains, the blue sky opening above, the silence and the clarity.

Yet look more closely at the text and you enjoy a different kind of wonder, akin to the one the author feels in reading every fig tree and macaque. Early on in the narrative Matthiessen writes of how rain "comes and goes." Roughly fifty pages, and many lifetimes, later, the sun "comes and goes." This stands for the changeable condition of the elements in the high mountains; everything is ephemeral. Yet you also notice, if you're paying attention, that the phrase itself keeps coming and going through the book and, a little later, "tears and laughter come and go." It hardly matters that "coming and going" is almost the first principle of Zen, the phrase you find in every Zen master's haiku; the point is that the words themselves tell you not to take the mood too seriously. "I don't trust my inner feelings," as Leonard Cohen writes in a late song, having lived as a Zen monk on a lonely mountain, "inner feelings come and go."

"There is no wisp of cloud—clear, clear, clear, clear," Matthiessen writes at another point on the high mountain. A less confident writer would have tried to decorate or vary the sentence, would never have had the courage to repeat the same simple word four times, as if to take you to a place where all words give out. "It is the precise bite and feel and sound of every step that fills me with life," Matthiessen writes elsewhere, and the reader might notice how it is the precise monosyllables—the strict bark of "bite and feel and sound"—that fill the prose with life.

You can enjoy *The Snow Leopard* without responding to any of this, and yet, if you are so inclined, *The Snow Leopard* offers a kind of handbook on how precision and modesty work, and how contemporary, immediate language can echo the sound of ancient verses. Perhaps my favorite moment in the entire work comes when Matthiessen writes, "I grow into these mountain like a moss. I am bewitched"; and then, after the two short, simple sentences beginning with "I," there comes a rolling sentence that takes in the

> blinding snow peaks and the clarion air, the sound of earth and heaven in the silence, the requiem birds, the mythic beasts, the flags, great horns, and old carved stones, the rough-hewn Tartars in their braids and homespun boots, the silver ice in the black river, the Kang, the Crystal Mountain.

In the very language, in other words, the "I" is subsumed in all the great forces around it, and everything becomes a single breath, in which the "I" disappears. Better yet, none of the immemorial presences that swallow up the "I" are without their shadow sides (the "requiem birds," the "black river," the Crystal Mountain, which has just been described as a "castle of dread") so that we never forget that one of Matthiessen's main companions on the journey is Death. The sentence enacts the very fading of the "I" into the mountain.

As the book concludes, we have learned something about the nature (you could say the folly) of expectation and the beauty of the truth that all expectations often cover up. And what of the snow leopard he had hoped to see? We see the snow leopard's prints, we feel its presence everywhere, but we realize that the sighting of the rare animal isn't important at all (the author has, in some ways, sighted the rare animal, more germane to his purposes, that is himself). We note that teachers may come where you don't look for them—in yellow-eyed men who seem to be demons—and that the temples that are full of wisdom in ancient lands are locked. We realize—and this, I think, is the most important point of *The Snow Leopard*, and begins to bring us back to Alex—how much every trip that really sustains us is in fact a journey home. The author, setting out, feels constantly the presence of some "inner garden" to which he's lost the key; by the time he comes down, something has been put to rest—or clarified, if only for a moment—and the author has, perhaps, something to bring back to his boy that probably he could never have shared with him if he'd stayed home.

Most of all he—and surely we, too—have learned that there are no happy endings, or endings at all; everything is in constant movement, we can't cling to any truth, and even the understandings that seemed so immortal near the Crystal Mountain are soon forgotten as "I trudge and pant and climb and slip and climb and gasp, dull as any brute" (every word a monosyllable again). Matthiessen appears to have learned nothing at all, as he descends, relieving himself on a dog who had attacked him a month before, failing to recognize a family he's already met, still cursing at others, not only himself. The people around him "hawk and piss and spit" and as he wanders back through the seasons, from winter to autumn and then into summer, back into the world of clocks, he is greeted by "fresh frog mud" and "sweet chicken dung."

And yet something has been registered, and the trip in search of the elusive animal that the author keeps just missing has taught us something that, for some readers at least, becomes a place, or a truth, they can never leave. And just before the end, at last, the story of Deborah Love's death is fully told, and in the telling is accepted. In the hard-won days Matthiessen spent close to the Crystal Mountain, sitting still, the "sound of rivers comes and goes and falls and rises, like the wind itself." And in the years since, readers and leaders and books have come and gone and fallen and risen, ceaselessly, and yet beneath all that, the mountain, the image of the leopard, the beauty of this tough-minded classic continue, quietly, to endure.

CHARLES JOHNSON

Prince of the Ascetics:

A Short Story

FROM *Shambhala Sun*

ONCE UPON A TIME, MY COMPANIONS AND I LIVED IN THE FOREST near the village of Uruvela on the banks of the Nairanjana River. We were known far and wide as five men who had forsaken worldly affairs in order to devote ourselves completely to the life of the spirit.

For thousands of years in our country, this has been the accepted way for the Four Stages of Life. First, to spend the spring of one's youth as a dedicated student; the summer as a busy householder using whatever wealth he has acquired to help others; the fall as an ascetic who renounces all duties at age fifty and retires into the forest; and the goal of the winter season is to experience the peace and wisdom found only in the Atma (or Self), which permeates all parts of the world as moisture seeps through sand. My brothers in this noble Fourth Stage of tranquility, which we had just entered, were Kodananna, Bhadiya, Vappa, and Assajii. We had once been family men, members of the Vaishya (trader) caste, but now owned no possessions. We lived, as was right, in poverty and detachment. We wore simple yellow robes and fasted often. Wheresoever we walked, always in single file, Vappa, a small man with a snoutlike nose, took the lead, sweeping the ground before us with a twig broom so we would not crush any living creatures too small to see. When we did not leave our ashram to make alms-rounds for food in Uruvela, we satisfied our hunger with fruit, but not taken off trees; rather we gathered whatever had fallen to the ground. Each day we wrote the Sanskrit word *"ahum,"* or "I," on the back of our hands so that we rarely went but a few moments without seeing it and remembering to inquire into the Self as the source of all things. People throughout the kingdom of Magadha affectionately called us *Bapu* (or "father") because they knew that we had just begun the difficult path described in the *Vedas* and *Upanishads*. The scriptures say that a fast mind is a sick mind. But we, my brothers and I, were slowly taming the wild horses of our thoughts, learning the four kinds of yoga, banishing the ego, that toadstool that grows out of consciousness, and freeing ourselves from the twin illusions of pleasure and pain.

But one day it came to pass that as we made our monthly rounds in the summer-gilded village, begging for alms, the merchants and women all looked the other way when we arrived. When Assajii asked them what was wrong, they apologized. With their palms up-turned, each explained how he had already given his monthly offering to a stunning young swami, a mahatma, a powerful sadhu who was only twenty-nine years old and had recently crossed the River Anoma that divided our kingdom from the land of the Shakya tribe. They said that just being in his presence for a few moments brought immeasurable peace and joy. And if that were not shocking enough, some were calling him *Munisha,* "Prince of the Ascetics."

"How can this be?" My heart gave a slight thump. "Surely you don't mean that."

A portly merchant, Dakma was his name, who was shaped like a pigeon, with bright rings on his fingers, puffed at me, "Oh, but he *is* such. We have never seen his like before. You—*all* of you—can learn a thing or two from him. I tell you, Mahanama, if you are not careful, he will put you five lazybones out of business."

"Lazybones? You call *us* lazybones?"

"As your friend, I tell you, this young man gives new meaning to the words 'sacrifice' and 'self-control.'"

Needless to say, none of this rested happily on my ears. Let it be understood that I, Mahanama, am not the sort of man who is easily swayed, but whatever serenity I had felt after my morning meditation was now gone, and suddenly my mind was capricious, like a restless monkey stung by a scorpion, drunk, and possessed by a demon all at the same time.

"This sadhu," I asked, helplessly, "where might we find him?"

Sujata, the unmarried daughter of a householder, with kind, moonlike eyes, stepped forward. "He lives at the edge of the forest by the river where the banyan trees grow. I have never seen *any* man so beautiful. Everyone loves him. I feel I could follow him anywhere. . . ."

Now I was in a mental fog. There was a dull pounding in my right temple as we trekked forthwith at a fast pace back into the forest. Vappa was sweeping his twig broom so furiously—he was as angry and upset as I was—that billowing clouds of dust rose up around us, and we must have looked, for all the world, like a herd of enraged, stampeding elephants. Soon enough we tracked down the brash young man responsible for our alms bowls being empty.

To my surprise, and yet somehow not to my surprise, the villagers had not lied. We found him meditating naked, except for a garland of beads, in a diagonal shaft of leaf-filtered light from the banyan tree above him. Straightaway, I saw that his posture in meditation was perfect, his head tilted down just so, leaving only enough space that an egg could be inserted between his chin and throat. He was twenty years younger than me, no older than one of my sons, his body gaunt and defined, his face angular, framed by a bell of black hair. He looked up when we approached, introduced ourselves, and pressed him to explain how he could have the nerve to install himself in *our* forest. In a sad, heavy way he exhaled, holding me with eyes that seemed melancholy, and said:

"I seek a refuge from suffering."

"Who," asked Bhadiya, cocking his head to one side, "are your teachers? What credentials do you have?"

"I have studied briefly with the hermit Bhagava. Then with Alara Kalama and Udraka Ramaputra, who taught me mastery of the third and fourth stages of meditation. But," he sighed, "neither intellectual knowledge nor yogic skills has yet led me to the liberation I am seeking."

I felt humbled right down to my heels. Those two venerated teachers were among the greatest sages in all India. Compared to *them,* my own guru long ago was but a neophyte on the path.

Twilight was coming on as he spoke, the blue air darkening to purple the four corners of the sky. A whiff of twilight even tinctured the shadows as he unfurled what I surmised was a bald-faced lie, a fairy tale, a bedtime story so fantastic only a child could believe it. Until a year ago, he said, he had been a prince whose loving father, Shuddodana, had sheltered him from the painful, hard, and ugly things of the world. The palace in which he was raised, with its parks, lakes, and perfectly tended gardens, gave you a glimpse of what the homes of the gods must look like. He was raised to be a warrior of the Shakya tribe, had a hundred raven-haired concubines of almost catastrophic beauty, and ate food so fine and sumptuous that even its rich aroma was enough to sate a man's hunger. He said he would have continued this voluptuous life of pleasure and privilege, for he had all that this world could offer, but one day while he and his charioteer, Channa, were out riding, he saw a man old and decrepit. On a different day he saw a man severely stricken with illness. On the third day he saw a corpse being carried away for cremation. And when he recognized that this fate awaited *him,* he could not be consoled. All satisfaction with the fleeting pleasures of his cloistered life in the palace left him. But then, on a fourth trip, he saw a wandering holy man whose equanimity in the face of the instability and impermanence of all things told him that *this* was the life he must pursue. And so he left home, abandoning his beautiful wife, Yoshodhara, and their newborn son, Rahula, and found his lonely way to our forest.

Once he had breathed these words, my companions begged to become his disciples. Kodananna even went as far as to proclaim that if all the scriptures for a holy life were lost, we could reconstruct them from just this one devoted ascetic's daily life. He had seduced them with his sincerity for truth-seeking. I, Mahanama, decided to remain with my brothers, but, to be frank, I had great misgivings about this man. He came from the Kshatriya caste of royalty. Therefore he was, socially, one *varna* (or caste) above us, and I had never met a member of royalty who wasn't smug and insensitive to others. Could only *I* see his imperfections and personal failures? How could he justify leaving his wife and son? I mean, he was not yet fifty, but he had forsaken his responsibilities as a householder. True enough, his family was well taken care of during his absence, because he was a pampered, upper-caste rich boy, someone who'd never missed a meal in his life but now was slumming among the poor, who could shave his waist-long beard, his wild hair, take a bath, and return to his father's palace if one day the pain and rigor of our discipline became disagreeable. I, Mahanama, have never had an easy life. To achieve even the simplest things, I had to undergo a thousand troubles, to struggle and know disappointment. I think it was then, God help me, that I began to hate *every* little thing about him: the way he walked and talked and smiled; his polished, courtly gestures; his refined habits; his honeyed tongue; his upper-caste education, none of which he could hide. The long and short of it was that I was no longer myself. Although I consented to study with him, just to see what he knew, I longed, so help me, to see him fail. To slip or make a mistake. Just *once,* that's all I was asking for.

And I *did* get my wish, though not exactly as I'd expected.

To do him justice, I must say our new teacher was dedicated, and more dangerous than anyone knew. He was determined to surpass all previous ascetics. I guess he was still a warrior of the Shakya tribe, but instead of vanquishing others, all his efforts were aimed at conquering himself. Day after day he practiced burning thoughts of desire from his mind and tried to empty himself of all sensations. Night after night he prayed for a freedom that had no name, touching the eighty-six sandalwood beads on his *mala* for each mantra he whispered in the cold of night, or in rough, pouring rain. Seldom did he talk to us, believing that speech was the great-grandson of truth. Nevertheless, I spied on him, because at my age I was not sure any teacher could be trusted. None could meet our every expectation. None I had known was whole or perfect.

Accordingly, I critically scrutinized everything he did and did not do. And what struck me most was this: It was as if he saw his body, which he had indulged with all the pleasures known to man, as an enemy, an obstacle to his realization of the highest truth, and so it must be punished and deprived. He slept on a bed of thorns. Often he held his breath for a great long time until the pain was so severe he fainted. Week after week he practiced these fanatical austerities, reducing himself to skin, bone, and fixed idea. My companions and I frequently collapsed from exhaustion and fell behind. But he kept on. Perhaps he was trying to achieve great merit, or atone for leaving his family, or for being a fool who threw away a tangible kingdom he could touch and see for an intangible fantasy of perfection that no one had ever seen. Many times we thought he was suicidal, particularly on the night he made us all sleep among the dead in the charnel grounds, where the air shook with insects, just outside

Uruvela. During our first years with him he would eat a single jujube fruit, sesame seeds, and take a little rice on banana leaves. But as the years wore on, he—being radical, a revolutionary—rejected even that, sustaining himself on water and one grain of rice a day. Then he ate nothing at all.

By the morning of December seventh, in our sixth year with him, he had fallen on evil days, made so weakened, so frail, so wretched he could barely walk without placing one skeletal hand on Bhadiya's shoulder and the other on mine. At age thirty-five, his eyes resembled burnt holes in a blanket. Like a dog was how he smelled. His bones creaked, and his head looked chewed up by rats, the obsidian hair that once pooled round his face falling from his scalp in brittle patches.

"Mahanama," he said. There were tears standing in his eyes. "You and the others should not have followed me. Or believed so faithfully in what I was doing. My life in the palace was wrong. This is wrong too."

The hot blast of his death breath, rancid because his teeth had begun to decay, made me twist my head to one side. "There must be . . ."—he closed his eyes to help his words along—"some Way between the extremes I have experienced."

I kept silent. He sounded vague, vaporish.

And then he said, more to himself than to me, "Wisdom is caught, not taught."

Before I could answer he hobbled away, like an old, old man, to bathe, then sit by himself under a banyan tree. I believe he went that far away so we could not hear him weep. This tree, I should point out, was one the superstitious villagers believed possessed a deity. As luck would have it, the lovely Sujata, with her servant girl, came there often to pray that she would one day find a husband belonging to her caste and have a son by him. From where we stood, my brothers and I could see her approaching, stepping gingerly to avoid deer pellets and bird droppings, and if my eyes did not deceive me, she, not recognizing him in his fallen state, thought our teacher was the tree's deity. Sujata placed before him a golden bowl of milk-porridge. To my great delight, he hungrily ate it.

I felt buoyant, and thought, *Gotcha.*

Vappa's mouth hung open in disbelief. Bhadiya's mouth snapped shut. Kodananna rubbed his knuckles in his eyes. They all knew moral authority rested on moral consistency. Assajii shook his head and cried out, "This woman's beauty, the delights of food, and the sensual cravings tormenting his heart are just too much for him to resist. Soon he will be drinking, lying, stealing, gambling, killing animals to satisfy his appetite, and sleeping with other men's wives. Agh, he can teach us nothing."

Disgusted, we left, moving a short distance away from him in the forest, our intention being to travel the hundred miles to the spiritual center of Sarnath in search of a better guru. My brothers talked about him like he had a tail. And while I cackled and gloated for a time over the grand failure of our golden boy, saying, "See, I *told* you so," that night I could not sleep for thinking about him. He was alone again, his flesh wasted away, his mind most likely splintered by madness. I pitied him. I pitied all of us, for now it was clear that no man or woman would ever truly be free from selfishness, anger, hatred, greed, and the chronic hypnosis that is the human condition. Shortly after midnight, beneath a day-old moon in a dark sky, I rose while the others slept and crept back to where we had left him.

He was gone, no longer by the banyan tree. Up above, a thin, rain-threaded breeze loosed a whirlwind of dead leaves. It felt as if a storm was on its way, the sky swollen with pressure. And then, as I turned to leave, seeking shelter, I saw faintly a liminal figure seated on kusha grass at the eastern side of a bodhi tree, strengthened by the bowl of rice-milk he had taken, and apparently determined not to rise ever again if freedom still eluded him. I felt my face stretch. I wondered if I had gone without food so long that I was hallucinating, for I sensed a peculiar density in the darkness, and the numinous air around him seemed to swirl with wispy phantoms. I heard a devilish voice—perhaps his own, disguised—demanding that he stop, which he would not do. Was he totally mad and talking to himself? I could not say. But for three watches of the night he sat, wind wheeling round his head, its sound in the trees like rushing water, and once I heard him murmur, "At last I have found and defeated you, *ahumkara,* I-Maker."

At daybreak, everything in the forest was quiet, the tree bark bloated by rain, and he sat, as if he'd just come from a chrysalis, in muted, early-morning light, the air full of moisture. Cautiously, I approached him, the twenty-fifth buddha, knowing that something new and marvelous had happened in the forest that night. Instead of going where the path might lead, he had gone instead where there was no path and left a trail for all of us. I asked him:

"Are you a god now?"

Quietly, he made answer. "No."

"Well, are you an angel?"

"No."

"Then what are you?"

"Awake."

That much I could see. He had discovered his middle way. It made me laugh. These rich kids had all the luck. I knew my brothers and I would again become his disciples, but this time, after six long years, we'd finally be able to eat a decent meal.

Author's note: The final six lines of dialogue are from the spiritual teachings of the late, great Eknath Easwaran.

JON D. LEVENSON

Chosenness and Its Enemies

FROM *Commentary*

FEW RELIGIOUS DOCTRINES HAVE ATTRACTED MORE VIRULENT criticism than the idea of the chosen people. Over the past several centuries alone, both Jews and non-Jews have judged this key tenet of classical Judaism to be undemocratic, chauvinistic, superstitious—in short, retrograde in every way that matters to the progressive mind.

Nor is it just progressives who have found it deficient. It, and Jews who still believe in it or otherwise decline to assimilate to prevailing norms, have been savaged by everyone from captains of capitalism to Soviet commissars. Henry Ford, to cite a famous example, sponsored the publication of the *Protocols of the Elders of Zion,* the notorious forgery originating in czarist Russia and alleging a Jewish plot to achieve global domination. Things have been no better on the other side of the political spectrum. The Soviet Union viciously persecuted the Jews, even issuing a book equating Zionism with racism and Nazism long before such moves became the hardy perennial of anti-Zionist invective.

Not to be outdone, President Charles de Gaulle of France, in a press conference not long after the Six-Day War of 1967, identified Jewish separateness not only as a reflection of the noxious character of the Jews themselves but as the cause of anti-Semitism in others. The Jews, de Gaulle observed, have long been "an elite people, self-confident and domineering"—and, presumably for that reason, guilty of "provoking ill will in certain countries and at certain times."

And yet, like the Jews themselves, the idea of the chosen people will not die. Those drawn to it, moreover, are not always detractors. Last year, for example, the distinguished social critic Charles Murray published in *Commentary* a much-discussed article in which he sought to explain what he called "the disproportionate Jewish accomplishment in the arts and sciences."[1] This record of achievement, he argued, correlates with the brute fact that "Jews have been found to have an unusually high mean intelligence as measured by IQ tests." Nor is this statistic simply a consequence of modern social history. Instead, Murray speculated, the higher average intelligence of Jews existed even in antiquity. And that raised a larger question, to which Murray offered a benignly provocative answer:

> Why should one particular tribe at the time of Moses, living in the same environment as other nomadic and agricultural peoples of the Middle East, have already evolved elevated intelligence when the others did not?
>
> At this point, I take sanctuary in my remaining hypothesis, uniquely parsimonious and happily irrefutable. The Jews are God's chosen people.

Whether or not Murray intended his concluding words in full seriousness, what is curious is how readily the old theological idea of the chosen people came to the mind of "this Scots-Irish Gentile from Iowa," as he described himself. Alas, many a Gentile thinker has been decidedly less positive. In a recent study of the ancient teaching and its role in modern anti-Semitism, the Israeli diplomat and political scientist Avi Beker presents a broad assortment of contempo-

[1] "Jewish Genius," April 2007.

rary attacks on the Jews that in one way or another echo the analysis put forward by Charles de Gaulle.[2] There is, for example, the acclaimed Greek composer Mikis Theodorakis, who not long ago told an interviewer that "today it is possible to say that this small nation is the root of all evil; it is full of self-importance and evil stubbornness." Asked by his (Jewish) interlocutor, "What is it that holds us Jews together?" Theodorakis—not coincidentally, the composer of the Palestinian national anthem—replied, "It is the feeling that you are the children of God. That you are the chosen."

And then there is José Saramago, the Portuguese writer and Nobel Prize laureate, who a few years ago described the Jews in perfervid terms as

> contaminated by the monstrous and rooted "certitude" that in this catastrophic and absurd world there exists a people chosen by God and that, consequently, all the actions of an obsessive, psychological, and pathological exclusivist racism are justified; educated and trained in the idea that any suffering that has been inflicted, or is being inflicted, or will be inflicted on everyone else, especially the Palestinians, will always be inferior to that which they suffered in the Holocaust.

As for the genealogy of this enduring set of attitudes, it stretches back all the way to early Christian writings that portray the Jews as a self-righteous and spiritually blind people, the enemies or even the murderers of God. In some of its inflections, it goes even further back, to Greco-Roman depictions of Jews as culturally inferior newcomers and misanthropes whose religion forbids them to show goodwill to outsiders. Theodorakis, for one, exhibits the influence of both

[2] *The Chosen: The History of an Idea, and the Anatomy of an Obsession.* Palgrave, 240 pp.

streams. He speaks of his grandmother's admonition to avoid the Jewish neighborhood on Easter because "the Jews put Christian boys in a barrel with knives inside. Afterward they drink their blood." But he also boasts: "They have only Abraham and Jacob, who were shadows, while we [Greeks] have Pericles."

But the hoary resonances of such bigotry should not mislead us. In focusing on the very *idea* of a chosen people, these modern anti-Semites break with the classical Christian tradition to reveal an indebtedness to Enlightenment notions of universalism. The Church, as Joel S. Kaminsky points out in a highly illuminating recent book, not only accepted the idea of a chosen people; it also claimed to *be* the chosen people.[3] As a New Testament letter ascribed to the apostle Peter puts it: "You are a chosen race, a royal priesthood, a holy nation, God's own people." Christianity, that is, did not claim to replace the people of Israel with an undifferentiated humanity; rather, with few exceptions, it claimed the status of Israel for itself exclusively.

Given the massive expansion of Christianity in the intervening centuries, it is easy to forget that the Enlightenment belief in a uniform humanity, loyal to reason alone and disregarding all claims of historical revelation and normative tradition, poses a formidable challenge to Christians as well as to Jews. Once upon a time, the question was, which is the real chosen people? For the past two centuries or so, the question has been, how can there be a chosen people at all?

Kaminsky's study, the work of a scholar of the Hebrew Bible, is exceptionally helpful in clarifying the first question—in which the second has perforce become entangled. For even ostensibly careful readers of the Bible fall captive to the historical animus against the doctrine of the chosen people. Among some Christian scholars, in-

---

[3] *Yet I Loved Jacob: Reclaiming the Biblical Concept of Election.* Abingdon Press, 242 pp.

deed, the traditional belief in the supersession of the Jews and of Judaism has often proved toxic, all the more so when melded with the Enlightenment commitment to universalism. Hence the common misconception that Christianity is open, inclusive, and universal, while Judaism is tribalistic, ethnocentric, and xenophobic.

Gerd Lüdemann, for example, a prominent German professor of the New Testament, writes that "the Nazis shamelessly directed ideas which were similar to those developed by Jews under Ezra and Nehemiah," two biblical leaders at the time of the Persian empire who strove to protect their endangered little community in Palestine from intermarriage. For her part, Regina Schwartz, an English-literature specialist at Northwestern, reads the Bible, and biblical chosenness, through the prism of today's invidious polarities of the "self" and the "Other":

> The Other against whom Israel's identity is forged is abhorred, abject, impure, and in the "Old Testament" vast numbers of them are obliterated. . . . The very idea that identity is constructed "against" suggests scarcity, as though there were a finite amount of identity itself, and so a space must be carved out for it and jealously guarded, like finite territory.

In countering such convergences of religious and antireligious bias, Kaminsky has his work cut out for him. He begins by situating the biblical concept of election in the narratives of fraternal rivalry in Genesis. The primordial example is the story of Cain and Abel. The favor that God shows Abel, Kaminsky argues, is not "primarily dictated by [the two brothers'] human behavior," as embodied in the offerings brought by each; rather, it results from "a mysterious divine fiat." Efforts by readers to figure out what Abel did right and Cain did wrong—efforts that were already under way in antiquity—do violence to the narrative, which is revealingly focused not on the favored (and doomed) younger brother but on the nonelect, on Cain. The key words are those God directs to the angry future fratricide:

> *Why are you distressed,*
> *And why is your face fallen?*
> *Surely, if you do right,*
> *There is uplift.*
> *But if you do not do right*
> *Sin couches at the door;*
> *Its urge is toward you*
> *Yet you can be its master.*[4]

The point for Kaminsky is this: "God's 'unfairness' in choosing some over others is not simply a benefit for the chosen or a detriment to the nonchosen." Rather, chosenness "was always about God's plan for the whole world, the elect and the nonelect alike." For the latter, the task is learning to "accept that God's blessing flows through the world in mysterious ways that, while merciful, are not, strictly speaking, equitable."

This is, to say the least, a much subtler vision than the drearily familiar picture of the chosen and the nonchosen facing off in deadly and inevitable opposition—a picture propounded by learned and unlearned enemies of chosenness alike. And if the little tale of Cain and Abel already sounds the themes that will characterize chosenness in the Hebrew Bible—God's mysterious favor, the dissension and

---

[4] Unless otherwise noted, all translations from the Hebrew Bible are taken from *Tanakh* (Jewish Publication Society, 1985). This passage presents difficulties at a number of points.

alienation this produces within the human family, the special obliga-
tions and suffering of the chosen one(s), the possibility of reconcili-
ation in the end—another version of the pattern appears in the figure
of Abraham.

Here one element in particular is worth stressing. In the literature of
postbiblical Judaism, the story of God's choice of Abraham is often
embroidered with accounts of Abraham's own surpassing merit,
most memorably as the son of an idol-maker who saw through the
false ideas of his inherited culture and reasoned his way to the
one true God. But as important as this tradition would become in
Judaism—and Islam—it has no source in Genesis. There, the singling-
out of Abraham comes as a bolt out of the blue, with no sense that
the future patriarch has done anything extraordinary to deserve it.

In the book of Deuteronomy, the same idea recurs, now trans-
posed to Abraham's Israelite descendants:

> For you are a people consecrated to the Lord your God: of
> all the peoples on earth the Lord your God chose you to be
> His treasured people. It is not because you are the most nu-
> merous of peoples that the Lord set His heart on you and
> chose you—indeed, you are the smallest of peoples; but it
> was because the Lord loved you and kept the oath He made
> to your fathers that the Lord freed you with a mighty hand
> and rescued you from the house of bondage, from the
> power of Pharaoh king of Egypt.[5]

Here, once again, Israel's special status derives not from any
special gifts or feats of its own. The chosen family—like, ideally, any

---

[5] I have replaced "favored" with "loved," the better to capture the sense of a
covenant.

family—begins in an act of love, a love that cannot be fully accounted for by a list of the beloved's attributes or a "scientific" argument for the beloved's uniqueness. There is something grandly unconditional in biblical chosenness, something that makes all rationalistic attempts to explain it seem cramped and uncomprehending.

But why should there be a division between chosen and non-chosen in the first place? If we are to understand the biblical vision in all its nuance and complexity, the context of family relations is essential and must not be hastily dismissed as primitive. For the God of the Hebrew Bible is nothing if not personal. He is not an abstract concept, a moral ideal, or a physical force. He is a personality, though a divine one, and His capacity for feelings is not an embarrassing impairment of that divinity but precisely that which makes it possible for Him to have relationships with human beings.

One of those feelings is love. As Kaminsky puts it: "No human lover loves his or her beloved in the same way he or she relates to all other people in the world. Nor does one love other families as much as one's own." As a judge, the biblical God is said to be impartial and impervious to bribery. But He is not only a judge: He is also a *father*. At the base of Jewish chosenness there stands neither an abhorrence of the Other nor the defensiveness engendered by "a finite amount of identity." Instead, there stands God's love for the people with whom He has entered into covenant and whom He has chosen to name as His own children—or, in a variant metaphor, as the bride to whom He has solemnly plighted His troth.

Detractors of the idea of a chosen people approach the matter from the opposite side. The subtle theology of God's surprising love and gracious election does not engage them. Their gaze is fixed instead on the plight of the *un*chosen, whom they see as the inevitable victims of Jewish ethnocentrism, racism, and malevolence. But Kaminsky points to an essential distinction that they miss. In the Bible, there are not two categories but at least three, which he names the elect, the nonelect, and the anti-elect.

That a group is nonelect does not necessarily mean that it is deficient, unworthy, or outside of God's care. The contrary idea derives mainly from the Christian tradition in which the "elect" are often synonymous with the "saved," and those who are not elect with the "damned"—the result being the long-standing and much-controverted question of whether there can be salvation outside the Church.

To be sure, traces of this dualistic system lie within Judaism itself, and specifically in the apocalyptic literature prominent among Jews about the time that Christianity emerged; remnants appear in later Jewish sources as well. But, on balance, both biblical and rabbinic thought affirm that the nonelect are deprived neither of dignity nor of the possibility of a portion in the world-to-come—the Jewish equivalent of "salvation."

In the Hebrew Bible, especially, it is all mankind, and not just the chosen, who in the famous words of Genesis are created "in the image of God." All belong to the same race—the human race—and descend, as the biblical account would have it, from the same parents. This alone shows how ugly and uncomprehending it is to brand ancient or modern efforts by Jews to maintain their peoplehood as the equivalent of Nazism or other forms of racism. Race, in the modern scientific or pseudoscientific sense of the word, is irrelevant to the Hebrew Bible.[6]

Chosenness, then, need not entail implacable enmity on anyone's part; nor are the unchosen the enemies of God or of the Jewish people. The Other has dignity while remaining the Other. He is not required, in the biblical view, to be brought low, to convert, least of all to die.

[6] See Hillel Halkin, "Jews and their DNA," in the September 2008 *Commentary*.

The anti-elect, however, are another matter, and much more challenging. By this term, Kaminsky means such groups as the sinful Canaanite nations, whom God enjoins Israel to annihilate in order to take possession of the promised land, and the Amalekites, a tribe that is reported to have savagely attacked the Israelites as they journeyed in the desert and that became an enduring symbol of murderous anti-Semitism. In both cases, "genocide" is a fair description of what God commands to be done.

But even here qualification is needed. "While some have compared the [Bible's] anti-Canaanite polemic to certain Nazi policies," Kaminsky writes, "no biblical text ever advocated the pursuit and slaughter of Canaanites who lived outside Canaan or fled its bounds." Moreover, archaeology has cast grave doubt on the claim that the Canaanites were indeed ever annihilated, a claim that is similarly undermined by a close reading of the biblical text. Today, in fact, many scholars see evidence for the proposition that Israel itself originated from a community of marginalized Canaanites.

The genocidal command is further attenuated if we juxtapose to the biblical text the relevant sources from later rabbinic literature. Kaminsky points to talmudic interpretations that propound a counternarrative in which genocide would have been averted had the Canaanites repented and sued for peace. Maimonides, the great medieval legal authority and philosopher, says the same thing about the Amalekites. Other talmudic passages declare that no currently living individuals or peoples can be identified with the Bible's abominated nations, in effect rendering the offending passages of historical interest only—except for the enduring lesson that Jews must shun the idolatrous practices associated with the Canaanites, be ever-vigilant to the lethal dangers symbolized by the Amalekites, and demonstrate exclusive devotion to their God.

Some things are gained when the idea of the chosen people is viewed from the vantage point of the anti-elect—but not so much as is asserted by their latter-day advocates and defenders. Meanwhile, much is lost.

The complicated dynamics of chosenness come together in their tightest and most highly developed form at the end of the book of Genesis, in the story of Joseph: a gem of biblical narrative and a highly sophisticated theological text. The favor received by the young Joseph, marked by the distinctive coat given him by his father, enrages his ten older brothers, nearly brings his life to an end, and results in his being sold into slavery in Egypt. Yet it is precisely his experience in Egypt—where he again meets with favor, first from his master, then from the warden of his prison, and finally from Pharaoh—that saves the lives of these same brothers when, beset by a worldwide famine, they come looking for food.

Where the first story of sibling rivalry in Genesis results in the murder of the favored son Abel and the exile of his older brother Cain, the final story offers a vision of potentially lethal rivalry defanged and turned to good, through the uncanny workings of providence and for the rescue of the entire family—indeed the entire world. At the end of the narrative, the younger brother, Joseph, is still in charge, his mysterious chosenness intact. His authority, however, is no longer a burden to his brothers but a blessing, and a family rent by strife has been reunited and become the recipient of immense favor of its own.

Kaminsky sees in this tale of familial discord and reconciliation a reflection on the wider issue of Israelite chosenness, which can work to the benefit not only of the chosen but of the unchosen, including those altogether outside the chosen family. Like Pharaoh in the Joseph story, Gentiles who are kindly disposed to the Israelites benefit richly. And here one is put in mind of the words of God's initial call to Abraham, assuring him that "all the families of the earth/Shall bless themselves by you" (or "be blessed through you").

Finally, the tale of Joseph is a tale of profound transformation within the chosen one himself. The protagonist, once a brash teen-ager who appears to accept his adolescent dreams as so many guar-antees of dominance, succeeds, not without much travail, in becoming a skilled courtier and administrator, able to keep his counsel, devise elaborate plans, and earn the appreciation of both his family and his lord.

In this perspective, the mere fact of chosenness provides no ex-emption from turmoil, peril, or the need for inner growth. To the contrary, it would seem to entail a high degree of suffering. And this, as Kaminsky points out, tells us something very important about the Hebrew Bible:

> The ability to sense one's chosenness and also to see one's character flaws is perhaps one of the greatest achievements of the Israelite religious mind. It creates a sense of ultimate meaning for one's nation, but it does so in ways that miti-gate movement toward an unfettered . . . triumphalism.

If Kaminsky centers his attention on the Bible, Avi Beker in *The Cho-sen* focuses on Jewish history, especially the history of anti-Semitism. His book is sweeping in its range and rich in examples and quota-tions, including the ones by Mikis Theodorakis and José Saramago cited earlier. But the paucity of social and historical context renders his discussion somewhat thin.[7]

Beker's handling of Christian theology is particularly weak. He writes that the apostle Paul in the New Testament "made a conscious and, in the event, historic decision to turn the new faith away from

---

[7] The manuscript could also have used a good fact-checker. For example, Beker quotes the reaction of the philosopher Martin Buber to the Israeli capture of the Western Wall in the Six-Day War—no small feat, since Buber had died two years earlier.

its Jewish origins," that Paul "treats the Jews like the devil," and that the "hatred first propagated by Paul" is still to be found among Christian anti-Semites.

This is simplistic if not wrongheaded. In his own mind, Paul was not turning away from Judaism or founding a new religion but following out the logical implications of living in a period when the biblical promises of messianic redemption were in the process of being fulfilled, especially the promises centered on the Gentiles. His arguments with Judaism were based, for the most part, on his reading of the Hebrew Bible, which he quotes abundantly and interprets using methods familiar to the Jews of the time. Yes, Paul thought that the God of Israel had done something new through the advent of Jesus that voided the Mosaic commandments (which never applied to the Gentiles anyway). It is also undeniable that his thinking about his fellow Jews was shifting and unstable, and that misreadings of it have fueled fierce theological anti-Semitism over the centuries. But that does not excuse a restatement of such misreadings as settled fact.

To his credit, Beker acknowledges the profound changes in Christian thinking that have occurred in the last decades and the ample presence today of devout Protestants and Catholics who repudiate the Church's historical teachings of contempt for the Jewish people. He also takes note of the positive effect that a profound immersion in the Bible has had on British and American statesmen, including Arthur Balfour, David Lloyd George (prime minister at the time of the Balfour Declaration committing Great Britain to the reestablishment of a Jewish homeland in Palestine), and Harry Truman. He might have added George W. Bush to the list. What this suggests is that even before the recent momentous changes in Church doctrine, a strong Christian faith did not necessarily entail anti-Jewish attitudes or policies.

· · ·

Beker's principal contention is that anti-Semitism is traceable primarily to jealousy over the Jews' unique status as the chosen people. This idea, too, has been around for a long time, having been propounded by no less than Sigmund Freud. In elaborating it, Beker notes that while Christianity and Islam have also insisted on being chosen, "only the Jews are condemned for continuing to claim the title." Actually, not quite: Muslim attacks on Christians for persisting in the claim of chosenness begin as early as the Qur'an itself. Nor, historically, has Christianity been welcoming of the Muslims' own assertion of specialness. For that matter, as I noted earlier, democratic societies with a strong investment in egalitarianism tend to look askance at all claims of chosenness. Among secular liberals in America, this is one source of the powerful prejudice against evangelicals and traditional Roman Catholics.

Still, the Jewish claim to be the chosen people does indubitably attract the greatest attention. Why it does so seems to me to have a simpler solution than jealousy.

Unlike most Christians and Muslims, Jews have for thousands of years constituted a small minority in almost every country in which they have lived; today, they continue to be a small minority everywhere except in Israel, which is itself a tiny minority in its Arab/Muslim region. When a group claiming chosen status is a vast majority, the idea of chosenness loses its social edge and can easily fade from mind. When a minuscule group makes the same claim, the majority may well resent it—all the more so when that majority adheres to a religion that sees itself as having superseded the one from which the claim derives. Add to this the fact that Judaism entails practices, like dietary laws and Sabbath observance, that continually draw attention to distinctions and render fraternization with members of the host culture difficult, and it is not hard to see how the non-Jewish mind would be drawn to dwell on the difference that being Jewish makes.

In any social system, whatever negative feelings already exist about a minority group will surely be exacerbated when that group claims to be nothing less than God's chosen. In democratic societies, where accidents of birth are thought to be subordinate to the self-determination of the individual, it can be all the more galling that God should be thought to have chosen a *people*—chosen, that is, not only arbitrarily but on the basis of family rather than individual merit. In this respect again, modern secular liberalism, however sworn to the ideal of tolerance, is as susceptible of bigotry as the most "benighted" religious tradition.

Given the animosity that the very idea of a chosen people generates in the modern West, it is hardly surprising that many Jews over the last two centuries have sought to reformulate their religion so as to downplay or eliminate the offending doctrine. Kaminsky notes the forthright statement of the Berlin Reform Congregation in the prayer book it adopted in 1844:

> [T]he concept of holiness and of a special vocation arising from this has become entirely foreign to us, as has the idea of an intimate covenant between God and Israel which is to remain significant for all eternity. Human character and dignity, and God's image within us—these alone are signs of chosenness.

Here, chosenness falls victim to death by redefinition and dilution: Because all mankind has become the chosen people, no people is singled out and thus none is really chosen.

Somewhat less radical is an approach taken by many Jews whereby chosenness is primarily defined as a special Jewish vocation to be, in words from the book of Isaiah, "a light unto the nations," spreading monotheism, social justice, loving-kindness, or their equivalents to the great masses of humanity that have not yet seen the light. This supposedly renders an inherently nonegalitarian doctrine more palatable to a culture in which inequality of any sort is deemed offensive. The general idea was well captured by Allan Bloom in *The Closing of the American Mind:*

> [T]he avant-garde (usually used in relation to art) and the vanguard (usually used in relation to politics) are democratic modes of distinguishing oneself, of being ahead, of leading, without denying the democratic principle. The members of the vanguard have just a small evanescent advantage. They now know what everyone will soon know.

Perhaps, indeed, some of the appeal of political progressivism to modern Jews is owing to its affinities with traditional notions of chosenness, now transposed into a very untraditional—and often explicitly antitraditional—key. But whether a stance of progressivism—of being not *above* everybody else, just *ahead* of everybody else—escapes the charge of elitism that so offends the egalitarian mind is open to much doubt. Nor, from the standpoint of Jewish identity, does it satisfy as a replacement for the concept of chosenness. For it is surely hard to justify the enormous sacrifices that the survival of Jewish identity has required over the centuries if the Jews' special status is both evanescent and about to become universally available.

Besides, according to traditional theology, much of what Jews are commanded to observe is not intended for Gentiles at any time; nor is it a light waiting to shine on the unknowing. It is, rather, the patrimony and the obligation of the Jewish people alone.

For all their differences, both Joel Kaminsky and Avi Beker steer clear of such contemporary apologetics and write as firm proponents of the classical idea of the chosen people. For Beker, Jewish differentness, despite the ready availability of conversion and assimilation, is inescapable. In this vein, he faults those of his fellow Israelis who imagine that redefining the Jews as a territorial people will cure the world of the longstanding disease of anti-Semitism. "Many Israelis fail to realize," he remarks, "how the features of the Chosen have made Israel the main object of anti-Semitism in the 21st century."

For Kaminsky, too, as we have seen, chosenness inevitably entails suffering, including the suffering inflicted on the chosen by the un-chosen. But he also stresses the possibility that election may work to the benefit of all, as part of a providential plan in which jealousy and enmity are not the last words. Can we, then, see the recent changes in Christian teaching as heralding an age in which the Jewish theology of chosenness will cease to be a neuralgic point? Will the different groups claiming the title of the biblical chosen people come to find, in that claim itself, a deep commonality and not just mutual rejection?

Perhaps; but perhaps not. What seems more certain is that, despite the determined efforts of so many, Jews and Gentiles alike, to do away with the idea of the chosen people, this ancient idea, like the Jewish people itself, is likely to be around for a long time to come—poorly understood, but hardly neglected.

PHILIP LEVINE

Words on the Wind

—Ford River Rouge

FROM *Georgia Review*

I'd walk up the hill through wild grasses
rich with milkweed and flags and make a nest
in the place I'd tamped down over the days
of decent weather. The view was something
terrifying and never the same:
on calm days the great plumes rose straight up
to insult the delicate nostrils of angels.
I was twenty-four and had no use
for the God of my fathers, no use for any-
thing spiritual. I believed in the deepest organs,
the liver, the kidneys, the heart, the lungs.
Nonetheless as I sat cross-legged drinking
chocolate milk words came on the wind.
Can you imagine God speaking to you
as you ate a little round store-bought pie
on a hilltop in Dearborn, where no Jews
were welcomed, where the wind came
in waves through the wild grasses
that had the guts to thrive? How I yearned
for the character of weeds and grass

that seemed more mysterious and grand
than the words the wind scattered through air
so fetid it was sweet. Noon, May 12,
1952. I wrote it on a calendar
at home and later threw the thing away.
You want those words, you who still believe,
who think the exact words are essential
to your salvation or whatever
it is you pray for? I'll take you there
on a spring day of wind and low gray sky,
a Dearborn day. We'll bring two quarts
of chocolate milk and little store-bought
pies—apple, cherry, or pineapple,
each worse than the other—and find the nest
of fifty years ago, and maybe we'll smoke
as all young men did, and lean back
into the flattened grass, and rest our heads
on the cold ground while we add our own
exhalations to the exquisite chaos
of the air, and commune with whoever.

WILFRED M. MCCLAY

Our Buried Sentiments

FROM *Touchstone*

A FEW YEARS AGO, A WOMAN WALKING HER DOG IN NOBLE, GEORGIA, stumbled on the remains of a human corpse. Investigators found many more corpses, eventually hundreds of them, which had been thrown out there by the Tri-State Crematory, a family owned business that received bodies from funeral homes in Georgia, Alabama, and Tennessee. Some of the corpses were "stacked like cordwood," as one observer said, while other "human bones, weathered white, were scattered through the woods like leaves, skulls mixed with leg bones in a ghoulish jumble," as *The New York Times* reported.

The story generated universal and sustained outrage around the country, but as the outrage mounted, I began to ask myself, "Why?"

Why such vehemence? Why, when so many Americans see nothing exceptional in the taking of a preborn life, when they are becoming inured to the warehousing of the elderly and infirm, when they regard the protection of embryonic life as itself a laughable proposition, when they routinely accept cremation, and the dismemberment of corpses for science, did this bizarre episode strike horror in so many?

And why, in this most Christ-haunted region of the South, not far from the home of Flannery O'Connor, was such opprobrium attached to the mistreatment of a body from which the spirit had departed, an inert "stiff" in which, literally, nobody was at home anymore? Why did those who took so low a view of the body that they were quite willing to have it disposed of by cremation, find this crematory's neglectful mistreatment to be, not merely regrettable, but an act of beyond-the-pale barbarity? Why draw the line here?

WE DO CARE

It was not a consumer-protection issue, in which the next of kin felt that they had not gotten what they paid for. No, the answer is something simpler, but also more profound.

It goes to the fact that there is something of primal importance about the way we treat the dead, and especially our ancestors. Nothing tells us more about a culture's regard for the human person, and its sense of itself as an entity persisting in time, than the character of its funerary rituals, its ways of acknowledging and remembering the dead.

We may be able to pretend to ourselves in twenty-first-century America that disposing of the dead is merely an elaborate form of taking out the trash, because there is "nothing there" but used-up protoplasm. But an incident like the one in Georgia puts such self-deceptions in a glaringly bright light, and undermines all our equivocations and sleights of hand.

We do in fact care what happens to the body. We can't help it. We still believe, viscerally, in the dignity of the human body. But we can mount no articulate defense of this belief. And so we have allowed ourselves through the practices we routinely employ to accept a diminution of one of life's most fundamental passages, and a violation of our elemental dignity, that amount to a negation of the human person himself.

As Robert Pogue Harrison has observed in his luminous book *The Dominion of the Dead,* civilization is built upon the awareness of our dead predecessors. "Only the dead can grant us legitimacy," he writes. "Left to ourselves we are all bastards." We bury the dead less to separate ourselves from them than to join ourselves to them. By burying them in our midst, we also humanize the grounds on which we ourselves live.

One might even say that burial has a certain civilizational priority, that what we make of the dead creates the foundation for what we make of ourselves. After all, as Harrison neatly puts it, "human beings housed their dead before they housed themselves."

Prehistoric nomads established permanent habitations of the dead, such as caverns, mounds, and barrows, and these were the chief settled landmarks and points of return, often also serving as shrines and sacred places with particular access to the spirit world. Only later did such men exchange their mobility for settled habitations, cities of the living built amid reminders of the dead. Which is why Lewis Mumford was right to proclaim that "the city of the dead antedates the city of the living" and is "the forerunner, almost the core, of every living city."

DANGEROUS PRACTICES

If this is true, then what are we to make of the fact, as Joseph Bottum has observed recently, that the modern city of San Francisco has proscribed the building of cemeteries and the interment of the dead inside its city limits? What does this tell us about the future of San Francisco, and us?

Will a civilization that comprehensively denies death by banishing every visible reminder be like a house without a foundation, destined to be blown away by the storms that will surely come? Will it be like a tree that has been deprived of its taproot, and is destined to wither and die for lack of nourishment?

Or will we be granted insight into the effect of separating ourselves from the bodies of our ancestors? Might the Tri-State Crematory episode provide just such a landscape-illuminating lightning bolt?

I think that it did, and that the rage, and the shudder of horror, so many felt at the news of the Georgia events disclosed a part of their souls that had not yet been anesthetized. Their reaction suggested that they knew, however dimly and unconsciously, that we have drifted into profoundly dangerous attitudes and practices.

Our disdain for the dead, and our desire to keep ourselves at the furthest possible distance from them, reflect back upon us. In this mirror we see clearly, if fleetingly, that we will need to remember where we came from if we are ever to understand, and ever to be able to explain cogently, why it is wrong to stack bodies like cordwood. For the measure we give is surely the measure we will receive.

Secularizations

FROM *First Things*

As WITH MOST ACADEMIC TRADITIONS, AND ESPECIALLY THOSE THAT are viewed as soft, there are orthodoxies and fashions, and sometimes sudden turns, that are conventionally described—following Thomas S. Kuhn's *Structure of Scientific Revolutions* of almost half a century ago—as paradigm shifts. Sociology is generally seen as one of those soft disciplines. From its once enormous popularity in the academy, it has in recent decades fallen upon hard times. As Peter Berger and others have argued, sociology did itself in by, among other things, its reckless abandonment of the intellectual discipline appropriate to being a discipline and its eagerness to make itself useful to sundry ideological and social causes. (See Berger's "Whatever Happened to Sociology?" in the October 2002 issue of *First Things*.)

Now a funny thing may be happening on the long road from the work of nineteenth-century Auguste Comte, commonly called the father of sociology. Comte envisioned a progression of three stages of history—from the theological to the metaphysical to the scientific. He left little doubt that these transitions were more or less inevitable and certainly the story of progress. If sociology was always a soft discipline compared to the hard sciences that it sought to emulate, the softest of the soft was the sociology of religion. There was a strong tendency to view religion as something vestigial, prescientific, and therefore premodern. Enter the well-known "secularization the-ory" that reigned almost unchallenged until the 1970s. In perhaps its most influential form, it was propounded by Max Weber (1864–1920) and, to put it too simply, claimed that there is a necessary connec-tion between modernity and religion: As modernity advances, reli-gion retreats. This near-inexorable process is called secularization.

As frequently discussed in these pages, secularization theory is now challenged on many fronts, and not least of all by Peter Berger, once one of its most influential proponents. The advocates of secu-larization theory had over many decades referred to "American excep-tionalism." This reflected the awareness that, if modernity necessarily entails secularization, it is something of a puzzle as to why the most modern of societies is also so vibrantly religious. Hundreds of books have been written in an attempt to explain American exceptional-ism. In recent years, however, the table has been turned, and the question of increasingly intense interest is "European exceptional-ism," meaning especially western and northern European secularity. Viewed in global terms, the American mix of modernity and religion seems to be the normal pattern. The interesting question is not why America is so religious but why Europe is so secular.

Here are at least some parts of the answer: the historical and cur-rent relationships between church and state, the impact of social pluralism, radically different understandings of the Enlightenment, different understandings of what it means to be an intellectual, dif-ferent institutional configurations for maintaining an intellectual tra-dition, and different ways in which the institutions of religion relate to factors such as class and ethnicity.

Let it readily be admitted that these ways of discussing the ques-tion can easily get mired in the gobbledygook of sociology talk. Some might feel more at home in addressing the differences between Europe and America in terms of the latter's providential purpose, and a good case can be made for doing so, but sociology doesn't do Divine Providence, which is just as well.

The new thinking about secularization does not reduce everything to an analysis of class or ethnic struggles, power rivalries, or economic dynamics. In her 2004 book *The Roads to Modernity*, for instance, the historian Gertrude Himmelfarb examines how the Enlightenment meant very different things in Europe and America. In America it was understood to be religion friendly, indeed religiously grounded, whereas in most of Europe it was a battle against the ancien régime, very much including the religious establishments. As Himmelfarb puts it, the Enlightenment in America took the form of "the politics of liberty" while in Europe it followed the French "ideology of reason." This is a persuasive analysis, to which it needs to be added that in the last half century the American intellectual class has turned decidedly toward the French understanding of the Enlightenment, a turn that is, underlying specific policies in dispute, a driving force in what are aptly called the "culture wars" in this country.

A great difference between Europeans and Americans is that Europeans are generally disposed to see religion more as a problem than as a solution. There are important caveats, to be sure, but the generalization holds. This is made evident in a number of ways. To take an obvious instance, there is the dramatic disparity between church attendance in Europe and the United States. In recent years, a number of scholars have challenged the claim, based on survey research of almost a century, that 40-plus percent of Americans go to church each week. Perhaps the statistics, gathered in various ways, are inflated, but the interesting question is why Americans who don't go to church regularly claim that they do. They *think* they should. For most Americans, it is the normal and approved thing to do. People are sometimes better understood by what they think they should do than by what they do. In Europe, going to church is to be in a self-understood minority; it is to take a stand, even to be countercultural.

In a new book coauthored by Peter Berger, Grace Davie, and Effie Fokas, *Religious America, Secular Europe?* the question is put this way: "Is secularization intrinsic or extrinsic to the modernization process? If Europe is secular because it is modern, then modernization and secularization acquire an organic link. If Europe is secular because it is European, then the reasoning becomes quite different. In light of the material presented in this book, we conclude that the latter is the much more likely option."

The authors draw on the work of Shmuel Eisenstadt, an Israeli sociologist, who has written extensively on "multiple modernities." What explains European exceptionalism with respect to religion? The answer is not modernity but, as Himmelfarb puts it, different roads to modernity. In America, as in almost all the rest of the world, there is no felt need to choose between religion and modernity. On the contrary, the relation between the two is benign if not mutually reinforcing. Needless to say, this is not the view that prevails in the more Europeanized sectors of America's intellectual class.

To be sure, religion in America is frequently of the type that sociologist Nancy Ammerman calls "Golden Rule Christianity"—do unto others as you would have them do unto you. This takes the edge off doctrinal and denominational disputes, and it can be understood as what Robert Bellah and others have called America's "civil religion." It is the source of the disputed virtue of tolerance, which, in the eyes of more orthodox Christians, is often decried as religious indifference—though it also makes possible the near-unanimous support for such national identity-markers as "In God We Trust" and "One Nation Under God." That support depends in large part on not inquiring too closely, and certainly not in a publicly aggressive manner, into the nature of the God affirmed.

Superficial critics of "Golden Rule Christianity" routinely deride it as superficial and a very poor substitute for what they propose as "authentic Christianity." It should not, I think, be treated so dismissively. You can do a lot worse than the Golden Rule as a maxim in support of social peace and cooperation. More important, most Americans do not center their spiritual lives on contemplating the national motto or the Pledge of Allegiance. For that, they have churches and synagogues—the bearers of much thicker religious traditions. This does not have to do, at least in the first place, with the distinction between public and private. Baptists, Lutherans, Methodists, and Catholics are publicly what they are. Indeed, belonging to a church is a mark of public acceptability, as is evident in numerous studies showing how immigrants quickly become more religiously affiliated in America than they were in their home country.

In this religio-cultural circumstance, Americans typically live at two levels of religious identity and affirmation. One is national ("In God We Trust"). The other, more deeply personal and communal, is lived in "the church of your choice." This is an experienced choice, and is thus a facet of modernity that is difficult to avoid in the American situation. In the sociological jargon, our religious connection is elective rather than ascribed. Even with those churches, such as the Catholic and Orthodox, that have a deep ecclesiology of being sacramentally incorporated into the Body of Christ and thus being more chosen than choosing, the need for choice and repeated choice is the norm. A tradition chosen is different from a tradition into which one is born and by which one is defined. A choice can always, at least hypothetically, be reversed. This is obviously in tension with the self-understanding of Catholic and Orthodox Christianity, but it is the American religious circumstance.

H. Richard Niebuhr wrote that the American contribution to ecclesiology was to add, to the European religious types of church and sect, the phenomenon of the denomination. A denomination is an elective association that assumes the appurtenances of the (uppercase) Church. The Catholic and Orthodox churches do not understand themselves to be denominations but the Church of Jesus Christ rightly ordered through time. For Catholics and Orthodox, one understands oneself to be baptized, and not usually by choice, into that one expression of the one Church. It is true that people also say they were "baptized Episcopalian" or "baptized Methodist." But that is a matter of institutional identity or even tribal loyalty rather than of a coherent ecclesiology, since other churches do not claim to be what the Catholic and Orthodox churches claim to be.

The European difference is most starkly posed by the French experience. The British sociologist David Martin contends that the absence of a successful Reformation in France set the stage for a brutal power struggle between religion and the state. By a "successful Reformation," he means chiefly a process of declericalization in which the Church is prepared to make an accommodation with the rising ambitions of the state along the lines of the "separation of church and state" in America. Grace Davie speaks of "the two protagonists in the struggle that dominates French history: on the one hand, an unreconstructed and hegemonic church and, on the other, a state that claims for itself moral as well as political authority. The ascendancy of one implies the decline of the other. This is a zero-sum game." It is the zero-sum that resulted in the victory of the state reflected in the French notion of *laïcité*, which is a harder version of what in America has been called the naked public square—public life under the control of the state and stripped of religious or religiously grounded references.

Of course, in the real world there are no pure types. The connections between modernity and choice, in both Europe and America, result in a pick-and-mix approach to religion. The French sociologist

Danièle Hervieu-Léger employs the term *bricolage*—which can be translated as "tinkering," as when a child assembles and reassembles the pieces of a Tinker Toy set or a Lego game. Among Catholics, this is referred to pejoratively as "cafeteria Catholicism." The American scholar Robert Wuthnow calls the phenomenon "patchwork religion."

A big difference between Europeans and Americans, however, is that the former usually do their tinkering in a private and unorganized manner, while Americans, with their propensity for organizing and association, are more likely to play *bricolage* within existing religious institutions, or to start yet another denomination. This is closely related to the way in which people say they are "spiritual but not religious." They resist taking their religion as a package deal, so to speak, insisting that it be tailored to what they describe as their "spiritual needs." This pattern is prominent among both Catholics and Protestants, as is evident in the increasing number of Catholics who church shop for a parish of their preference, and the growing number of renewal movements, such as Opus Dei, Regnum Christi, and the Neocatechumenal Way. It should be noted that these and other movements are also very much at the center of Catholic renewal in European countries, not least of all in France.

In addition to the idea of "believing without belonging," Davie also speaks of "vicarious religion." This is evident in the ways that Europeans view the religiously committed as substitutes or surrogates in practicing the religion that they generally favor but do not want, for whatever reason, to practice themselves. They do not want to be personally involved in the church but want it to be there in time of need (usually associated with death and dying) or as an institution of moral continuity in the society. For instance, in Germany people pay 8 percent of their income tax to the support of the church, which, given tax rates in Germany, can be a sizable sum. They can opt out of the system by registering themselves *konfessionslos*—but the interesting thing is that most people do not.

"Vicarious religion" also helps explain the death of mainline Protestantism in this country, which was recently addressed by Joseph Bottum in the August/September 2008 issue of *First Things* ("The Death of Protestant America: A Political Theory of the Protestant Mainline"). Fifty years ago it was thought to be a question of great public moment when an Episcopal bishop such as James Pike publicly denied the existence of hell, heaven, or of God himself.

The Episcopal Church was undoubtedly the culturally elite church of the Protestant Establishment, and people who themselves had little interest in heaven, hell, or God felt themselves betrayed when it failed to do its vicarious duty in upholding what Christians are supposed to believe. Establishment Protestantism was failing to do its duty. It was letting down the side, with unforeseen consequences for the society as a whole, and that worried people who expected the churches to do their believing for them.

Of course, there were many others who celebrated the mainline collapse as liberation from what is derisively called traditional morality. Fifty years later, it is hard to find anyone in America, apart from spiritually inclined gay activists and their allies in the media, who thinks that what is happening in the Episcopal Church has a serious bearing on the future of the country.

Vicarious religion is different in Britain. Most sociologists addressing the secularization issue depict Britain as being somewhere midway between the European and the American situations. But England today, and Scotland historically, has a long tradition of an officially established church. Americans are frequently puzzled by the way in which an affirmation of heresy or virtual apostasy by a bishop of the Church of England can still raise an enormous media ruckus in Britain. After all, it has been more than a half century since Church of England bishops have been writing sympathetically about "the death of God" and other theological frivolities. And yet, perverse episcopal eruptions still generate great public controversy, with everybody getting into the act, including professed atheists (who form upward of 20 percent of the population, as compared with 5 percent in America).

Davie's idea of vicarious religion is useful. One notes in passing that some have suggested that the death of the Protestant mainline in this country might be succeeded by the ascendancy of Catholicism as the country's establishment religion. That suggestion could be tested by the public reaction if a few Catholic bishops publicly repudiated what are understood to be key articles of faith or, for instance, attempted to ordain women to the priesthood. Unlike the Church of England, however, the Catholic Church is under international control and not a national property. In fact, there is still a substantial part of the population that is not sure the Catholic Church really belongs here at all. The media treatment of the sex-abuse crisis, beginning in 2002, depicted it as entirely an internal problem of the Church with few, if any, implications for the larger society.

That having been said, however, vicarious religion is alive and well in America. There are undoubtedly many non-Catholics, and also lapsed Catholics—or, as some cleverly say, "collapsed Catholics"—who would be greatly disturbed if the Church failed to keep up their side by continuing to teach what they are not sure they believe, or are sure they do not believe. A Jewish friend remarks, "'The Catholic Church is the church we mean when we say *Church*.' If it goes, that's the whole game." It is not as it is in England, where the nation pays the church to do its vicarious religion, but somebody has to maintain standards, and the Catholic Church in America is the chief, maybe the only, candidate for the job. That at least is how some view the convergence of the role of vicarious religion between Europe and America.

Yet another way of thinking about secularization is described as the move "from obligation to consumption." In Europe, it is said, religious institutions are like public utilities. Like gas or electrical utilities, they are maintained for all but not all are expected to use them equally. Closely connected is the rational-choice theory advocated by Rodney Stark and others. These are interesting heuristic ideas that help to joggle the mind but may be of limited intellectual utility in understanding the dynamics of secularization. America is presumably the preeminent "consumer society." One might say that Americans typically "consume" more religion than do Europeans, but how far do you get by asking, "How much religion have you consumed this week?" Especially when the religion in play is Christianity, which emphasizes giving rather than getting. As in worship and in love of God and neighbor.

According to rational-choice theory, state-subsidized European churches are overstuffed with bureaucrats and professionals who live off the establishment, whereas American churches are subjected to the rigors of the marketplace. Thus Europeans view their churches as public utilities rather than, as in America, rival companies. In the language of Walter McDougall, that intrepid historian of this country, Americans are, even in religion, a "nation of hustlers." (Also in the good sense of "hustler," he adamantly insists.) Yet others have suggested that America is more vibrantly religious not because Americans are necessarily more religious but because Americans are simply more sociable. As almost everybody since Tocqueville has underscored, Americans have a penchant for association and the building of voluntary associations. Europeans are—and this goes back centuries—more inclined to let the state or other authorities make the important decisions for them. This might be viewed as the "vicarious authority" dimension of "vicarious religion."

José Casanova of Georgetown University pushes the question back further, arguing that there is no one thing properly called *secularization*. Secularization theory, he says, is composed of "three very different, uneven, and unintegrated propositions." First, there is *secularization* understood as differentiation, in which secular spheres of society are increasingly distinguished from religious institutions and norms. Then there is what most people probably mean by *secularization:* a decline in religious beliefs and practices. Finally, there is *secularization* as the marginalization of religion, pushing it almost totally into the private sphere of life. While the first and the third of these may seem pretty much the same thing, it is surely true that discovering what people actually believe and why they believe it is not as susceptible to the kinds of structural analyses of which sociologists are fond.

The authors of *Religious America, Secular Europe?* seem at points to be curiously favorable to the more unitary government school systems of Europe, where, unlike America, "religion" or "world religions" is a staple in the curriculum. The result, they suggest, is that controversial questions such as creationism, intelligent design, and sexual morality are taught in their proper educational slot ("religion") rather than being allowed to disrupt the educational curriculum. This is unpersuasive. As with religious-studies departments in American universities replacing departments of theology, the study of religion in general is a poor substitute for the study of religion that is believed and lived in the particular. Even if the Supreme Court permitted religion to be taught in American government schools, a following of the European pattern would seem to be but a further instance of the secularization that Casanova describes as differentiation and marginalization.

Here again the difference between public utility and rival firms is pertinent. In America, the rival firms in the religious formation of children are the home, the churches, and explicitly religious schools. I expect that serious studies focused on this question would demonstrate that the American way of competition better serves religious vitality and, not incidentally, the pluralism that most consider a strength of this society. The "separation of church and state" is often taken to absurd extremes, but, in removing the teaching of religion from the public utility that is the government school system, it is not without its blessings. The absurd extremes typically involve the exclusion of any favorable reference to a particular religion, especially if it is to a majority religion, which is presumed to offend those of other religions or of no religion. The presumably offended are usually not consulted, it being decreed by the enforcers of secularism that they *should* be offended, even if they aren't.

And so the sociological arguments about the nature and causes of secularization go 'round and 'round. The political scientist John Madeley sees European exceptionalism as deeply rooted in the history of the continent. The history is that of a triad of church, state, and nation. "First, the church inherited part of its claim to universal dominion from the Roman Empire; then, after centuries of strain between religious *sacerdotum* and secular *regnum,* this claim was successfully tested and set aside by ever more powerful dynastic states and empires in the early-modern period; and, finally, from approximately 1800, the claim of the nation to be the unique font of sovereignty and political authority has progressively been pressed."

The triadic contest continues, however, in some peculiar ways. Jerry Z. Mueller has recently written in *Foreign Affairs* that the European Union is, in fact, the triumph of nationalism, with each nationally defined member state provided security for its national self-expression without the dangers of going to war with another European state. In Poland, it is hard to differentiate religion, state, and nation, since the story of Poland is the story of Catholicism, and its existence has depended—and some would say still depends—on that solidarity of identity. In Finland, unlike most European countries, almost all children are baptized in the official Lutheran Church. Otherwise, in terms of professed belief and practice, Finland is not so very unlike other European countries. Does baptism signify incorporation into the Finnish nation or incorporation into the Body of Christ? Or both? And in post-Soviet

Russia, the Russian state and Holy Orthodoxy are forging a single sovereignty that, logically enough, is aggressively hostile to religious minorities. Are these instances of secularization?

In 2004 there was a grand brouhaha over whether the preamble of the European Constitution should include a specific reference to Christianity. Both John Paul the Great and the present pope, among many others, entered the ring. Grace Davie says the controversy turned on the difference over whether a preamble is to speak of the past or the future. She writes, "If a preamble is concerned with historical fact, then the reference must be specific—Christianity has had a huge and lasting influence in the formation of Europe. It is willful to pretend otherwise. But if a preamble is an inspiration for the future, the answers might well be different, or at least there are different questions to consider. Much of the confusion surrounding this highly controversial issue lay in the fact that Europeans omitted to consider the precise nature of the preamble that they were trying to write." If they were not confused, and if they did intend a preamble addressing the future, would Christianity have been mentioned? Davie does not say, although it would seem to have a strong bearing on what is meant by the secularization of Europe.

Jürgen Habermas, among the most influential of European social theorists and a person with whom Benedict XVI has entered into public conversation, has written: "Christianity, and nothing else, is the ultimate foundation of liberty, conscience, human rights, and democracy. . . . We continue to nourish ourselves from this source. Everything else is postmodern chatter." Needless to say, this was not the view of those who managed the campaign for the European Constitution.

I have omitted in this essay, mainly because it is omitted in the literature under discussion, some more melancholy accounts of the European circumstance—as set forth in the work of Bernard Lewis, George Weigel, Bat Ye'or, and, at a much more popular level, Mark

Steyn. They depict Europe as a dying continent: dying culturally, spiritually, and, perhaps most decisively, demographically. The nations of Europe have a birthrate far below replacement level, and, according to demographers, many have passed the point of no return, meaning that it is nearly impossible, from a statistical viewpoint, that native populations will maintain their numbers into the next generation or two. This situation is exacerbated by the fast-growing number of unassimilated and culturally aggressive Muslim immigrants, leading some writers to warn that Europe will, in the not-too-distant future, be replaced by "Eurabia." Most of these writers see a strong connection between secularization and demographic disaster. Without a deeply grounded—usually meaning a religiously grounded—hope for the future, the case for having children is gravely weakened.

The social scientists writing in *Religious America, Secular Europe?* do refer, usually in passing, to the Muslim and demographic challenges, but they seem to believe that, one way or another, Europe will muddle through. The record of history suggests that there is a great deal to be said on behalf of muddling through, but this apparent insouciance is less than entirely plausible.

Nonetheless, the arguments surveyed in the book and related literature are an encouraging sign of fresh thinking in the social sciences about the nature and causes of secularization. It is not likely that grand systematic schemes like those of Comte or Weber will emerge out of these debates, which is perhaps just as well. What is emerging is a renewed and thoroughly multicultural understanding of *homo religiosus*—the creature in the gutter who, despite every effort, cannot help but see in the muck the reflection of the stars and thus recognize (in the fine phrase of Berger's) "signals of transcendence."

The important task of a renewed sociology of religion is to help us understand how, both individually and in social structures, *homo religiosus* accommodates that irrepressible vision within all the other things that he knows to be true and important.

ROBERT PINSKY

The Procession

FROM *Agni*

At the summit of Mauna Kea, an array of antennae
Sensitive to the colors of invisible light.

The antennae sidle heavily on motors to measure
Submillimeter waves across the cold universe,

In patterns choreographed by an astronomer's hand
At a computer in Massachusetts, in real time:

A system of waves and removes and extremes
Devoted to the wavering, remote nature of things.

Your soul: your father Adam known as Vishnu
And Lakshmi your mother known also as Eve,

Both of them smaller than the width of a hair
Are riding astride matched tortoises along a road

Nine microns wide, following another Eve
And another Adam in a long procession

Of mothers and fathers, Lakshmis and Vishnus
With you their child Cain and their child Abel.

Innumerable their names and doings, innumerable
Their destinies and remote histories and tongues.

Somewhere among them your ancestor the slave
Also your ancestors the king the thief the stranger.

The immense agonies of my tiny span of life:
A pause as one tortoise in the chain lifts his foot

To tread the emanation of a dead star, still alive
And afire when the procession first set out.

Everyone alive the outcome of a rape,
Everyone alive the outcome of a great love.

Cain and Abel, Heloise and Abelard, mostly
Anonymous they travel a filament of light

To cross the Nothing between the galaxies
Into the pinhole iris of your mortal eye.

At the heart of each telescope on Mauna Kea,
An aperture finer than a hair on Vishnu's head.

On every hair on each Vishnu's head, a procession
Of tiny paired tortoises crossing a galactic distance.

In the skull of each tortoise in the long procession,
A faceted jewel attuned to a spectral channel

Where endlessly Kronos eats us his children, suffering
By nature each of us in a certain sliver of time.

MELISSA RANGE

Scriptorium: The Lindisfarne Gospels

FROM *Image*

Before the stepwork and the fretwork,
before the first wet spiral leaves the brush,
before the plucking of the geese's quills,
before the breaking of a thousand leads;

before the curving limbs and wings
of hounds, cats, and cormorants
knot into letters, before the letters knot
into the Word, Eadfrith ventures from his cell,

reed basket on his arm, past Cuthbert's grave,
past the stockyard where the calves' cries bell,
and their blood illuminates the dirt as ink
on vellum, across the glens and woods

to gather woad and lichens, to the shores
to gather shells. The earth, not the cell,
is his scriptorium, where he might see
the interlace of branch and twig and leaf;

how green bleeds brown when fields are plowed;
how green banks blue where grass gives way to sea;
how blue twists into white in swirling lines
purling through the water and the sky.

Before the skinning of a hundred calves,
before the stretching and the scraping of their hides,
before the boiling vinegar, the toasting lead,
the bubbling orpiment and verdigris,

before the glair cracks from the egg,
before the monk perfects his recipe—
egg white, oak-gall, iron salt, mixed
in a tree-stump, some speculate—

to make the pigments glorious to the Lord,
before Eadfrith's fingers are permanently stained
the colors of his world—crimson, emerald,
cerulean, gold—outside the monastery walls,

in the village, with its brown hounds
spooking yellow cats stalking green-black birds,
on the purple-bitten lips of peasants
his gospel's corruption already sings forth

in vermilion ink, firebrands on a red calf's hide—
though he will be long dead before the Vikings sail,
and two centuries of men and wars
will pass before his successor Aldred

pierces Eadfrith's text with thorn,
ash, and all the other angled letters

of his gloss. Laced between the lines of Latin,
the vernacular proclaims, in one dull tint,

a second, shattering illumination,
of which Eadfrith was not unaware:
this good news is for everyone,
like language, like color, like air.

RICHARD RODRIGUEZ

The God of the Desert

FROM *Harper's Magazine*

ON THE FLIGHT FROM LONDON I SIT OPPOSITE A RUMBLE SEAT where the stewardess places herself during takeoff. The stewardess is an Asian woman with a faraway look. I ask how often she makes this flight. Once or twice a month. Does she enjoy Israel? Not much. She stays in a hotel in Tel Aviv. She goes to the beach. She flies back. What about Jerusalem? She has not been there. What is in Jerusalem?

The illustrated guidebook shows a medieval map of the world. The map is round. The sun has a beard of fire. All the rivers of the world spew from the mouth of the moon. At the center of the world is Jerusalem.

Just inside the main doors of the Church of the Holy Sepulchre, tourists seem unsure how to respond to a rectangular slab of marble resting upon the floor. Lamps and censers and trinkets hang suspended above the stone. We watch as an old woman approaches. With some effort, she gets down on her knees. I flip through my book: *This marble represents the Stone of Unction where Jesus's body was anointed. This is not original; this stone dates from 1810.* The old woman bends forward to kiss the pale stone.

I have come to the Holy Land because the God of the Jews, the God of the Christians, the God of the Muslims—a common God— revealed Himself in the desert. My curiosity about an ecology that joins three desert religions dates from September 11, 2001, from prayers enunciated in the sky over America on that day.

Most occidental Christians are unmindful of the orientalism of Christianity. Over two millennia, the locus of Christianity shifted westward—to Antioch, to Rome, to Geneva, to the pale foreheads of Thomistic philosophers, to Renaissance paintings, to glitter among the frosts of English Christmas cards. Islam, too, in the middle centuries, swept into Europe with the Ottoman carpet, but then receded. Only to reflux. Amsterdam, Paris are becoming Islamic cities.

After centuries of Diaspora, after the calamity of the Holocaust in Europe, Jews turned once more toward the desert. Zionists did not romanticize the desolate landscape. Rather, they defined nationhood as an act of planting. The impulse of the kibbutz movement remains the boast of urban Israel: to make the desert bloom.

The theme of Jerusalem is division. Friday. Saturday. Sunday. The city has been conquered, destroyed, rebuilt, garrisoned, halved, quartered, martyred, and exalted—always the object of spiritual desire; always the prize; always the corrupt model of the eventual city of God. Recently, the government of Ariel Sharon constructed a wall that separates Jerusalem from the desert, Jerusalem from Bethlehem, Easter from Christmas.

Jerusalem was the spiritual center of the Judaean wilderness. It was Jerusalem the desert thought about. It was Jerusalem the prophets addressed. Jerusalem was where Solomon built a temple for the Lord and where God promised to dwell with His people. Jerusalem was where Jesus died and was resurrected. It was from Jerusalem Muhammad ascended to heaven during his night journey.

My first impression of the city is my own loneliness: oil stains on the road, rubble from broken traffic barriers, exhaust from buses, the drift of cellophane bags. At the Damascus Gate an old woman sits on the pavement, sorting grape leaves into piles—some kind of leaves. It is hot. Already it is hot. Late spring. It is early morning. There is a stench of uncollected garbage, and the cats, light and limp as empty purses, slink along the blackened stone walls. Shopkeepers are unrolling their shops.

I turn into the courtyard of the Church of the Holy Sepulchre, the site of Christ's burial and resurrection. A few paces away, within the church, is Golgotha, where Jesus was crucified. Golgotha, the Place of the Skull, is also, according to Jerusalem tradition, the grave of Adam. Jerusalem is as condensed, as self-referential, as Rubik's Cube.

I wait in line to enter the Sepulcher, a freestanding chapel in the rotunda of the basilica. A mountain was chipped away from the burial cave, leaving the cave. Later the cave was destroyed. What remains is the interior of the cave, which is nothing. The line advances slowly until, after two thousand years, it is my turn. I must lower my shoulders and bend my head; I must almost crawl to pass under the low opening.

I am inside the idea of the tomb of Christ.

I return many times to the Church of the Holy Sepulchre and form in my mind an accommodation to its clamorous hush, to the musk of male asceticism—indeed, I form a love for it that was not my first feeling, though my first impression remains my last: emptiness.

I wait for Haim Berger in the lobby of a hotel in Ein Bokek, one among an oasis of resorts near the Dead Sea. The lobby is a desert of sand-colored marble. The lobby's temperature is oppressively beige—it would be impossible to cool this useless atrium. My cell phone rings. It is Maya, the director of the agency attached to my hotel in Jerusalem. Haim will be late one hour. Look for him at ten o'clock.

I watch a parade of elderly men and women crossing the lobby in bathing suits to catch a shuttle to the sulfur baths. They are so unself-conscious about their bodies, they seem to walk in paradise.

I believe I am waiting for someone in shorts and boots and aviator glasses, driving a Jeep. A Volkswagen pulls up and parks haphazardly. A man bolts from the car. He is willowy of figure, dressed all in white, sandals, dark curly hair. He disappears into the hotel; reemerges. We wait side by side.

I cannot go to the desert alone. I am unfit for it. The desert requires a Jeep. It requires a hat and sunglasses and plastic liters of warm water it is no pleasure to drink. It requires a guide. It requires a cell phone.

Just now the man dressed in white begins patting his pockets, searching for his chiming cell. "*Ken . . . Shalom, Maya,*" I hear him say. Then, turning toward me, "Ah."

Haim Berger is full of apology. He has taken his wife to an emergency room. Yes, everything is all right. Just a precaution. There is an Evian bottle for me in the car. We will switch to the Jeep later.

Within ten minutes, I am standing with Haim on the side of a highway. We look out over a plain, over what once was Sodom and Gomorrah. Haim asks if I know the story. Of course I know the story. Which nevertheless does not stop him from telling it. We might be standing near where Abraham stood when "Abraham saw dense smoke over the land, rising like fumes from a furnace."

I ask Haim if he is religious. He is not.

All three desert religions claim Abraham as father. A recurrent question in my mind concerns the desert: Did Abraham happen on God or did God happen on Abraham? The same question: Which is the desert, or whom? I came upon a passage in 2 Maccabees. The passage pertains to the holiness of Jerusalem: *The Lord, however, had not chosen the people for the sake of the Place, but the Place for the sake of the people.* So God happened on Abraham. Abraham is the desert.

An old man sits at the door of his tent in the heat of the day.

Between that sentence and this—within the drum of the hare's heart, within the dilation of the lizard's eye, God enters His creation.

The old man, who is Abraham, sits at the door of his tent and becomes aware of three strangers standing nearby. They arrive without the preamble of distance. The nominative grammar of Genesis surpasses itself to reveal that one of these travelers is God or perhaps all three are God, like a song in three octaves. Abraham invites the Three to rest and to refresh themselves. In return, God promises that in a year's time Abraham's wife, who is long past childbearing, will hold in her arms a son.

Abraham's wife, Sarah, in the recesses of the tent, snorts upon hearing the prognostication; says, not quite to herself: *Oh, sure!*

God immediately turns to Abraham: *Why does Sarah laugh? Is anything too marvelous for God?*

Sarah says: *I am not laughing.*

God says: *Yes you are.*

In 1947 a Bedouin goatherd lost a goat and climbed the side of a mountain to look for it. The boy entered a cave—today the cave is known worldwide among archaeologists as Cave Number One. What the boy found in the cave—probably stumbled upon in the dark—were broken clay jars that contained five sheepskin scrolls. Four of the scrolls were written in Hebrew; one in Aramaic. More scrolls were subsequently found by other Bedouin and by scholars in caves nearby. The discovered scrolls—including a complete copy of the Book of Isaiah—are the oldest known manuscript copies of books of the Bible.

The scrolls date to the second century B.C. Scholars believe the Jewish sect of Essenes, of the protomonastic community of Qumran, hid the texts we now know as the Dead Sea Scrolls. No one remembers whether the goatherd found his goat.

Haim is not religious, but he offers to tell me a curious story: Last year he took a group of students into a mountainous part of the desert. He had been there many times. He had previously discovered markings on rocks that seemed to indicate religious observance; he believes the markings are ancient.

On the particular day he describes—it was the winter solstice—as the group approached a mountain, they saw what appeared to be a semicircle of flame emanating from the rock face, rather like the flame from a hoop in the circus. Haim knew it was a trick of the light, or perhaps gases escaping from a fissure in the rock. He walked before the mountain in an arc to observe the phenomenon from every angle. He repeats: He was not alone. They all saw it. He has photographs. He will show me the photographs.

Haim's love for the desert dates from his military service. His Jeep broke down. He cursed the engine. He slammed the hood. He took a memorable regard of the distance. Since that day, he has become intimate with the distance; he has come to see the desert as a comprehensible ecosystem that can be protective of humans.

Haim has tied a white kerchief over his hair.

Haim says: Bedouin know a lot. Bedouin have lived in the desert thousands of years. Haim says: If you are ever stranded in the desert—*Are you listening to me? This may save your life!*—in the early morning, you must look to see in which direction the birds are flying. They will lead you to water.

Haim stops to speak with admiration of a bush with dry, gray-green leaves. "These leaves are edible." (Now I must sample them.) "They are salty, like potato chips." (They are salty.)

Of another bush: "These have water. If you crush them, you will get water. These could save your life." He crushes a fistful of leaves and tears spill from his hand.

The child of Abraham and Sarah is named Isaac, which means "He Laughs." Sarah proclaims an earthy Magnificat: *God has made laughter for me, and all who hear of it will laugh for me.* From the loins of these two deserts—Abraham, Sarah—God yanks a wet, an iridescent caul—a people as numerous as the stars. From the line of Sarah, royal David. From King David's line will come Jesus.

One's sense of elision begins with the map. Many tourist maps include the perimeters of the city at the time of Herod's temple, the time of Christ. *This once was. Built over the site. All that remains. This site resembles. This is not the room of the Last Supper; this is a Crusader structure built over the room, later converted to a mosque—note the mihrab, the niche in the wall.*

The empty room is white—not white, golden. *Is the air really golden?* As a child in Omaha, my friend Ahuva was ravished by the thought—told to her by an old man in a black hat—that the light of Jerusalem is golden. An ultra-Orthodox boy wanders into the room (a few paces from this room is the Tomb of King David, the anteroom to which is dense with the smell of men at prayer; upstairs is a minaret); the boy is eating something, some kind of bun; he appears transfixed by a small group of evangelical Christian pilgrims who have begun to sing a song, what in America we would call an old song.

I am kneeling in the early morning at St. Anne's, a Romanesque church built in the twelfth century. The original church was damaged by the Persians; restored in the time of Charlemagne; destroyed, probably by the Caliph Hakim, in 1010. The present church was built by the Crusaders. Sultan Salah-ed-Din captured the city in 1192 and converted the church to a madrasa. The Ottoman Turks neglected the structure; it fell to ruin. The Turks offered the church to France. The French order of White Fathers now administers St. Anne's. Desert sun pours through a window over the altar.

Not only is the light golden, Ahuva, but I must mention a specific grace. Each afternoon around four o'clock, without fail, the most delightful breeze comes upon Jerusalem, I suppose from the Mediterranean, miles away. It begins at the tops of the tallest trees, the date-palm trees; shakes them like feather dusters; rides under the bellies of the lazy red hawks; snaps the flags on the consulate roofs; lifts the curtains of the tall windows of my room at the hotel—sheer curtains embroidered with an arabesque design—lifts them until they are suspended perpendicularly in midair like the veil of a bride tormented by a playful page, who then lets them fall. And then lifts. And then again.

I walk around the wall of the city to the Mount of Olives, to a Christian sensibility the most evocative remnant of Jerusalem, for it matches—even including the garbage—one's imagination of Christ's regard for the city he approached from Bethany, which was from the desert. The desert begins immediately to the east of Jerusalem.

All the empty spaces of the Holy City—all courts, tabernacles, tombs, and reliquaries—are resemblances and references to the emptiness of the desert. All the silences of women and men who proclaim the desert God are references and resemblances to this—to the Holy City, to the hope of a Holy City. Jerusalem is the Bride of the Desert.

The desert prowls like a lion. I am fatigued from the heat, and I look about for some shade and a bottle of water. Having procured both at an outdoor stand (from a young man whose father kneels in prayer), I grow curious about an entrance I can see from the courtyard where I rest. Perhaps it is a chapel. An old man is sitting on the steps near the entrance. I approach him. What is this place?

The Tomb of Mary, he answers.

Inside the door I perceive there are steps from wall to wall, leading downward. I can discern only the flickering of red lamps below, as if at the bottom of a well. When I reach the level of the tomb, an Orthodox priest throws a switch and the tomb is illuminated. It is a shelf of rock. The legend of the Dormition of Mary and the Catholic doctrine of the Assumption—neither of which I understand very well—lead me to wonder whether this is a spurious site. I decide I will accept all sites in this junk room of faith as true sites. I kneel.

A couple of years ago the bone box of James, the brother of Jesus, was raised from the shady world of the antiquities market. I believe the box has been discredited (dust not of the proper age within the incising of the letters). Authenticity is not my point. The stone box is my point. For it creates emptiness. Jerusalem is just such a box—within its anachronistic walls—a city of ossuaries, buried, reburied, hallowed, smashed, reconstructed, then called spurious or probable in guidebooks.

I have brought five guidebooks to Jerusalem, my Pentateuch: The Archaeological. The Historical. The Illustrated. The Practical. The Self-Absorbed. Each afternoon, when I return to my hotel, I convene a colloquy among them—the chatter of guidebooks. I read one and then another.

The closed nature of the city frustrates my interest. My mind is oppressed by the inaccessibility of the hive of empty chambers, empty churches, empty tombs. The city that exists is superimposed in some meaty way over the bone city I long to enter. The streets are choked and impassible with life; the air stifling, the merchandise appalling. I feel feverish, but I think it is only the heat. I make the rounds of all the gates to the Temple Mount until at last I find the entrance that Israeli security will let me through—the passageway for infidels.

The sun is blazing on the courtyard. Even the faithful have gone away. Elsewhere the city is vertiginously sunken—resentments and miracles parfaited. Here there is a horizontal prospect.

The Al-Aqsa Mosque and the Dome of the Rock have been closed to non-Muslims since my last visit. I stand outside the shrine and try to reconstruct the interior from memory—the pillars, tiles, meadows of carpet. The vast Muslim space is what I remember. Islamic architecture attempts the sublime feat of emptiness. It is the sense of emptiness enclosed that is marvelous. The dome is the sky that is made. The sky is nothing—the real sky—and beggars have more of it than others.

Muslims own Jerusalem sky. This gold-leafed dome identifies Jerusalem on any postcard. The conspicuous jewel. Jews own the ground. The enshrined rock was likely the foundation for the Holy of Holies of Solomon's temple, the room that enclosed the Ark of the Covenant. The Rock is also the traditional site of the near-sacrifice of Isaac by Abraham. God commanded Moses to commission Bezalel the artisan to make the Ark. The Book of Exodus describes two golden cherubim whose wings were to form above the Ark a Seat of Mercy—a space reserved for the presence of the Lord. The architecture for the presence of God has been conceptualized ever after as emptiness.

The paradox of monotheism is that the desert God, refuting all other gods, demands acknowledgment within emptiness. The paradox of monotheism is that there is no paradox—only unfathomable singularity.

May I explain to you some features of the shrine?

A man has approached as I stand gazing toward the dome. He looks to be in his sixties; he is neatly dressed in a worn suit. The formality of syntax extends to his demeanor. Obviously he is one of the hundreds of men, conversant in three faiths, who haunt the shrines of Jerusalem, hoping to earn something as informal guides.

No thank you.

This is the Dome of the Rock, he continues.

No thank you.

Why are you so afraid to speak to a guide? (The perfected, implicating question.)

I am not afraid. I don't have much time.

He lowers his eyes. *Perhaps another time.* He withdraws.

My diffidence is purely reflexive. One cannot pause for a moment on one's path through any of the crowded streets or souks without a young man—the son, the nephew, the son-in-law of some shopkeeper—asking, often with the courtliness of a prince, often with the stridency of a suitor: *May I show you my shop?*

Emptiness clings to these young men as well—the mermen of green-lit grottoes piled with cheap treasure—men with nothing to do but fiddle with their cell phones or yawn in their unconscious beauty and only occasionally swim up to someone caught in the unending tide of humanity that passes before them.

May I show you my shop?

No thank you.

Behind the wall of my hotel in East Jerusalem are a gasoline station and a small mosque. The tower of the mosque—it is barely a tower—is out-fitted with tubes of green neon. Five times in twenty-four hours the tubes of neon flicker and sizzle; the muezzin begins his cry. Our crier has the voice of an old man, a voice that gnaws on its beard. I ask everyone I meet if the voice is recorded or live. Some say recorded and some say real.

I believe God is great. I believe God is greatest.

The God of the Jews penetrated time. The Christian and the Muslim celebrated that fact ever after with noise. In the medieval town, Christian bells sounded the hours. Bells called the dawn and the noon and the coming night.

In the secular West, church bells have been stilled by discretion and by ordinance. In my neighborhood of San Francisco the announcement of dawn comes from the groaning belly of a garbage truck.

No one at the hotel seems to pay the voice any mind. The waiters serve. Cocktails are shaken and poured. People in the courtyard and in the restaurant continue their conversations. The proprietress of the place turns a page of the book she is reading.

At four o'clock in the morning, the swimming pool is black. The hotel is asleep and dreaming. The neon ignites. The old man picks up his microphone to rend our dream asunder.

It is better to pray than to sleep.

The voice is not hectoring, it is simply oblivious. It is not like one's father, up early and dressing in the dark; it is like a selfish old man who can't sleep. The voice takes its permission from the desert—from the distance—but it is the modern city it wakes with enforced intimacy.

The old man's chant follows a tune; it is always the same tune, like a path worn through a carpet. And each day the old man becomes confused by the ornamental line—his voice is not agile enough to assay it. His voice turns ruminative, then puzzled. Finally, a nasal moan:

Muhammad is the prophet of Allah.

River Jordan water runs between my toes—a breathtakingly comfortable sensation. I have taken a bus tour of Galilee; the bus has stopped at the Yardenit Baptism Site, which resembles a state picnic grounds. I watch a procession of Protestant pilgrims in rented white smocks descend some steps into the comfortable brown water.

Protestantism is the least oriental of the desert faiths. Protestants own little real estate within the walls of Jerusalem. They own nothing of ancient squabbles between the Holy Roman Empire, the Byzantine Empire, the Ottoman Empire. Protestants are free to memorialize sacred events without any compulsion to stand guard over mythic ground.

For example, the traditionally venerated site of Christ's baptism is near Jericho. After the Six-Day War in 1967 that location was declared off-limits to tourists. And so this place—Yardenit—of no historical or religious significance, was developed as a place to which Christians might come for baptism ceremonies. The faith of evangelical pilgrims at Yardenit overrides the commercialism that attaches to the enterprise *(Your Baptism videotaped by a professional)*. One bank or the other, it is the same river, and pilgrims at Yardenit step confidently into the Bible.

Distance enters Abraham's seed with God's intimacy. A birth precedes the birth of Isaac. There is domestic strife of God's manufacture. For God also arranges that Sarah's Egyptian servant, Hagar, will bear Abraham a son. That son is Ishmael; the name means "He Listens." Sarah soon demands that Abraham send Hagar and her son away. *I cannot abide that woman. She mocks me.*

So Hagar and Ishmael are cast into the desert of Beersheba as Abraham and Sarah and the camels and tents and servants and flocks flow slowly away from them like a receding lake of dust.

Abruptly Haim tells me to stop. Listen! The desert has a silence like no other, he says. Do you hear a ringing in your ear? It is the bell of existence.

Not far from here, in Gaza, missiles are pitched through a blue sky. People who will be identified in news reports this evening as terrorists will shortly be killed or the innocent will be killed, people who even now are stirring pots with favored spoons or folding the last page of the morning paper to line the bird's cage.

I hear. What do I hear? I hear a truck shifting gears on a highway, miles away.

God hears the cry of Ishmael: God finds Hagar in the desert and rescues her dying child by tapping a spring of water—a green silk scarf pulled from a snake hole. God promises Hagar that Ishmael, too, will be a nation. From Ishmael's line will come the Arab tribes, and from the Arab tribes the Prophet Muhammad.

Mahdi, my Palestinian guide, pulls off the main road so I can see the Monastery of the Temptation in the distance. (Mahdi has been telling me about the years he lived in Riverside, California.) The monastery was built upon the mountain where Christ was tempted by Satan to consider the Kingdoms of the World. And here are we, tourists from the Kingdoms of the World, two thousand years later, regarding the mountain.

A figure approaches from the distance, surrounded by a nimbus of moisture. The figure is a Bedouin man on foot. A young man but not a boy, as I first thought. He is very handsome, very thin, very small, very dusty, utterly humorless. He extends, with his two hands, a skein of perhaps twenty-five bead necklaces. He speaks English—a few words like "beads." *Camel,* he says. *For your wife, your girlfriend.*

This is camel, he says again, fingering some elongated beads. I ask him who made the necklaces. His mother.

There is no sentimentality to this encounter. Sentimentality is an expenditure of moisture. The Bedouin's beseeching eyes are dry; they are the practice of centuries. He sits down a short distance away from us while we contemplate the monastery. He looks into the distance, and, as he does so, he becomes the desert.

Moses, Jesus, Muhammad—each ran afoul of cities: Moses of the Court of Egypt, Jesus of Jerusalem, Muhammad of Mecca. The desert hid them, came to represent a period of trial before they emerged as vessels of revelation. Did they, any of them, experience the desert as habitable—I mean in the manner of Haim, in the manner of the Bedouin?

After he fled Egypt, Moses took a wife; he took the nomadic life of his wife's people as a disguise. Moses led his father-in-law's flock across the desert to Mount Horeb, where God waited for him.

As a boy, Muhammad crossed the desert in Meccan caravans with his uncle, Abu Talib. Muhammad acquired the language of the Bedouin and Bedouin ways. As a middle-aged man, Muhammad was accustomed to retire with his family to a cave in the desert to meditate. During one such retreat Muhammad was addressed by God.

The Jews became a people by the will of God, for He drove them through the desert for forty years. God fed the people Israel with manna. Ravens fed Elijah during his forty days in the desert. After his ordeal of forty days, Jesus accepted the ministrations of angels. Such supernatural nourishments of the body suggest a reliance on God rather than an embrace of the desert.

In *The Desert Fathers,* Helen Waddell writes that the early Christian monks of the desert gave a single intellectual concept to Europe—eternity. The desert monks saw the life of the body as "most brief and poor." But the life of the spirit lies beyond the light of day. The light of day conceals "a starlit darkness into which a man steps and becomes suddenly aware of a whole universe, except that part of it which is beneath his feet."

There are people in every age who come early or late to a sense of the futility of the world. Some people, such as the monks of the desert, flee the entanglements of the world to rush toward eternity. But even for those who remain in the world, the approach of eternity is implacable. *The glacier knocks in the cupboard, / The desert sighs in the bed* was W. H. Auden's mock-prophetic forecast. He meant the desert is incipient in the human condition. Time melts away from us. Even in luxuriant weather, even in luxuriant wealth, even in luxuriant youth, we know our bodies will fail, our buildings will fall to ruin.

If the desert beckons the solitary, it also, inevitably, gives birth to the tribe. The ecology of the desert requires that humans form communities for mutual protection from extreme weathers, from bandits, from rival chieftains. Warfare among Arab tribes impinged often upon the life of the Prophet Muhammad. In response to the tyranny of kinship, Muhammad preached a spiritual brotherhood—discipleship under Allah—that was as binding as blood, as expansive as sky.

The Christian monastic movement in the Judaean wilderness reached its peak in the sixth century, by which time there were so many monks, so many monasteries in the desert (as many as eight hundred monks in some of the larger communities), it became a commonplace of monastic chronicles, a monkish conceit, to describe the desert as a city.

· · ·

I am driving with Mahdi through Bethlehem, then several Bedouin settlements to the east, leading into the desert. The road narrows, climbs, eventually runs out at the gates of Mar Saba, a Greek Orthodox monastery.

A monk opens the gate. Mahdi asks in Arabic if we may see the monastery. The monk asks where we are from. The monk then takes up a metal bar, which he clangs within a cast-iron triangle.

Waiting in the courtyard below is another monk. He greets us in English. Obviously four bangs, or however many, on the contraption upstairs summons English. The monk's accent is American. He, too, asks where I am from. He is from St. Louis.

We are first shown the main church. The church is dark, complexly vaulted, vividly painted. We are told something of the life of St. Saba, or Sabas, the founder of the monastery. Saba died in A.D. 532. "He is here," the monk then says, ushering us to a glass case in a dark alcove, where the saint lies in repose. "The remains are uncorrupted."

The monk carries a pocket flashlight that he shines on the corpse of the saint. The thin beam of light travels up and down the body; the movement of the light suggests sanctification by censing. The figure is small, leathern, clothed in vestments. This showing takes place slowly, silently—as someone would show you something of great importance in a dream.

We ask about another case, the one filled with skulls. They are the skulls of monks killed by Persians in A.D. 614. One has the impression the young monk considers himself to be brother to these skulls, that they remain a part of the community of Mar Saba, though no longer in the flesh. One has the impression grievance endures.

The monk next leads us to the visitors' parlor. No women are allowed in the monastery. In this room the masculine sensibility of the place has unconsciously re-created a mother's kitchen. The monk disappears into a galley; he returns with a repast that might have been dreamed up by ravens: tall glasses of lemonade, small glasses of ouzo, a plate of chocolates. The lemonade is very cool and we ask how this can be without electricity. Butane, the monk answers. For cooking and refrigeration.

The monk's patience is for the time when we will leave. Until this: "What has brought you to the Holy Land?"

I have come to write about the desert religions, I reply. I am interested in the fact that three great monotheistic religions were experienced within this ecology.

"Desert religions, desert religions," the monk repeats.

Then he says: "You must be very careful when you use such an expression. It seems to equate these religions."

I do mean to imply a common link through the desert.

"Islam is a perversion," he says.

A few minutes later, the monk once more escorts us through the courtyard and to the stone steps. He shakes my hand and says what I remember as conciliatory, though it may not have been: "The desert creates warriors."

Haim makes his living conducting tours of the desert. He is, as well, a student and an instructor at Ben-Gurion University of the Negev, where we stop briefly to exchange vehicles.

Haim invites me into his house; he must get some things. Haim's wife is also a graduate student at the university. There are some pleasant drawings of dancers on the walls. The curtains are closed against the desert. Mrs. Berger returns while I am waiting. She is attractive, blond, pregnant, calm. "You turned on the air-conditioning," she says to Haim—not accusatorily but as a statement of (I assume unusual) fact. "I have to gather some things," he replies. I ask if I may see the photograph of the mountain.

"Ah, Haim's mountain." Mrs. Berger conveys affection, indulgence.

Haim goes to his computer, pulls up the images: the mountain from the distance. Closer. Closer. The suggestion of a rectangular shape, I hesitate to say the shape of tablets; nevertheless that is how it appears. It is difficult to ascertain the scale. Yes, I can see—along the top and side of the rectangular shape there are what appear to be flames.

Haim carries several filled grocery bags out to the Jeep. We leave Mrs. Berger standing in the dark kitchen. *Goodbye.*

Stephen Pfann looks to be in his forties. His hair is white; he wears a beard. He has large, pale eyes of the sort one sees in Victorian photographs. It is because of his resemblance, in my imagination, to a Victorian photograph that I attribute to him the broad spirit of Victorian inquiry. Stephen's discourse has a dense thread-count, weaving archaeology, geology, history, theology, also botany, biology. Stephen's teenage children seem adept at reining him in when he is kiting too high. Stephen and his wife, Claire, administer the University of the Holy Land, a postgraduate biblical institute in Jerusalem. Stephen says he would be willing to take me to Qumran. He suggests an early-morning expedition and promises, as well, an Essene liturgy at sunrise.

My imagination runs away: prayers within a cave. Clay lamps, shadows. Some esotericism in the liturgy and a sun like the sound of a gong.

On the appointed morning, Stephen picks me up at my hotel. As it is already bone-light, I presume we have missed the sunrise. But, in fact, we are reciting psalms on a level plain beneath Cave Number One as the sun comes up over Arabia, over Jordan, over the Dead Sea. The light is diffuse, though golden enough. The texts remark the immensity of creation. (I am thinking about a movie I saw. An old man—Omar Sharif—whispers as he dies: "I join the immensity.")

We have been joined here by several others, two Pfann children, a forensic pathologist connected with the University of the Holy Land.

Stephen mentions "the umbilicus," by which term he means the concentration of God's intention on this landscape. Underfoot is a large anthill—a megalopolis—then a satellite colony, then another, then another, the pattern extending across the desert floor.

The old woman leans forward to kiss the pale stone.

We begin our climb to Cave Number One. The air has warmed. Pfann, in his stride, points at minute flora; his daughter nods and photographs them. Pfann and his children are as nimble as goats. "Is everyone all right?" Pfann calls backward.

I am not all right. I am relegated at several junctures to using both hands and feet. The good-natured pathologist climbing ahead of me is watchful and discreet with his helping hand, all the while recounting the religious conversion that brought him to the Holy Land.

The cave is not cool, by the way. A smell of bat dung. I hear Stephen saying something about the rapidity of the transfer of heat molecules from one substance to another. (The dryness of the cave preserved the scrolls.) I am perspiring. I am making toe marks in the dust.

Hundreds of thousands of years ago, water receded from this cave. Two thousand years ago, an Essene—probably an Essene—filled a basket with grating clay jars and climbed to this cave to hide the holy scrolls against some intimation of destruction. Sixty years ago, a Bedouin goatherd, muttering goat curses—an old man now if he lives—came upon five clay vats spilling revelation.

The community of Qumran was destroyed by Roman legions in A.D. 68.

· · ·

The desert resembles dogma: It is dry, it is immovable. Truth does not change. Is there something in the revelation of God that retains—because it has passed through—properties of desert or maleness or Semitic tongue? Does the desert, in short, make warriors? That is the question I bring to the desert from the twenty-first century.

The Semitic God is God who enters history. Humans examine every event that pertains to us for meaning. The motive of God who has penetrated time tempts us to imperfect conjecture. When armies are victorious, when armies are trodden in the dust, when crops fail, when volcanoes erupt, when seas drink multitudes, it must mean God intends it so. What did we do to deserve this? King David psalmed for the vanquishing of his enemies, did he not? There is something in the leveling jealousy of the desert God that summons a possessive response in us. *We are His people* becomes *He is our God.* The blasphemy that attaches to monotheism is the blasphemy of certainty. If God is on our side, we must be right. We are right because we believe in God. We must defend God against the godless. Certitude clears a way for violence. And so the monk's dictum—the desert creates warriors—can represent centuries of holy war and sordid prayer and an umbilicus that whips like a whirlwind.

In Afghanistan's central plateau, there were two mountain-high Buddhas. For centuries, caravans traveling the Silk Road would mark them from miles away. The Bamiyan Buddhas were destroyed by the Taliban in 2001; their faces are now anvils, erasures. An inscription from the Koran was painted beside the alcove of the larger Buddha: *The just replaces the unjust.* Just so do men destroy what belief has built and they do it in the name of God, the God who revealed Himself in the desert, the desert that cherishes no monuments, wants none. *There is no God but God.*

On July 16, 1945, the first nuclear weapon was tested in the American desert. The ape in our hearts stood still. Wow.

The desert creates warriors, by which construction St. Sabas meant (for it was his construction) that the monk discerns his true nature in the desert—his true nature in relation to God—and the discernment entails learning to confront and to overcome the temptations of human nature. In that sense a warrior.

The desert creates lovers. St. Sabas desired the taste of an apple. The craving was sweeter to him than the thought of God. From that moment Sabas forswore apples. The desire for apples was the taste of God.

Desert is the fossil of water. (Haim has been at great pains to point this out—striations in mesas and the caverns water has bored through mountains of salt, and salt is itself a memory of water.) Is dogma a fossil of the living God—the shell of God's passage—but God is otherwise or opposite? Perhaps it is that the Semitic tongues are themselves deserts—dry records of some ancient fluency, of something feminine that has withdrawn. The Semitic tongues descend from Shem, son of Noah, survivor of the Flood. Abraham was of Shem's line. Perhaps the Semitic tongues, inflected in the throat, recall water, are themselves oases?

I have often heard it observed by critics of the desert religions that monotheism would have encouraged in humankind a different relationship to nature if the Abrahamic God had revealed Himself from within a cloak of green. The desert encourages a sense of rebuff and contest with the natural world. Jesus cursed the recalcitrant fig tree right down to firewood.

Consider Las Vegas and Dubai—two modern desert cities constructed upon an intention to distract. Las Vegas casinos banish clocks, admit neither night nor day. Dubai has wagered its financial future on a time zone that lies conveniently between the markets of Asia and Europe. Both cities defy the desert through exertions of fantasy; both cities pour cooled air. Fountains of electric light tumble and splash in reassuring displays of human will. For thousands of years humans have flaunted their will over nature. What we call global warming now leaves many in the world anticipating a nostalgia for ice, for zero. The ecology least threatened by the work of man is desert, the flowing desert.

The desert's uninhabitability convinces Jew and Christian and Muslim that we are meant for another place. Within the deserts of the Bible and the Koran, descriptions of Eden, descriptions of the Promised Land, resemble oases. For Jews, Eden was predesert. For Christians and Muslims, paradise—a reconciliation with God—is postdesert.

In the Koran, paradise is likened to *gardens underneath which rivers flow.* For Christians, paradise is an urban idea, a communion, a city of God. The commendation of the body in the ancient rite of Christian burial prays that angels may come to lead the soul of the departed to the gates of the holy city Jerusalem.

I purchase for five shekels a postcard scene of Jerusalem in the snow—black-and-white—the sky is dark but Jerusalem shines swan, a royal city.

I follow Haim a quarter of a mile to a grove of untrimmed date-palm trees. I have seen their like only in ancient mosaics, the muted colors, the golden dust. In their undressed exuberance these palms resemble fountains. But they are dry; they prick and rattle as we thread our way among them. We could just as easily have walked around, couldn't we? I suspect Haim of concocting an oasis experience. But his glance is upward, into the branches of some taller trees. Haim is hoping for what he calls a lucky day. If it is Haim's lucky day, we will see a leopard. Recently, a leopard entered the town of Beer-Sheva. Haim suspects the creature may be lurking here.

But it is not Haim's lucky day. We continue up an incline, alongside a muddy riverbed. Winged insects bedevil my ears. We walk around a screen of acacia trees, at which Haim steps aside to reveal:

a waterfall, a crater filled with green water! There are several Israeli teenagers swimming, screaming with delight as they splash one another. A tall African youth stands poised at the edge of the pool.

This Ethiopian Jew (we later learn) has come to this desert from another. He has come because the Abrahamic faith traveled like particles of desert over mountains and seas, blew under the gates of ancient cities, and caught in the leaves of books. Laughter, as spontaneous as that of his ancestress Sarah, echoes through the canyon as the boy plunges into the stone bowl of water. Displaced water leaps like a javelin.

John the Baptist wrapped himself in camel hide. He wandered the desert and ate the desert—honey and locusts and Haim's gray leaves. John preached hellfire and he performed dunking ceremonies in the River Jordan. People came from far and wide to be addressed by the interesting wild man as "Brood of Vipers." When watery Jesus approached flaming John and asked for baptism, John recognized Jesus as greater than he. It was as though the desert bowed to the sea. But, in fact, their meeting was an inversion of elements. John said: *I baptize only with water. The one who comes after me will baptize with Spirit and fire.*

Desert is, literally, emptiness—its synonyms desolation, wasteland. To travel to the desert "in order to see it," in order to experience it, is paradoxical. The desert remains an absence: The desert is this place I stand multiplied by infinite numbers—not this place particularly. So I come away each night convinced I have been to the holy desert (and have been humiliated by it) and that I have not been to the desert at all.

Just beyond the ravine is a kibbutz, a banana plantation, a university, a nuclear power plant. But, you see, I wouldn't know that. The lonely paths Haim knows are not roads. They are scrapings of the earth. Perhaps they are tracks that Abraham knew, or Jesus. Some boulders have been removed and laid aside. From the air-conditioned van or from the tossing Jeep or through binoculars, I see the desert in every direction. The colors of the desert are white, fawn, tawny gold, rust, rust-red, blue. When the ignition is turned off and the Jeep rolls to a stop, I pull the cord that replaces the door handle; the furnace opens; my foot finds the desert floor. But the desert is distance. Nothing touches me.

Many nights, I return to my hotel with the desert on my shoes. There is a burnt, mineral scent in my clothing. The scent is difficult to wash out in the bathroom basin, as is the stain of the desert, an umber stain.

Standing, scrubbing my T-shirt, is the closest I get to the desert. The water turns yellow.

I tell myself I am not looking for God. I am looking for an elision that is nevertheless a contour. The last great emptiness in Jerusalem is the first. What remains to be venerated is the Western Wall, the ancient restraining wall of the destroyed Second Temple.

After the Six-Day War, the Israeli government bulldozed an Arab neighborhood to create "Western Wall Plaza," an emptiness to facilitate devotion within emptiness—a desert that is also a well.

I stand at the edge of the plaza with Magen Broshi, a distinguished archaeologist. Magen is a man made entirely of Jerusalem. You can't tell him anything. Last night at dinner in the hotel garden, I tried out a few assertions I thought dazzling, only to be met with Magen's peremptory *Of course.*

Piety, ache, jubilation, many, many classes of ardor pass us by. Magen says he is not a believer. I tell Magen about my recent cancer. If I asked him, would he pray for me here, even though he does not believe? *Of course.*

Western Wall Plaza levels sorrow, ecstasy, cancer, belief. Here, emptiness rises to proclaim its unlikeness to God, who allows for no comparison. This is His incomparable Temple. It does not resemble. It is all that remains.

No writing! You cannot write here. A woman standing nearby has noticed I carry a notebook. I have a pen in my hand. The woman means on the Sabbath, I think. Or can one never write here? It is the Sabbath.

"He is not writing anything," Magen mutters irritably, waving the woman away.

PATTIANN ROGERS

I Hear and Behold God in Every Object, Yet Understand God Not in the Least

FROM *Portland*

> For God so loved the order of things that He gave
> his only begotten Son that whosoever believes in
> him should not perish . . .

SO JESUS SAID, ACCORDING TO JOHN. GOD SO LOVED THE WORLD, loved the order of things, loved the earth, loved the order of the earth, loved us as creatures born of the order of things, born of the stars and the order of the stars, born of the earth born of the stars, made of the stars, made of the earth.

I fall into the beauty of that song and momentarily I am saved. I do not perish. I agree with Walt Whitman: *I hear and behold God in every object, yet understand God not in the least.*

Maybe the creative order of the universe—those massive stars, the supernovae, those super stars smelting in their nuclear furnaces all the elements from which every body in the universe is composed, the planets gathering those elements to become themselves, the earth slowly forming, core and mantle, mountains rising, tectonic plates shifting, the great oceans of the earth churning for billions of years until the first flickering grip of life begins, those first, daring, determined, primordial creatures coming and coming—maybe the processes of this order resulted ultimately in the birth of a certain child who came to be called the Christ. Perhaps the universe brought forth in love this child who uttered those words. Maybe this was the way it happened—the order of things, the universe, the love embodied in creation bringing forth this fruit. I don't know how it happened. But here it is, our earth and the heavens, those words, the story of that life, that resounding message. And isn't it true that love enhances, gives health and energy, causes the capacity for good to expand, is kin to joy, a cousin to reverence, while hate hinders, withers its host, promotes destruction, brings anger and misery, nurtures the well-being of nothing?

Love is a creative force in the physical world. We are agents of love and its witnesses.

Jesus Christ could not have lived without love, the Christ story could never have been conceived by anyone without love, the words themselves would never have existed without love, and without the words and a speaker of words this story could not have been told. *God is love,* He is said to have said. Maybe love was what was there before the beginning, before the Big Bang. Maybe love is the creative power within the order of things. Maybe love is the way of the universe. I could take the beauty of that into my heart.

Consider the lilies of the field, how they grow: they neither toil nor spin, and yet I say to you that even Solomon in all his glory was not arrayed like one of these. Those words of beauty were placed in their order by a poet in love with the earth. *Not one sparrow falls to the ground that God is not aware.* Those words of honor were composed by a poet in love with the life of the earth. *The meek shall inherit the earth.* Who better to receive with love the order of the earth?

Maybe a child born of love who then loves wholly, purely, perfectly, with all his heart and all his soul and all his mind, can walk on water, can give sight to the blind, can rise again from the dead, can be this attuned with the creative love within the order of things. That child, the gift of the universe, would be love in human form. Maybe this is how love conceived itself.

I am in love with the life of the earth, the hundred budding eyes seeking light in a water-buried nest of tadpoles, a tomato on the vine basking from blossom to ripe red, in love with our enormous, frightening sun and all creatures basking in the light of its being, a green anole invisible on a green leaf, a yellow-striped garter snake curled on a smooth stone, in love with the fragrance of a river when a summer evening begins to cool and the cicadas and crickets strike up their buzz and jingle in the poplars and shore grasses. I'm in love with the cosmic heaven, its terrible, haunting glory, its racing explosions and dangerous maelstroms of burning rocks and dusts and great arcs of glowing gases, in love with the silence of that same sky above midnight snow, the white land and its barren shadows drenched in the pale blue stillness of the moon; in love with the order of things, crystals adhering piece by icy piece, a single, widening furl of campfire smoke, electrons and atoms, ocean currents and the rhythmic currents of blood through the bodies of living creatures and the rhythmic currents and waves of a veering flock of ricebirds over the fields, the sweep of porpoises veering through the swell of ocean waves; and our own creations, the written language of musical scores, bells and drums, wax whistles and pianos, hot-air balloons, bicycles, Rollerblades, calculus, arboretums, *Voyager I* and *Voyager II,* and all voyagers traveling to the constant night of the ocean floors or to the airless glacier peaks of mountains or into the realms of the nano world, actors, artists, acrobats, archivists, a quilt spread on the grass, supper on a quilt spread on the grass, in love with our words alone in an otherwise wordless universe (as far as we know), in love with *as far as we know,* in love with *amen.*

All of us want to be loved unconditionally. We crave that love. We are born craving to be loved unconditionally. Some of us become warped and crippled from the lack of that love, some of us become stunted, some of us sicken, some of us die from the lack of that love. Maybe the health and vibrancy of the universe too depends on a love like that. Maybe the creation is not finished. Maybe the creation, in its ongoing shifting and changing, altering and evolving, requires a robust strength that love alone can provide, a love given freely and unconditionally throughout the coming and going of stars and mountains and suns and planets, in the coming and going of life. We know we are a source of love. We know we have the ability to receive and to give love, to sustain by giving love. We can love the order of the world, receive and acknowledge with love its gifts of life and beauty and one another. We can express love to a universe that requires it, give love despite fear, despite horror and grief, despite suffering, despite our ignorance, love unconditionally despite death. Each of us can give that gift as we are able. I want this gift to be received. I want to participate in the creation in this way now; wherever *now* might be, in place, in time, among the countless and the far beyond.

AMANDA SHAW

Contemptus Mundi
and the Love of Life

FROM *First Things*

JUST DOWN THE ROAD FROM THE LIVELY PIAZZA BARBERINI IS A
Capuchin church, Santa Maria della Concezione. Practically every
Roman street corner boasts some little church, supported—or some-
times squashed—between the hotels and high-rises that have sprouted
up over the centuries. And, more often than not, these unassuming
churches shelter some almost-forgotten treasure: the prison cell of
St. Paul, the grill of St. Laurence, a darkened Caravaggio canvas,
Michelangelo's unfinished tomb. Ancient treasures, whose saints and
artists have long since passed to their reward, but that linger in re-
membrance: *Remember, man, that you are dust, and to dust you shall
return.*

But the rose-colored Capuchin church, once more popular than
even the catacombs, has a unique appeal. The crypt below is lavishly
decorated with the bones of more than four thousand friars from
three centuries of Franciscan mendicancy. It's not so morbidly spec-
tacular as one would expect. There is a certain monastic peace that
settles on the pilgrim as he makes his way through the Crypt of the
Skulls and the Crypt of the Pelvises, past the Crypt of the Leg and
Thigh Bones, and finally into the Crypt of the Three Skeletons, with
shoulder-bone flowers and stars adorning the corridor vaults between.

It is an extraordinary memento mori, provoking somber thoughts about somber matters. Yet, somewhat incongruously, the Capuchin bone crypt came to mind as I attended a wedding on this year's Feast of the Presentation. I've been to plenty of weddings, all quite joyful and lovely, but this one was different—it was the final profession of two Sisters of Life, members of a vibrant order founded in 1991 by New York's John Cardinal O'Connor. Each sister knelt before the mother superior, placed her young hands in those wise and experienced ones, and vowed to live perpetually in poverty, chastity, and obedience, committed to protecting human life in all its stages. "If you are faithful to these vows," said Mother Agnes, "I promise you, in the name of God, eternal life."

A bold promise, to be sure, but a bold offering too: These women were giving nothing less than their whole lives to Christ. And yet they weren't claiming to do Great Things or offer Great Sacrifices or be famous and heroic. Instead, the liturgy echoed the deep-rooted Dominican rite of profession: *What do you seek?—God's mercy and yours.* "Seek and you shall find," the Scriptures promise; God never withholds his mercy. The secret of the spiritual life is not such a secret after all.

A final profession is a wedding. The veil is that of a bride, and the long, white habit of the sisters—modeled after the Dominican robe— has always reminded me of a wedding gown. As the sisters processed in, carrying lit candles for the feast, they chanted the words of David: *The Bridegroom is here; go out and welcome him.* Later, after they had made their vows before the altar, the presiding archbishop blessed their rings and placed them on their fingers, a sign of perpetual covenant with the Lord. And throughout, the packed congregation—family and friends, religious sisters and mothers with children, those who have given and those who have received—took part in the prayers and hymns.

A final profession is a wedding, but at times it also seems like a funeral. *Nunc dimittis servum tuum, Domine,* intoned the choir before Mass. *Secundum verbum tuum in pace.* Simeon's canticle was appropriate for the day's feast, but it resonated, too, with the occasion. In a sense, the professed sisters were dying to the world; they were offering up the normal cares and pursuits that we take for granted— home, family, ambitions—not because these are bad or dangerous but because they are not enough. And though the veiled women have chosen to be set apart for Christ, they are hardly alone. The Capuchin crypt reminds me of that, and so does the Litany of Saints. *SS. Francis and Clare . . . SS. Dominic and Catherine . . . St. Elizabeth Ann Seton . . . Bl. Teresa of Calcutta, pray for us.* All the while, the newly professed lie prostrate before the altar, a posture of total vulnerability and submission. The next time they will be outstretched like this will be at their funeral Mass, when they go forth to meet their Bridegroom: *Lord, now you let your servant go in peace; your word has been fulfilled.*

A wedding and a funeral, life and death, the here and hereafter: What should the innocent bystander, who stumbled in by chance and barely knows the sisters, make of all this? *Regnum mundi et omnem ornatum saeculi contempsi,* chants the choir; *I have had contempt for the kingdom of this world, and all temporal adornments.* These lines, taken from the breviary's Common for Holy Women, are hard— almost inhuman. How can such worldly contempt be a human goal, especially for one who calls herself a Sister of Life? Can contempt for the world encompass love for the world? Or can I simply blame overzealous Augustinians, who pit the flesh and the world harshly, even speciously, against the spirit and the City of God?

One thing is certain: *Contemptus mundi* is no new trend in Christianity. In his commentary on the Psalms, St. Augustine testified, "My soul, which in the contempt of this world seems to men as it were to die, shall live not to itself, but to him." Third-century bishop Eucharius wrote an elegy entitled *De Contemptu Mundi,* as did

St. Bruno, the eleventh-century founder of the Carthusians. St. Bernard of Cluny composed a three-thousand-line *contemptus mundi* poem in the following century, and Pope Innocent III issued a similar lament with the dour subtitle "On the Misery of the Human Condition." *Contemptus mundi,* in the Middle Ages, was a flourishing genre. As Thomas à Kempis, spokesman for so much of medieval spirituality, declared, "This is the highest wisdom: through contempt of the world, to strive for the kingdom of heaven."

This ascetic tradition did abate somewhat in modern thought, but it didn't disappear. The Renaissance humanists Petrarch and Erasmus both titled works *De Contemptu Mundi,* and Sir Philip Sidney—hardly a monk or mendicant—began one of his sonnets with the now familiar plea: *Leave me, O love which reachest but to dust, / And thou, my mind, aspire to higher things.* Even at the brink of the twentieth century, Pope Leo XIII taught, "No man can be high-souled, kind, merciful, or restrained who has not learned self-conquest and a contempt for this world when opposed to virtue."

What is the modern, life-affirming Christian supposed to conclude? Perhaps it is just poetic overstatement, or a bit too much fervor for the ascetic ideal. Or, seeing that most of the authors were writing to protest corruption in Church and society, perhaps *mundi* needs qualification: It is not the world as God's physical creation that is contemptible; rather, it is the evil that has crept in and fashioned the City of Man, in hostility to God's loving Providence. As Leo crucially noted, we should condemn this world "when it is opposed to virtue."

Still, this interpretation of *contemptus mundi* doesn't quite harmonize with the Sisters of Life, who, to put it simply, aim to affirm life's value, from conception until natural death. Hardly a purely transcendent vision of reality, and hardly a celestial mission. They love life in its physicality, and, imitating Christ, they love it in its frailty. *I have had contempt for the kingdom of this world,* the choir chanted at the profession, yet that is not the final word: *Because of the love of my Lord Jesus Christ, whom I saw, whom I loved, in whom I believed, and whom I worshipped.*

Etymologists may quibble, but I cannot help hearing *tempus*—time—veiled in our word "contempt." The incarnate Lord calls man to see this world for its temporality, to glimpse its anticipation of eternity, and to grasp its crucial role in redemption. *In the fullness of time, God sent forth his son:* Eternity broke through time, that we might become sons and share in eternity.

Time is exile, but time is also hope. "Detachment" might be an apt synonym for such contempt: The detachment that allows man to embrace the simplicity of the stable and the solitude of the cross; to say *not my will, but thine, be done.* The detachment that frees the Christian to hope for heaven. The sisters live this detachment visibly and radically. Their white cotton habit and heavy blue scapular, however attractive as religious attire, can scarcely be called temporal adornment; and, if the liturgy of profession is a wedding, it is an obviously spiritual one. "Almost otherworldly," someone remarked afterward, as we shared in a donated feast, lovely enough for the finest bride. Almost ethereal—"yet," one of the young sisters interjected, "so very real." And isn't that exactly how the banquet of the Lamb, which this celebration anticipates, ought to be? *The Bridegroom is here; go out and welcome him.*

They are on the way. We are on the way. And sometimes—dazzled by a speck of eternity—we wonder why we cannot be there now. As Pope Benedict muses in *Spe Salvi,* "It would be like plunging into the ocean of infinite love . . . plunging ever anew into the vastness of being, in which we are simply overwhelmed by joy." When we taste the raindrop, here and now, it is tempting to want the sea. Then the words of George Herbert, begging to be swept off to paradise, come back to chide:

Thus far Time heard me patiently,
Then chafing said. This man deludes:
What do I here before his door?
He doth not crave less time, but more.

It is, perhaps, an eschatological uncertainty principle: You cannot demand heaven and be ready for it at the same time; the overeager stargazer needs more time on earth. But there is more to it, a deeper theology. The troparian for the Presentation, sung at the profession of the sisters, proclaims: *Rejoice, O Virgin Theotokos, Full of Grace! / From you shone the Sun of Righteousness, Christ our God, / Enlightening those who sat in darkness!* I have sometimes wondered how Mary, in whom time met eternity, must have felt after her son's ascent into heaven. She, of all women, was prepared to enter her reward, and yet God entrusted her to John and willed that she remain behind. "Blessed is the womb that bore you, and the breasts that you sucked," said a woman in the crowd, but Jesus replied, "Blessed rather are those who hear the word of God and keep it!"

Mary did both. The Church calls her the Gate of Heaven not only because she gave birth to the Messiah but also because she lived her entire life in reverence to his will. She presented the divine Word to Simeon and Anna at the Temple; and she presented him to the disciples, in living witness, after his death and resurrection. I imagine Christ would have taken Mary with him into heaven, had she asked. But it is unthinkable that she, who marked her life by pure *fiat,* would have foregone the chance to continue channeling his love to earth. "The theme of spiritual sacrifice is fused with that of *light,*" said John Paul II, speaking on Candlemas to a gathering of consecrated men and women: "This Child, Simeon prophesies, will be a 'light for the Gentiles, the glory of Israel,' but also a *sign of contradiction.* The Virgin appears as a candlestick bearing Christ, the 'Light of the world.'"

A candlestick on earth and a candlestick in heaven: This is the role of all the blessed. When the pilgrim walks through the Capuchin bone crypt and is reminded of those who have gone before—those many Christians who, we hope, lived in fidelity to God's will—there is an unmistakable peace: *If you are faithful to these vows, I promise you eternal life.* For some, like the Capuchin friars or Sisters of Life, God's will is the life of radical adherence to the gospel, of selling all that one has and following him. But, as the Litany of Saints reminds, God's path for each of his children is personal and unique: *SS. Joachim and Anne . . . SS. Augustine and Monica . . . St. Gianna Beretta Molla.* What unites all these holy men and women is their commitment to living in the world, in the Lord, and for the world, for the Lord.

This is the real life of love—and, therefore, the real love of life.

FLOYD SKLOOT

Ezra Pound in a Spring Storm
—Amity, OR, 2006

FROM *Hudson Review*

The night we sold our house a storm blew in
from the Coast Range, whirling as if enraged
by what we had done. I saw lights vanish
from the valley below, heard the woods hiss
around us in the first drizzle, and a pack of deer
rush east across the hill's crest to flee a volley
of hail. In a lull between squalls, drenched oak
like wild horses shook rain from their leaves,
bearded irises thrashed in a swirl of crosswind
beneath my window, and keening sounds rose
from within the woods that I first took to be cries
from the heart of the land itself. Why not?
After fourteen years here, I thought nothing
would surprise me.

But then in a sudden shaft
of moonlight, cursing as he lurched over slick
leaves and steadied himself with a moss-covered
maple branch, Pound made his way upslope
from a thicket of blackberry vines. Beard biblical,
voice blazing, he stopped to glare at me.
How could'st thou leave thy cottage in the woods?

. . .

I knew there would be inspectors testing water
and septic, roof and foundation, but Pound
probing my mind had never crossed my mind.
Would he care that aging parents drew us back
to the city, or that the time had come for younger
bodies to tend this land?
                              I saw he was lost
in memory, mourning his days with Yeats,
their cottage in the woods. *Gone forever,*
he had written in a fit of nostalgia. Yet not.

As I reached for him, Pound raised his branch,
or perhaps the giant fir looming above him
swayed as he spoke, and it was the voice
of the mad prophet from his late Cantos.
What thou lovest well is thy true heritage.

The glow he dwelt in faded with a shift of wind
and I saw him swallowed by his own shadow.
No, by his cape flung across his face
as he drew nearer, hair ruffling like a mane.
I had time only to tell him I would never leave
this place no matter where I lived.
But he was already all motion, a storm
departing, deaf to everything.
                              Backed by
distant thunder, his voice became a flicker
of lightning all around me. Then came
stillness I would take with me everywhere.

MEIR SOLOVEICHIK

Why Beards?

FROM *Commentary*

BECAUSE OF A BEARD, A PAPACY WAS LOST. THAT IS THE STORY OF Johannes Bessarion, a fifteenth-century cardinal and convert from Greek Orthodoxy who strove to reunite Eastern and Western Christianity. Extraordinarily influential among the Catholic hierarchy, Bessarion was widely thought to be a likely successor to Pope Nicholas V. But at the conclave following Nicholas's death, a serious personal flaw was pointed out: retaining an Eastern Orthodox custom shunned by Rome, Bessarion still sported a full beard. As the historian Mark Zucker tells it:

> Not only did this result in Bessarion's loss of the pontifical throne, but his beard was later to cause him even greater humiliation and suffering. For a slight breach of etiquette during an embassy to Louis XI in 1471, the French king pulled him by the beard, an insult so serious and so upsetting that it is said to have brought about his death, from shame and grief, a year later.

To anyone familiar with Talmudic tales, Bessarion's story cannot help bringing to mind another, much earlier episode of contested religious leadership. It seems the sage Rabban Gamliel, the *nasi* or religious head of post–Temple Jewry, was temporarily relieved of his position on account of what his colleagues considered a heavy-handed exercise of authority. The rabbis' ultimate choice of a successor was Elazar ben Azaryah, a brilliant scion of prestigious lineage. But Elazar, too, had a flaw, though the opposite of Bessarion's: being only eighteen years old, he did not yet have the full growth of facial hair expected of a Jewish religious leader. Fortunately, according to the Talmud, a miracle was wrought overnight, and Elazar awoke to find himself the owner of a long white beard. The story concludes that he was wont to say of himself: "Behold, I am akin to a man of seventy years."

The contrast between these two tales highlights the truth behind at least one popular visual stereotype of traditional Jews, and particularly of rabbis. Indeed, the Jewish penchant for beards as a cultural marker traces all the way back to the Bible. In the book of Chronicles, we read of the insult visited upon a group of David's servants who had been sent to comfort the Ammonite king Hanun on the death of his father. Suspecting the delegation of having come on a mission of espionage, Hanun

> took David's servants, and shaved them, and cut off their garments in the middle to their hips, and sent them away. Then there went certain persons, and told David how the men had been treated. And he sent to meet them: for the men were greatly ashamed. And the king said, "Stay at Jericho until your beards are grown, and then return."

Nor was this ancient Jewish horror of barefacedness a merely cultural phenomenon; it was intimately connected with a religious commandment. "Do not cut the edges of your beard," the Bible explicitly instructs, adding elsewhere: "The edges of your beard you shall not destroy." This ban was considered by the rabbis to be among the 365 prohibitions in the Torah, and breaking it as serious a sin as the consumption of pork. And so it has remained ever since.

Why? And, given the force of the prohibition, how is it that, as cursory inspection confirms, so many devout Jews today in fact go beardless?

The second question is the more quickly dispensed with: many traditionalist Jewish men have availed themselves of an ancient exegetical exception. In forbidding shaving, the biblical text, as we have just seen, employs two different verbs, enjoining the Israelites first not to "cut" the beard and then not to "destroy" it. In order to reconcile this seeming ambiguity, the Talmud argues that the one truly forbidden action is razoring—that is, a method that both shears the facial hair and thoroughly removes it. Alternative approaches, such as trimming (cutting but not destroying) or, at the other end of the spectrum, using tweezers (destroying but not actually cutting), are permitted.

Basing themselves on this ruling, yeshiva students in Europe would commonly use a depilatory cream (which destroys but not by cutting) in order to burn the whiskers off the face. The cream was quite painful, and if left on too long could remove skin as well as hair. Thankfully, in twentieth-century America, a new technology appeared: electric shavers. Although some halakhic authorities have opposed the use of such devices, others have permitted them on the grounds that, since they are known not to cut as close as a razor, they do not actually "destroy."

Be all that as it may, the careful reader of the Bible and the Talmud cannot but conclude that the spirit of the law, if not the letter, is quite clear: Jewish men are encouraged to have beards. Again the question is: why? To help answer it, we can turn to another ancient society—one in which beardlessness was quite common, and especially among priests and royalty.

The practice of shaving makes its first appearance in the Bible in connection with the story of Joseph, who as a young man was sold by his brothers into slavery in Egypt, where he was subsequently imprisoned on false charges. The ruler of Egypt, learning of the young Israelite's knack for dream interpretation, orders him released from his prison cell and taken to the palace. And so, as we read in Genesis, Joseph "was shaved, and his clothes were changed, and he was brought before Pharaoh."

In Egypt, then, one might appear in public, and certainly in high or royal society, only in a barefaced state. As the historian Lisbeth Fried has written:

> In contrast to the majority of peoples in the ancient Near
> East, for the ancient Egyptians, at least from the time of the
> Old Kingdom (2686–2181 B.C.E.), the custom among men
> was to shave beard and mustache, and wear a false goatee
> on special occasions. Foreigners can be distinguished from
> native Egyptians in many Egyptian tomb paintings by the
> presence of full beards.

Why were the Egyptians so ardent on the subject of hair removal? In *The Beginning of Wisdom,* a study of the biblical book of Genesis, Leon Kass points out that *the* defining cultural feature of ancient Egypt was its obsession with achieving immortality. One sees this quite dramatically, he notes, in the practice of mummification, a ritual that the Egyptians believed would allow the corpse to traverse the underworld in a living and vital state. Kass's point is vividly illustrated in the description of the mummification procedure offered by the Greek historian Herodotus. It involved the removal of the brains and all internal organs and then "covering the corpse with natron for 70 days," washing it, and wrapping it "from head to toe in bandages of the finest linen anointed with gum." According to other sources, the procedure culminated in the pronouncement of a blessing: "You will live again, you will live for ever. Behold, *you are young again for ever*" (emphasis added).

Wherever we look, writes Kass, "we see in Egypt the rejection of [bodily] change and the denial of death." Shaving was a key element in this rejection. "No shaggy outlines or blemishes mar the perfectly smooth look. What appears to be an unveiling [of the human face] is actually also a veiling of age and disorder." With this in mind, it begins to seem no accident at all that the Hebrew Bible, which steadily sets itself against pagan practices of every kind, should have positively enjoined the opposite practice—that is, the wearing of beards—thus visibly and deliberately repudiating the false blessing of eternal youthfulness and underscoring the fact of our eventual and inevitable mortality. In biblical Hebrew, the very word for beard, "*zakan,*" shares a root with "*zaken,*" an elderly person.

Moving forward in time from the ancient world, a different but no less instructive contrast with Jewish law and custom is offered by the tradition of shaving that developed in the Catholic priesthood— the same tradition that would cost Johannes Bessarion the papacy. Here the key element was the ideal not of youthfulness but of celibacy. Indeed, as Zucker notes, it was one and the same pope, Gregory VII (1073–1085), who by decree "enforced not only celibacy among the clergy but shaving as well."

To be sure, a desire to differentiate Christians from both bearded Jews and bearded Muslims must have played a part in the development of this practice. But at least as great a part seems to have been played by the association of beards with ordinary human carnality.

Explaining the religious virtue of shaving, the medieval scholar Guglielmus Durandus argued that

> cutting the hair of the beard . . . denotes that we ought to cut away the vices and sins which are a superfluous growth in us. Hence we shave our beards that we may seem purified by innocence and humility, and that we may be like the angels who remain always in the bloom of youth.

If, by contrast, the Jewish faith has always found religious value in facial hair, it is because Jews are not expected to embody angelic innocence.

This is hardly to say that Jews do not believe in immortality. Traditional Judaism has always embraced the doctrine of the immortality of the soul and the ultimate resurrection of the dead. But immortality for Jews also lies elsewhere than in the eternity of one's body or of one's spirit. Rather, it lies in one's children, and in the legacy of Jewish faith passed on to those who follow.

"For I love him," God says of Abraham in Genesis, "because he will command his children and household after Me, and they will keep the ways of the Lord, performing justice and righteousness." The same moral, minus the explicitly religious precept, informs a famous Talmudic tale about the sage Honi:

> One day, as he was walking on the road, he saw a man planting a carob tree. He asked him, "How long will it take this tree to bear fruit?" The man replied, "Seventy years." He asked, "Are you quite sure you will live another seventy years to eat its fruit?" The man replied, "I myself found fully grown carob trees in the world; as my forebears planted for me, so am I planting for my children."

By forbidding Jews to destroy their hair, the Bible warns them away from seeking the siren song of eternal youth. By encouraging Jews to grow beards, it reminds them that they will not be young forever, that they must prepare the ground for those who come after, just as their fathers did for them. In acknowledging their mortality, Jews are instructed to eschew aspiring to the condition of disembodied angels—for, as a Midrash memorably instructs, angels cannot become parents who will instruct their children in the ways of the Lord:

> R. Yehoshua ben Levi said: When Moses ascended on high, the ministering angels spoke before the Holy One: "Sovereign of the universe! What business has one born of woman among us?" He answered them: "He has come to receive the Torah." They said to him, "That secret treasure—you desire to give it to flesh and blood?!" The Holy One said to Moses: "Return them an answer." He then spoke before them: ". . . What is written therein? . . . 'Honor your father and your mother.' Do you have fathers and mothers?" Immediately they conceded to him.

Similarly, for Judaism, it is not the young or the celibate who are most worthy to be revered, but rather those who have already raised children and, even better, been blessed with grandchildren. Discussing this aspect of Jewish identity, Rabbi Joseph Soloveitchik observes the curious fact that, of the three biblical patriarchs, Jacob, the last of the three, is the one commonly referred to by the Midrash as "the old one," despite the fact that both his father Isaac and his grandfather Abraham lived longer than he. The reason, Soloveitchik suggests, is that it was Jacob/Israel who truly created the Jewish people and embodied the principle of its continuity. This he did most strikingly when, leaping over the gulf of the generations, he gathered his son Joseph's two children to himself, declared them "mine, no less than [my sons] Reuben and Simeon," and blessed them by saying that they would be "called by the name of my forefathers Abraham and Isaac [and] grow into a great people."

Such is the authority of old age. Embroidering the same idea in a different context, the Midrash goes so far as to hint that physical manifestations of age are the indispensable substance from which we weave the moral fabric of society:

> Until Abraham, there was no old age, so that one who wished to speak with Abraham might mistakenly find himself speaking to [his son] Isaac, or one who wished to speak with Isaac might mistakenly find himself speaking to Abraham. But when Abraham came, he pleaded for old age, saying, "Master of the universe, You must make a visible distinction between father and son, between a youth and an old man; *so that the old man may be honored by the youth.*" God replied, "As you live, I shall begin with you." So Abraham went off, passed the night, and arose in the morning. When he arose, he saw that the hair of his head and of his beard had turned white. He said, "Master of the universe, if You have given me white hair as a mark of old age, [I do not find it attractive]." "On the contrary," God replied, "'the hoary head is a crown of glory.'" (Proverbs 16:31, emphasis added)

Which brings us to today, and to American society. Ours is decidedly not an age of Abrahams, Jacobs, or of youthful Elazars proud to be regarded as men of seventy. On the contrary, it is one in which the external signs of aging are avoided at all costs, youth is worshipped, and immortality is sought not in children but in Botox. Like the ancient Egyptians, we, too, go to our embalmers to be told: "Behold, you are young again for ever."

Even for those who forgo trips to the dermatologist and plastic surgeon, our infatuation with youth remains embedded in daily habit. Yale University's Stephen Carter, the author of *Reflections of an Affirmative-Action Baby* (1991), once complained that American blacks had fought for decades for the right to be called "Mr." and "Mrs.," only to discover that such basic marks of respect had become obsolete across the board.

Writing in a similar vein of our culture of "perpetual adolescence," Joseph Epstein observes on the basis of old newsreel films that even baseball games used to be attended by adults dressed "in a suit and a fedora or other serious adult hat." Now, "informality has been institutionalized" to the point where captains of industry dress like children. If, Epstein writes, it was once assumed that life had a beginning, a middle, and an end, and that "the middle—adulthood— was the lengthiest and most earnest part, where everything serious happened and much was at stake," today "the ideal almost everywhere is to seem young for as long as possible."

Epstein's words have helped me understand an interesting incongruity that I face again and again. According to the Talmud, a Jewish male becomes an adult at the age of thirteen, a female at twelve. And there was indeed a time, not so long ago, when the notion of a thirteen-year-old as an adult seemed perfectly sensible—when hungry mouths depended on a newly minted teenager finding a job, learning a trade, preparing to leave the care of his parents, and, soon enough, starting a family of his own. This was hardly peculiar to Jews. "How quickly the Depression generation was required to mature!" Epstein writes. "How many stories one used to hear about older brothers going to work at eighteen or earlier, so that a younger brother might be allowed to go to college, or simply to help keep the family afloat!"

No longer. Today, thanks in large part to our increasing wealth and the luxury it provides, the idea of a twelve- or thirteen-year-old adult seems ludicrous. There is thus always a touch of the comic in the air when a rabbi, facing the grinning bar-mitzvah boy before him, refers to him as a "man." He is, after all, clearly still a child, one who has perhaps worked hard to prepare for this Sabbath day but mostly looks forward to hanging out afterward with his friends and returning to a life in which his every care and financial concern is seen to by his parents.

Like all other communities in America, Jews have reaped the benefits of an age of affluence and extended youthfulness, and Orthodox Jews, of whom I am one, are hardly an exception in this regard. The affluence is without question a great blessing, but within it there can be found a loss and even a potential curse—one that is nowhere more evident than at an Orthodox wedding. Typically such events are lavish and expensively catered affairs, and why not: Judaism stresses continuity, and a wedding is the happiest moment in a Jewish life. But inevitably there comes a moment when the groom and his extended family, followed by the bride's family and the bride herself, proceed down the aisle, and the crowd, having remained seated and chatting away as grandparents in their seventies or eighties have walked haltingly to their places, rises reverently before the young couple, beautiful and handsome, young and radiant.

While there may be a good reason for this relatively new practice, standing up for the bride and groom is not required by Jewish law; standing for the elderly, at any time, and any place, is a biblical obligation. The same chapter of Leviticus that instructs male Jews to grow a beard insists that we "rise before the aged, and glorify the face of an elder." Is it possible—or probable—that even traditional Jews, whose very appearance ought to teach them to revere the aged, have forgotten why weddings are so special to Judaism: because we plant for those who come after us, just as those who preceded us planted on our behalf?

I, too, am a creature of the culture of extended youthfulness, and not just because I do not have a beard. I regularly call men twice my age by their first name (although I draw the line at men whom I do not yet know). And when I take my children to see the Mets play at Shea stadium, I certainly do not dress the way men dressed in the newsreels described by Epstein.

Nevertheless, and for the sake of my children, I hope that I will internalize the lesson embodied by the Jewish penchant for beards and reinforced by the Jewish religious system in general. I hope that I will have the strength to resist the sundry temptations of our benign American Egypt and embrace the path of Abraham, the man chosen by God to found a family that from generation to generation would communicate to the world the principles of justice and righteousness. And I hope I will also remember Joseph Epstein's admonition—that there is no quicker route to senility than through the all-consuming and utterly futile effort to stay young forever.

JOHN UPDIKE

The Writer in Winter

FROM *AARP*

YOUNG OR OLD, A WRITER SENDS A BOOK INTO THE WORLD, NOT himself. There is no Senior Tour for authors, with the tees shortened by twenty yards and carts allowed. No mercy is extended by the reviewers; but then it is not extended to the rookie writer, either. He or she may feel, as the gray-haired scribes of the day continue to take up space and consume the oxygen in the increasingly small room of the print world, that the elderly have the edge, with their established names and already secured honors. How we did adore and envy them, the idols of our college years—Hemingway and Faulkner, Frost and Eliot, Mary McCarthy and Flannery O'Connor and Eudora Welty! We imagined them aswim in a heavenly refulgence, as joyful and immutable in their exalted condition as angels forever singing.

Now that I am their age—indeed, older than a number of them got to be—I can appreciate the advantages, for a writer, of youth and obscurity. You are not yet typecast. You can take a distant, cold view of the entire literary scene. You are full of your material—your family, your friends, your region of the country, your generation—when it is fresh and seems urgently worth communicating to readers. No amount of learned skills can substitute for the feeling of having a lot to say, of *bringing news*. Memories, impressions, and emotions from your first twenty years on earth are most writers' main material; little that comes afterward is quite so rich and resonant. By the age of forty, you have probably mined the purest veins of this precious lode; after that, continued creativity is a matter of sifting the leavings. You become playful and theoretical; you invent sequels, and attempt historical novels. The novels and stories thus generated may be more polished, more ingenious, even more humane than their predecessors; but none does quite the essential earth-moving work that Hawthorne, a writer who dwelt in the shadowland "where the Actual and Imaginary may meet," specified when he praised the novels of Anthony Trollope as being "as real as if some giant had hewn a great lump out of the earth and put it under a glass case."

This second quotation—one writer admiring a virtue he couldn't claim—meant a lot to me when I first met it, and I have cited it before. A few images, a few memorable acquaintances, a few cherished phrases, circle around the aging writer's head like gnats as he strolls through the summertime woods at gloaming. He sits down before the word processor's humming, expectant screen, facing the strong possibility that he has already expressed what he is struggling to express again.

My word processor—a term that describes me as well—is the last of a series of instruments of self-expression that began with crayons and colored pencils held in my childish fist. My hands, somewhat grown, migrated to the keyboard of my mother's typewriter, a portable Remington, and then, schooled in touch-typing, to my own machine, a beige Smith-Corona expressly bought by loving parents for me to take to college. I graduated to an office model, on the premises of *The New Yorker* magazine, that rose up, with an exciting heave, from the surface of a metal desk. Back in New England as a freelancer, I invested in an electric typewriter that snatched the letters from my fingertips with a sharp, premature *clack*; it held, as well as a black ribbon, a white one with which I could correct my many errors. Before long, this clever mechanism gave way to an even more highly evolved device, an early Wang word processor that did the typing itself, with a marvelous speed and infallibility. My next machine, an IBM, made the Wang seem slow and clunky and has been in turn superseded by a Dell that deals in dozens of type fonts and has a built-in spell checker. Through all this relentlessly advancing technology the same brain gropes through its diminishing neurons for images and narratives that will lift lumps out of the earth and put them under the glass case of published print.

With ominous frequency, I can't think of the right word. I know there *is* a word; I can visualize the exact shape it occupies in the jigsaw puzzle of the English language. But the word itself, with its precise edges and unique tint of meaning, hangs on the misty rim of consciousness. Eventually, with shamefaced recourse to my well-thumbed thesaurus or to a germane encyclopedia article, I may pin the word down, only to discover that it unfortunately rhymes with the adjoining word of the sentence. Meanwhile, I have lost the rhythm and syntax of the thought I was shaping up, and the paragraph has skidded off (like this one) in an unforeseen direction.

When, against my better judgment, I glance back at my prose from twenty or thirty years ago, the quality I admire and fear to have lost is its carefree bounce, its snap, its exuberant air of slight excess. The author, in his boyish innocence, is calling, like the sorcerer's apprentice, upon unseen powers—the prodigious potential of this flexible language's vast vocabulary. Prose should have a flow, the forward momentum of a certain energized weight; it should feel like a voice tumbling into your ear.

An aging writer wonders if he has lost the ability to visualize a completed work, in its complex spatial relations. He should have in hand a provocative beginning and an ending that will feel inevitable. Instead, he may arrive at his ending nonplussed, the arc of his intended tale lying behind him in fragments. The threads have failed to knit. The leap of faith with which every narrative begins has landed him not on a far safe shore but in the middle of the drink. The failure to make final sense is more noticeable in a writer like Agatha Christie, whose last mysteries don't quite solve all their puzzles, than in a broad-purposed visionary like Iris Murdoch, for whom puzzlement is part of the human condition. But in even the most sprawling narrative, things must add up.

The ability to fill in a design is almost athletic, requiring endurance and agility and drawing upon some of the same mental muscles that develop early in mathematicians and musicians. While writing, being partly a function of experience, has few truly precocious practitioners, early success and burnout are a dismally familiar American pattern. The mental muscles slacken, that first freshness fades. In my own experience, diligent as I have been, the early works remain the ones I am best known by, and the ones to which my later works are unfavorably compared. Among the rivals besetting an aging writer is his younger, nimbler self, when he was the cocky new thing.

From the middle of my teens I submitted drawings, poems, and stories to *The New Yorker*; all came back with the same elegantly terse printed rejection slip. My first break came late in my college career when a short story that I had based on my grandmother's slow dying of Parkinson's disease was returned with a note scrawled in pencil at the bottom of the rejection slip. It read, if my failing memory serves: "Look—we don't use stories of senility, but try us again."

Now, "stories of senility" are about the only ones I have to tell. My only new experience is of aging, and not even the aged much want to read about it. We want to read, judging from the fiction that is printed, about life in full tide, in love, or at war—bulletins from the active battlefields, the wretched childhoods, the poignant courtships, the fraught adulteries, the big deals, the scandals, the crises of sexually and professionally active adults. My first published novel was about old people; my hero was a ninety-year-old man. Having lived as a child with aging grandparents, I imagined old age with more vigor, color, and curiosity than I could bring to a description of it now.

I don't mean to complain. Old age treats freelance writers pretty gently. There is no compulsory retirement at the office, and no athletic injuries signal that the game is over for good. Even with modern conditioning, a ballplayer can't stretch his career much past forty, and at the same age an actress must yield the romantic lead to a younger woman. A writer's fan base, unlike that of a rock star, is postadolescent, and relatively tolerant of time's scars; it distressed me to read of some teenager who, subjected to the Rolling Stones' halftime entertainment at a recent Super Bowl, wondered why that skinny old man (Mick Jagger) kept taking his shirt off and jumping around. The literary critics who coped with Hemingway's later, bare-chested novel *Across the River and into the Trees* asked much the same thing.

By and large, time moves with merciful slowness in the old-fashioned world of writing. The eighty-eight-year-old Doris Lessing won the Nobel Prize in Literature. Elmore Leonard and P. D. James continue, into their eighties, to produce best-selling thrillers. Although books circulate ever more swiftly through the bookstores and back to the publisher again, the rhythms of readers are leisurely. They spread recommendations by word of mouth and "get around" to titles and authors years after making a mental note of them. A movie has a few weeks to find its audience, and television shows flit by in an hour, but books physically endure, in public and private libraries, for generations. Buried reputations, like Melville's, resurface in academia; avant-garde worthies such as Cormac McCarthy attain, late in life, best-seller lists and *The Oprah Winfrey Show.*

A pervasive unpredictability lends hope to even the most superannuated competitor in the literary field. There is more than one measurement of success. A slender poetry volume selling less than a thousand copies and receiving a handful of admiring reviews can give its author a pride and sense of achievement denied more mercenary producers of the written word. As for bad reviews and poor sales, they can be dismissed on the irrefutable hypothesis that reviewers and book buyers are too obtuse to appreciate true excellence. Over time, many books quickly bloom and then vanish; a precious few unfold, petal by petal, and become classics.

An aging writer has the not insignificant satisfaction of a shelf of books behind him that, as they wait for their ideal readers to discover them, will outlast him for a while. The pleasures, for him, of bookmaking—the first flush of inspiration, the patient months of research and plotting, the laser-printed final draft, the back-and-forthing with Big Apple publishers, the sample pages, the jacket sketches, the proofs, and at last the boxes from the printers, with their sweet heft and smell of binding glue—remain, and retain creation's giddy bliss. Among those diminishing neurons there lurks the irrational hope that the last book might be the best.

LEON WIESELTIER

Ring the Bells

FROM *The New Republic*

FOR A LONG TIME I DID NOT HEAR THE BEAUTY OF CHURCH BELLS; or more accurately, I did not wish to hear it. They sounded only like Christianity, which in my early years was a vexing triumphalist sound—the pealing of history, from which my honor as a Jew required me to recoil. When the tintinnabulations of the Church of St. Francis Xavier on Avenue O reached my ears, they brought the message that I was a member of a minority. I was not acquainted with the liturgical schedule of the church, with the practical reason for the ringings—though I might have surmised, based on my own experience of the aesthetically nullifying effects of the repetitions of ritual, that Christians who heard the bells religiously, in their ancient role as a signaling device, also did not attend to their beauty. When the bells sounded, it was a time for prayer, not for music. Art demands detachment, but religion forbids it. (There is an old joke about two jazz musicians walking along a street when a huge bell falls out of a church steeple and crashes disastrously behind them. "What was that?" one asks, with alarm. "F sharp," the other replies.)

Still, no soul is only Jewish or only Christian, and eventually the beauty got to me. And then I had another problem. It happened in graduate school, when life is slow enough for spiritual incidents. I was loitering in the magnificent little cloister at Magdalen College.

It was a late afternoon in an Oxford autumn, and the yellow spears of the waning sun were landing in the severe stone geometries of the place and striking the walls like friendly lightning. Suddenly I heard the harmonies of a choir rehearsing evensong—a piece by Byrd, I later learned—in an adjoining chapel. Fixed by the lights and the sounds, I was overcome, and elated by, an unfamiliar contentment, and I thought: This is Christian beauty and I want it. I was shocked by the thought. I remember thinking also that we, I mean the Jews, have nothing like this. This was another variety of minoritarian torment. Soon the joy passed, perhaps because the singing ceased, and my confusion passed with it. As I strolled home along Addison's Walk, I got it clear in my mind that Christianity may in some of its expressions be beautiful, but beauty is not Christian. Religious or cultural or national definitions of beauty are conceptual mistakes. So I returned, you might say, to my senses. And the next day I returned to Magdalen to consult the chapel schedule, so that I might hear the choir again.

I was reminded of the evolution of my relationship to the ravishments of other traditions when I read about the controversy at Harvard about the broadcast of the Muslim call to prayer in Harvard Yard. It was sounded from the steps of Widener Library—where a great Jewish scholar once spent many decades in the groundbreaking study of early Islamic philosophy—for several days during Islam Awareness Week. (Is anybody not aware of Islam?) The sound of the *adhan* in the quads startled many people, and provoked ferocious opposition. An editorial in the *Crimson* denounced it as an infringement upon the liberty of others, who were forced to listen to an affirmation of a faith in which they do not believe. What troubled the eloquent authors of the editorial was the text of the summons, which included the words "I bear witness that there is no lord except God" and "I bear witness that Mohammed is the Messenger of God." "This puts the *adhan* in a different class of expression than, say, the sounding of church bells or the displaying of a menorah," they maintained, "because it publicly advances a theological position." Indeed it does, though it is important to add that almost all of the alleged victims of this aural coercion could not understand a word of it. For all they knew, they were listening to a recipe for kanafi. And the menorah is, in its fiery silence, a religious symbol of a religious holiday, even if most American Jews prefer to think of the occasion historically or commercially. Is the sight of it, therefore, an optical coercion? As for church bells, see above. Moreover, the secular integrity of the setting was long ago surrendered. In the middle of it stands an imposing Christianish chapel, which, despite its hospitality to people of all faiths, could never be mistaken for a synagogue or a mosque. Years ago I was among a company of Jews—I think it included the dean of the faculty, though I may be mistaken—who festively carried a Torah through Harvard Yard, and this was no more "halacha at Harvard" than the *adhan* is "sharia at Harvard." Even before there was multiculturalism, there was respect for human variety and pleasure in it. An open civil space will always be cacophonous. There will be affirmation and alienation, sometimes even within a single individual; and there will be indifference, which is in its way one of the accomplishments of pluralism. When I was at college, the arrival of spring was reliably announced by the defiant blasting of "Sympathy for the Devil" from dorm-room loudspeakers turned toward the campus. I did not share the theological position that it advanced, but I was exhilarated. In a Dionysian frenzy I played Frisbee until dark.

There are also other controversies of diversity at Harvard: one of the university gyms has been restricted for six hours a week for the use of Muslim women whose religious observance does not permit them to work out in the company of men. As a matter of principle, this troubles me—I believe in integration, and in the challenges that the experience of integration presents to the insularity of traditional identities (Woodrow Wilson once remarked that the purpose of a college education is to make a man as much unlike his father as possible), and the customization of places according to identity can be carried to absurd and unfair lengths; but these Muslim women would not be at Harvard if they, too, did not in some way believe in integration, and it seems humane to allow their abs some respite from the pressure. But the *adhan,* like the church bells, sounds magnificently American to me. Indeed, the ringing of the bells began, long before democracy, in a protodemocratic moment, in 313, when the Edict of Milan established the "Peace of the Church" and the persecution of Christians in the Roman Empire came to an end, and Christians could be summoned publicly to prayer. And who was Constantine compared to Lincoln? As I write, the bells of Lincoln's church across the street from my office are chiming, and sweetening yet another hour of this Jew's day.

RICHARD WILBUR

A Measuring Worm

FROM *The New Yorker*

This yellow striped green
Caterpillar, climbing up
The steep window screen,

Constantly (for lack
Of a full set of legs) keeps
Humping up his back.

It's as if he sent
By a sort of semaphore
Dark omegas meant

To warn of Last Things.
Although he doesn't know it,
He will soon have wings,

And I, too, don't know
Toward what undreamt condition
Inch by inch I go.

The Wanderer

FROM *Tricycle*

> Master Sheng Yen has dedicated his life to spreading
> the teachings of Chan Buddhism in China and in
> the West. In this excerpt from his new autobiogra-
> phy, *Footprints in the Snow*, Master Sheng Yen tells
> the story of his arrival in New York and how he
> learned to live without a home.

AFTER I RESIGNED FROM MY POST AS AN ABBOT IN TAIWAN, DR. C. T.
Shen (a cofounder of the Buddhist Association of the United States)
brought me back to New York to spread the dharma there. My re-
turn to the United States did not restore me to my former position
of strength, however. There was no room for me to live at the Temple
of Great Enlightenment, which was occupied by nuns. I stayed at
Shen's villa, named Bodhi House, on Long Island, and traveled back
and forth to the city. But I wanted to move out because I was too far
away from my students. Shen told me, "If you move out, I can no
longer take good care of you."

"That's okay," I said. "I will wander."

I had no money for rent, so I slept in front of churches or in
parks. I learned how to get by from three of my students, who had
experience living on the street. They taught me to find discarded

fruit and bread in back of convenience stores and food markets. They showed me that I could make a little money here and there from odd jobs, sweeping up shops or tending a pretzel stand. I learned that I could store my things in a locker at Grand Central Terminal and wash clothes at a Laundromat. My students pointed out the fast-food restaurants that were open twenty-four hours, and they told me that I could spend my nights at these places, resting and drinking coffee.

I wandered through the city, a monk in old robes, sleeping in doorways, nodding with the homeless through the night in coffee shops, foraging through Dumpsters for fruit and vegetables. I was in my early fifties, no spring chicken, but I was lit from within by my mission to bring the dharma to the West. Besides, what did it matter? The lessons Dongchu had taught me made it a matter of indifference to me whether I slept in a big room or a small room or in the doorway of a church.

Some people may have felt pity for me, but I didn't pity myself. I didn't feel that I was unlucky. Some people feared me and worried that I would ask for money or other help. I decided it was best not to call on anyone, although I did accept some offers of help. I spent nights at the apartments of my followers. Master Haolin welcomed me and let me stay at his monastery in Chinatown. But I did not want to stay there too long, because I did not know if I would be able to repay him for this service. I preferred to wander.

This may strike some of you as strange—that a friend and fellow monk would let me leave his monastery to live out on the street. But Haolin had a very small place without much income. When I lived there, it was an added burden on him. If he was wealthy and had a big place I would have felt differently about imposing on his hospitality.

I think that being out on the streets was a good thing, because it taught me not to rely on anyone and pushed me to find my own place to propagate Chan. There is a long tradition of bodhisattvas enduring difficulties as they spread the dharma. Shakyamuni Buddha taught that to be a great practitioner, a bodhisattva, you do not look toward your own happiness and security. You only wish for sentient beings to cease suffering. In India, Buddhist monks had to travel to areas without Buddhism, and they would inevitably encounter resistance. When they arrived in China, Confucianism and Taoism were dominant, and the Confucians wanted to keep the Buddhists out, especially the monastics. Shakyamuni Buddha believed that if you could withstand difficulties, you would be able to inspire others and thus influence them. Ordinary people just want life to be smooth, without problems. But Buddhist practitioners have a different attitude. They are ready to endure many difficulties if they are in the service of transforming others.

How do we endure hardship? Master Mazu taught that it is necessary to have a mind of equanimity. This means always maintaining a calm, stable mind, which is not ruled by emotion. When you encounter success, you don't think that *you* created it. Don't get too excited or proud of yourself. Your success happened for a reason and came to pass because of many people and circumstances. If you work hard at something but find that too many obstacles prevent you from accomplishing it, you may have to give up. In that case, you shouldn't get depressed. Conditions aren't right. Perhaps this will change, perhaps it won't. *You* are not a failure. Becoming upset only causes suffering.

Keeping a mind of equanimity, though, does not mean being inactive or passive. You still need to fulfill your responsibilities. Master Xuyun said, "While the business of spreading Buddha's teachings is like flowers in the sky, we ought to conduct them at all times. Although places for the practice [monasteries, retreat centers] are like the reflection of the moon in the water [referring to the fact that they are illusory and impermanent], we establish them wherever we go." This means that these jobs are illusory, but we still need to do them. Sentient beings are illusory, but we still need to help deliver them. A place of practice is like the reflection of the moon in the water. It's not real, but we still build monasteries so we can deliver sentient beings. This is our responsibility. We must try our best to fulfill our responsibilities, without being attached to success and failure.

Chan masters apply the mind of equanimity in all aspects of their lives. If they don't, they are not truly Chan masters. In my time of wandering, I kept a mind of equanimity. I didn't think of myself as homeless. I thought of Master Hanshan (1546–1623), who lived on Tiantai Mountain. He used the sky as his roof, the earth as his bed, the cloud as covers, a rock as a pillow, and the stream as his bathtub. He ate vegetables if vegetables were available. If rice and vegetables were available in a monastery, he ate that. If nothing was available, he ate tree leaves or roots. He felt free and wrote beautiful poems.

> Beneath high cliffs I live alone
> swirling clouds swirl all day
> inside my hut it might be dim
> but in my mind I hear no noise
> I passed through a golden gate in a dream
> my spirit returned when I crossed a stone bridge
> I left behind what weighted me down
> my dipper on a branch click clack

When you have nothing, you are free. When you own something, then you are bound to your possessions. I felt very happy. I did not feel that I had no future. In fact, I felt my future was rich and great indeed because I had students. I still had a mission to fulfill. I just did not know where I would sleep at night. I knew that I was much better off than homeless people, who really did not have anything and were without a future. And I knew that I would not wander forever.

My life is very different now. I have met with world leaders and given a keynote address in the General Assembly Hall at the United Nations. My disciples include high-level officials in Taiwan. I was received as a VIP in motorcades in mainland China and Thailand. I am venerated by my followers. People feel that if they don't treat me this way, it's not right, but it does not make any difference to me whether they treat me this way or not. I am famous today but tomorrow, when I can no longer do what I do now, I will be forgotten. How many people have their names remembered in history? Fame, like wealth and power, is illusionary. So a mind of equanimity is necessary in all circumstances.

There is a Chinese saying that goes: "After experiencing wealth and property, it is hard to return to poverty." This is true if you don't have a mind of equanimity. If you can maintain a mind of equanimity, you are free, no matter what the conditions.

Contributors' Notes

Diane Ackerman is the author of many books of poetry and non-fiction, including *The Zookeeper's Wife, An Alchemy of Mind, A Natural History of the Senses,* and *Jaguar of Sweet Laughter: New and Selected Poems.* Ms. Ackerman has received many prizes and poems, but the one that tickles her most is having a molecule named after her (*dianeackerone*), a sex pheromone in crocodiles.

Mary Jo Bang is the author of six collections of poetry, including *Elegy,* which won the National Book Critics Circle Award. Her most recent collection, *The Bride of E,* appeared in September 2009. She has received a grant from the Guggenheim Foundation and a Hodder Fellowship from Princeton University. A graduate of the M.F.A. program at Columbia University, she teaches at Washington University in St. Louis.

Rick Bass is the author of twenty-two books of fiction and nonfiction, including a new memoir, *The Wild Marsh.* A previous memoir, *Why I Came West,* was nominated for a National Book Critics Circle Award.

David Berlinski has taught mathematics and philosophy at universities in the United States and France. He is the author of

A Tour of the Calculus, The Advent of the Algorithm, Newton's Gift, and other books. A senior fellow at the Discovery Institute and a former fellow at the Institute for Applied Systems Analysis and the Institut des Hautes Études Scientifiques, Berlinski writes frequently for *Commentary* and other journals.

Joseph Bottum is the editor of *First Things.* His books include *The Fall & Other Poems* and *The Pius War.*

Nicholas Carr's latest book is *The Big Switch: Rewiring the World, from Edison to Google.*

Judith Ortiz Cofer's books include *A Love Story Beginning in Spanish* (poems), *Woman in Front of the Sun: On Becoming a Writer* (essays), *The Meaning of Consuelo* (a novel), and others. She is the Regents' and Franklin Professor of English and Creative Writing at the University of Georgia.

Billy Collins's latest book of poems is *Ballistics.* He served as U.S. poet laureate from 2001–2003.

Christi Cox is the editor of *Snow Lion: The Buddhist Magazine* and has written for *Tricycle, Yoga Journal,* and other magazines. She edits books for authors such as the Dalai Lama and is completing her own book, *The Dalai Lama Spends the Night: And Other True Tales of Hope, Despair, and Spiritual Transformation.*

Louise Glück's many books of poetry include *Averno, Seven Ages, Vita Nova,* and *The Wild Iris* (Pultizer Prize for Poetry, 1993). She served as U.S. poet laureate from 2003–2004.

Seamus Heaney was born in County Derry in Northern Ireland. *Death of a Naturalist,* his first collection, appeared in 1966, and since then he has published poetry, criticism, and translations that have established him as one of the leading poets of his generation. In 1995 he was awarded the Nobel Prize for Literature.

Jane Hirshfield's many books of poems include *After*; *Given Sugar, Given Salt*; and *The Lives of the Heart*.

Paula Huston is the author of *Daughters of Song*, *The Holy Way: Practices for a Simple Life*, *By Way of Grace: Moving from Faithfulness to Holiness*, and *Forgiveness: Following Jesus into Radical Loving*, and the coeditor of *Signatures of Grace*.

Pico Iyer is the author of several books about faith and crossing cultures in the modern world, including *Video Night in Kathmandu: And Other Reports from the Not-So-Far East*, *The Lady and the Monk: Four Seasons in Kyoto*, *The Global Soul: Jet Lag, Shopping Malls, and the Search for Home*, and *Abandon*. His most recent book, *The Open Road*, describes thirty-three years of talks and travels with the Fourteenth Dalai Lama.

Charles Johnson, a 1998 MacArthur Fellow, is the S. Wilson and Grace M. Pollack Endowed Professor of English at the University of Washington in Seattle. His fiction includes *Faith and the Good Thing*, *Dreamer*, and *Middle Passage* (winner of the National Book Award). He is also the author of many short story collections and nonfiction books.

Jon D. Levenson is the Albert A. List Professor of Jewish Studies at Harvard Divinity School and the coauthor (with Kevin J. Madigan) of *Resurrection: The Power of God for Christians and Jews*.

Philip Levine's many books of poetry include *Breath*, *The Mercy*, *The Simple Truth* (Pulitzer Prize for Poetry, 1995), and *What Work Is* (National Book Award for Poetry, 1991).

Wilfred M. McClay has been SunTrust Bank Chair of Excellence in Humanities at the University of Tennessee at Chattanooga, where he is also a professor of history, since 1990. His books include *The Masterless: Self and Society in Modern America,* which won the Merle Curti Award of the Organization of American Historians, and *Figures in the Carpet: The Human Person in the American Past.*

Richard John Neuhaus, who died on January 8, 2009, was founding editor of *First Things* and the author of many books, including *The Naked Public Square: Religion and Democracy in America, The Catholic Moment: The Paradox of the Church in the Postmodern World,* and *As I Lay Dying: Meditations Upon Returning.*

Robert Pinsky is the author of many books of poems, including *Gulf Music* and *Jersey Rain,* as well as a translation of Dante's *Inferno.* He served as U.S. poet laureate 1997–2000.

Melissa Range's poems have appeared in *The Georgia Review, The Paris Review,* and *Image.* She has received a Rona Jaffe Foundation Writers' Award, a "Discovery"/*The Nation* award, and a writing fellowship from the Fine Arts Work Center in Provincetown, Massachusetts.

Richard Rodriguez is a contributing editor at *New America Media* in San Francisco, and writes for various publications in the United States and Europe. He is the author of the autobiographical book on class, ethnicity, and race, *Hunger of Memory, Days of Obligation: An Argument with My Mexican Father;* and *Brown: The Last Discovery of America.* He has received a George Foster Peabody Award, the Frankel Medal from the National Endowment for the Humanities, and the International Journalism Award from the World Affairs Council of California.

Pattiann Rogers has published twelve books of poetry, the most recent being *Wayfare, Firekeeper: Selected Poems (revised and expanded)*, and *Generations*. Among other awards, Rogers has received two NEA grants, a Guggenheim Fellowship, five Pushcart Prizes, and the Literary Award from the Lannan Foundation.

Amanda Shaw is an assistant editor at *First Things*.

Floyd Skloot's *Selected Poems: 1970–2005* won the 2009 William Stafford Memorial Poetry Award from the Pacific Northwest Booksellers Association. Skloot has also published three memoirs, four novels, six collections of new poems, and a collection of essays.

Meir Soloveichik is associate rabbi at Congregation Kehilath Jeshurun in New York and a doctoral candidate in the philosophy of religion at Princeton University.

John Updike, who died on January 27, 2009, was a novelist, poet, short story writer, and essayist, and the holder of many major awards, including the Pulitzer Prize, the National Book Award, the National Medal of Arts, and the National Humanities Medal.

Leon Wieseltier is the literary editor of *The New Republic* and the author of *Kaddish*.

Richard Wilbur, though long retired from teaching, serves once a week as Simpson Lecturer at his alma mater, Amherst College. He is the author of many books of poems, including *Collected Poems: 1943–2004*; *Mayflies: New Poems and Translations* (2000); and *New and Collected Poems* (Pulitzer Prize for Poetry, 1989). His translations of *Le Cid* and *The Liar* by Corneille were published in 2009.

Master Sheng Yen, who died on February 3, 2009, was a teacher in the Chan school of Buddhism and the author of more than fifty books, including *Footprints in the Snow: The Autobiography of a Chinese Buddhist Monk*. At the time of his death he had 3,000 students in the United States and more than 300,000 students in Taiwan.

Philip Zaleski is the editor of the Best Spiritual Writing series. His most recent books include *Prayer: A History* (with Carol Zaleski) and a revised edition of *The Recollected Heart*.

Other Notable Spiritual Writing of the Year

Amittay, Ayelet, "Living Kaddish," *Tikkun,* January/February.

Berry, Wendell, "Faustian Economics," *Harper's Magazine,* May.

Byassee, Jason, "Not Your Father's Pornography," *First Things,* January.

Caldecott, Stratford, "Angels in the Architecture," *Second Spring,* no. 8.

Cording, Robert, "Gift," *Ploughshares,* Spring.

Dalby, Liza, "There Is Much We Do Not Know About the Feelings of Butterflies," *Shambhala Sun,* July.

Duncan, David James, "Ikkyū at the Wind-Eye," *The Sun,* December.

Frazier, Ian, "Native," *Portland,* Summer.

Gordon, Mary, "A Burning Soul," *Portland,* Spring.

Guttierez, Eric, "Crossing Rivers," *Harvard Divinity Bulletin,* Winter.

Halkin, Hillel, "The Translator's Paradox," *Commentary,* June.

Harris, Lisa Ohlen, "Wild Olive Shoot," *The Journal,* Spring/Summer.

Herlihy, John, "The Holy Mountain of Athos," *Sophia,* Summer.

Kadetsky, Elizabeth, "Modeling School," *Antioch Review,* Spring.

Levine, George, "The Heartbeat of a Squirrel," *Raritan,* Summer.

Norris, Kathleen, "Psyche, Soul, and Muse," *Image,* Fall.

Ozeki, Ruth L., "The Art of Losing," *Shambhala Sun,* March.

Padel, Ruth, "Learning to Make an Oud in Nazareth," *The New Yorker,* October 27.

Reno, R. R., "The End of the Road," *First Things,* October.

Smythe, Allison, "The Significance of Place," *Relief,* vol. 2, no. 1.

Stanton, Edward F., trans., "Four Letters of St. Teresa of Avila," *Tiferet,* no. 7.

Ward, Michael, "C. S. Lewis and the Star of Bethlehem," *Books & Culture,* January/February.

Waterston, Ellen, "The Old Hackleman Place, An Obituary," *Oregon Quarterly,* Summer.

Wiman, Christian, "From a Window," *The Atlantic,* July/August.

Wright, Charles, "The Evening Is Tranquil, and Dawn Is a Thousand Miles Away," *The New Yorker,* June 30.